Praise for *Learning to Lead* and Rev. Dr. Willard W. C. Ashley's Work

"Persuasive [and] compelling.... Provides a contemporary leadership model that integrates emotional, physical and spiritual aspects of humanity, thereby offering future leaders the tools needed to pursue personal growth and realize self-fulfillment."

—**Yvonne Simons**, executive director, the Anne Frank Center, USA

"Helps spiritual leaders ... develop their leadership gifts in the crucible of caring, crisis, community and congregational environments. Your investment in walking through this book will bring gracious and generous returns as you identify and implement the lessons offered by gifted, wise and tested leaders."

—**Rev. Dr. Thomas R. De Vries, MDiv, DMin**, general secretary, Reformed Church in America

"Should be on the shelf of every religious leader.... A great resource."

—*Manna: The Voice of Living Judaism*

"Draws on a wealth of experience and provides a compendium of realistic scenarios.... A comprehensive resource for clergy, pastoral counselors and caregivers of all faiths."

—*Catholic Library World*

"This highly recommended resource will provide clergy with a practical guide grounded in hard-earned experience [and] will also offer congregations a tool for self-assessment."

—*Congregational Libraries Today*

"Practical.... Comprehensive and ... well systematized.... I suggest it be compulsory on every minister's bookshelf."

—*Insights*

"A valuable and comprehensive resource for faith communities."

—*New York Disaster Interfaith Services Newsletter*

Learning *to* Lead

Other Professional Resources from SkyLight Paths

Professional Spiritual & Pastoral Care
A Practical Clergy and Chaplain's Handbook
Edited by Rabbi Stephen B. Roberts, MBA, MHL, BCJC

Disaster Spiritual Care
Practical Clergy Responses to Community,
Regional and National Tragedy
*Edited by Rabbi Stephen B. Roberts, BCJC, and
Rev. Willard W. C. Ashley Sr., MDiv, DMin, DH*

How to Be a Perfect Stranger, 5th Edition
The Essential Religious Etiquette Handbook
Edited by Stuart M. Matlins and Arthur J. Magida

The Perfect Stranger's Guide to Funerals and Grieving Practices
A Guide to Etiquette in Other People's Religious Ceremonies
Edited by Stuart M. Matlins

The Perfect Stranger's Guide to Wedding Ceremonies
A Guide to Etiquette in Other People's Religious Ceremonies
Edited by Stuart M. Matlins

Show Me Your Way
The Complete Guide to Exploring Interfaith Spiritual Direction
By Howard A. Addison

Learning *to* Lead

Lessons in Leadership for People of Faith

Edited by Rev. Willard W. C. Ashley Sr., MDiv, DMin, DH

Walking Together, Finding the Way®

SKYLIGHT PATHS®
PUBLISHING
Nashville, Tennessee

Learning to Lead:
Lessons in Leadership for People of Faith

© 2013 by Willard W. C. Ashley

Library of Congress Cataloging-in-Publication Data

Learning to lead : lessons in leadership for people of faith / edited by Rev. Willard W. C. Ashley, Sr.
    p. cm.
Includes bibliographical references and index.
ISBN 978-1-59473-432-8
1. Christian leadership. I. Ashley, Willard W. C., 1953-
BV652.1.L435 2012
253—dc23
                         2012027689

10 9 8 7 6 5 4 3 2

Cover Design: Kelley Bureau and Gloria Todt
Cover Art: ©Michel Boubin/iStockphoto
Manufactured in the United States of America

SkyLight Paths Publishing is creating a place where people of different spiritual traditions come together for challenge and inspiration, a place where we can help each other understand the mystery that lies at the heart of our existence.

SkyLight Paths sees both believers and seekers as a community that increasingly transcends traditional boundaries of religion and denomination—people wanting to learn from each other, *walking together, finding the way.*®

SkyLight Paths, "Walking Together, Finding the Way," and colophon are trademarks of LongHill Partners, Inc., registered in the U.S. Patent and Trademark Office.

Walking Together, Finding the Way®
Published by SkyLight Paths® Publishing
A Division of LongHill Partners, Inc.
An Imprint of Turner Publishing Company
4507 Charlotte Avenue, Suite 100
Nashville, TN 37209
Tel: (615) 255-2665
www.skylightpaths.com

This book is dedicated to my family, friends, faculty colleagues, students, mentors, patients, and the congregations who allowed me to be their partner in ministry:

Tanya Pagán Raggio-Ashley, MD—Thank you for your love, support, and dedication as a wife, friend, and colleague.

Willard W. C. Ashley Jr.—Thank you for the many lessons you taught me about being a leader as your dad. What a blessing to have you as a son.

Annette Ashley, Tina Ashley, and Eunice Walden—You continue to be my inspiration. You keep before me the lessons our parents taught us. Thank you.

Phyllis Harrison-Ross, MD—Your leadership encouraged me to embrace my call to be a strong ethical leader in academia, mental health, and the larger community. The world is a better place because of you.

Rabbi Stephen B. Roberts—Without you, this book would not have happened! Thank you for being there from the inception to the completion of this book. Thank you for being a good friend in times of need. I owe the success of this book to you. Many thanks.

Joanne Noel, DMin—Thank you for reading the draft and offering editorial suggestions.

New Brunswick Theological Seminary—Thank you for your support, suggestions, and spiritual strength during the process of editing this book. To President Gregg Mast, the trustees, administration, faculty, staff, students, and field educators: thank you for granting me tenure.

Artie Raggio Jr.—My late brother-in-law, who died too young. He was quiet, yet a strong and compassionate leader.

Contents

Introduction

Rev. Willard W. C. Ashley Sr., MDiv, DMin, DH

The Purpose of This Book

Two questions continually arise in congregations, spiritual retreats, faith-based seminars, seminaries, universities, conflict mediation sessions, and gatherings of people of faith. First, "How do we prepare spiritual leaders in an ever-changing environment?" Second, "What are the most critical lessons for people of faith to know about being a leader?" The first question addresses methodology, and the second question explores content. This book attempts to answer both questions with the use of theory, practical methodologies, and case studies. The contributors to this book are experts in their field and excel in both theory and practice. It is also the purpose of this book to add a diverse set of scholarly voices to the work of theological field educators.

This book will provide the reader with an opportunity to hear some of the voices that shape the current theories and practices in theological education. *Learning to Lead* is an invitation to reflect on the current state of spiritual leadership, affirm what has worked; challenge what is abusive, harmful, or outdated; and offer the latest thinking in the practice of spiritual leadership. It is my intention and the focus of this book to help people who hold leadership positions in faith-based institutions, whether as ordained clergy, seminarians, or lay leaders. People who do not hold leadership positions can benefit from reading this book to understand some of the joys and challenges of spiritual leadership and learn how spiritual leaders are prepared. *Learning to Lead* reflects my experience of thirty years in pastoral ministry, twenty-eight years in theological education, and twenty years in pastoral care, which includes eleven units of clinical pastoral education (CPE) and graduate certificates in marriage and family therapy and psychoanalysis.

Why This Book?

This book is an affirmation of field education and contextual learning as a methodology to help prepare spiritual leaders. Dr. George Sinclair, director of field education at Andover Newton Theological School (ANTS), considered one of the pioneers of field education, was obsessed with the work of preparing men and women for ministry. Years ago when I was a student and then in the 1980s when I was the assistant dean of students and director of recruitment at ANTS, his passion rubbed off on me. That passion grew when I served as a field educator in the 1990s in the field education program at Princeton Theological Seminary. Yet again my passion was stoked when the director of field education at New York Theological Seminary asked me in 1997 to give a lecture to educators in the field on supervisor certification. My passion to prepare men and women for ministry continued to be fueled during the time spent flying from Newark, New Jersey, to Raleigh, North Carolina, every other week to teach twelve doctor of ministry candidates who were enrolled at Drew Theological Seminary. Finally, in 2008 my passion found an institutional home at New Brunswick Theological Seminary, where I have served as director of field education, associate professor, and most recently acting dean of the seminary.

Colleagues have written and edited excellent books on the subjects of field education, contextual learning, and preparing spiritual leaders. Because this book is intended to be multifaith and diverse, it offers a wider range of perspectives. In addition, this book reflects the most up-to-date thinking by a team of international, cross-cultural, multifaith scholars and practitioners.

The challenge before us as theological educators remains to provide quality education, on-the-job training, contextual learning, supportive nurture, transformative experiences, and to teach people of faith the joys of being lifelong learners, especially those who have been called to serve as spiritual leaders. What complicates this task is the reality that seminaries are not the only avenues for learning how to do ministry. People have options and choices, both good and bad.

Clergy of all faiths are not the only ones to engage in ministry. The reality is we need to continue to ask the larger questions "How do we prepare persons who hold leadership positions in our faith-based institutions?" and "How do we groom the next generation of spiritual leaders?" Seminary is one answer. However, it is not the only answer. Seminaries are trying to answer the same questions. New economic and social realities challenge how seminaries prepare clergy and stay in step with the emergence of the army of lay leadership. Our communities' and trauma response efforts following disasters have taught us that we must collaborate with multiple faiths and work side by side with ordained and lay leadership. Disaster response work makes it clear that we cannot afford to live on our own geographic, social, political, or theological islands void of any meaningful interactions with other faiths. Ministry requires collaboration. What is the formula or key to effectively preparing a community composed of multiple faiths to do ministry? What universals can we extract?

Who Should Read This Book?

This book is multifaith and cross-cultural and offers an international team of contributors. Readers from various faiths and multiple cultures will find this book to be an excellent resource. Clergy, seminarians, faith-based executives, lay leaders, and people of faith can use this book to explore how to prepare spiritual leaders. We expect theological educators to use this book.

The book was written for clergy, lay leaders, and academics and aims to find content suitable for their needs. The contributors are sensitive to gender-specific terms. To be inclusive, in most cases, instead of the word "church," "temple," or "synagogue," we use the word "congregation." Instead of the word "religion," we use the broader term "spirituality." We expect people from various faiths will find universal truths and practical suggestions about the business of doing ministry and what some faith traditions call "contextual theology."

How to Use This Book

This book was not designed for you to read in one sitting from cover to cover. It was designed for people of various faiths to use as a teaching tool, as a conversation starter at retreats or congregational gatherings, and as a resource guide and educational textbook for seminarians, clergy, and people who hold leadership positions in faith-based institutions. You may find it helpful to read a chapter as needed to respond to a specific situation. It is a great text to read together as a multifaith group and then discuss various topics. Try reading select sections of the book to help address issues or concerns that you experience as a congregational leader. The book offers a number of evaluative tools to critique and check your own spiritual leadership practices or those of your congregation or other spiritual leaders.

Organization of the Book

Learning to Lead is divided into four sections to answer four questions. The contributors to the first section answer the question "What are the foundations of spiritual leadership?" The contributors of this section offer both solid theory and practical suggestions as to the psychology, mechanics, systems, friendships, and aspirations that drive spiritual leaders.

The second section answers the question "How do you evaluate spiritual leadership?" This section examines the practices of both individuals and congregations. The contributors to part II acknowledge the multitudinous changes in society along with the adjustments or outright changes required by individuals and congregations to stay current.

The third section explores the question "How do you care for others?" The contributors argue that pastoral care is the foundation for good spiritual leadership. In this section the reader is confronted with challenges that are both systemic and individual choices. It is here that the contributors examine the results of spiritual leaders who do harm to others. The contributors to part III lay out the issues along with sacred and secular solutions.

The fourth section answers the question "How do you collaborate with specific spiritual leaders?" This section is not meant to be an exhaustive treatment of the question, but rather a glimpse into how to work with specific faith groups. The contributors to part IV offer resources for further reading to provide more insights into their particular faith traditions.

Basic Assumptions

First, spiritual leadership values community and collaboration. We do not work alone. Our starting point of conversation or assumptions include that we:

- Find and engage good people who also love to do ministry.
- Invest in their success.
- Be available to offer feedback and help.
- Learn their strengths and limitations as well as our own.
- Practice good self-care.
- Never stop learning.
- Listen more than we talk.
- Lead with love.
- Embrace constructive criticism.
- Do not take ourselves too seriously.
- Laugh, dance, and keep the faith.
- Rely on family, friends, sages, elders, mentors, and humor to keep us sane or at least grounded.

All the while keep in mind that this is not about you. Our role is to help others to grow, succeed, and do effective ministry.

Second, it is a basic assumption of this book that both men and women were created to hold leadership positions in faith-based institutions. Exclusion from positions of spiritual leadership based on gender, race, class, or sexual orientation is a topic about which not all people of faith agree. Even among the contributors of this book there may not be a consensus. Nevertheless, a basic assumption of this book is that spiritual leaders collaborate with a wide range of people and faith-based organizations to bring healing, justice, and support to multiple communities.

Third, we are stewards of the earth. Good stewardship is green, environmentally friendly, socially responsible, and collaborative.

Fourth, there are universals in the practice of spirituality that hold us accountable and may be summed up as "Do no harm." To this end, what is important to know as a starting point in working with spiritual leaders is that both lay leaders and clergy of all faiths believe in the power of spirituality as an answer to the question "How do we think, behave, relate to others, and draw closer to our higher power?" In addition, both believe that there is a way to be human that honors the key concepts of their respective faiths. After those two beliefs you may find tons of differences among various faiths, lay leaders, and clergy, whether those differences are real, imagined, or created. This is not to dishonor or diminish the value of ordination for faiths (like my own) that ordain clergy and make a distinction between lay and ordained. Instead, we want to affirm that there are some universals in helping spiritual leaders develop the skills to lead.

Fifth, change is constant. Spiritual leaders must be equipped to acknowledge, critique, evaluate, lead, and embrace change. We must help faith-based institutions and individuals overcome their anxieties and unrealistic resistances to change. Thus, leadership must be adaptive. We often lead under pressure, within ongoing changes in circumstances.

Sixth, spiritual leaders are both born and made. Thus, we create educational opportunities and supervised on-the-job training for both lay leaders and clergy.

Seventh, spiritual leaders must understand the theories and practices of working with groups. So much of what we do as spiritual leaders involves groups, boards, interfaith gatherings, meetings, support ministries, teaching, rallies, banquets, public theology, and healing events. Some clergy (myself included) argue that our public worship is a form of group therapy. We find many of the curative factors from traditional group therapy in the worship experience. This is not to discourage anyone from going to group therapy with a licensed professional. We need both.

As the editor, I do apologize in advance for not offering a chapter on the theory and practice of groups. Know that there are numerous excellent books on the topic. You would do well to read a few or take a course on the subject. You cannot escape group work as a spiritual leader.

A Field Educator's Perspective

My observation over a lifetime is that our transformative experiences shape us as spiritual leaders. Allow me to further assert that spiritual leaders, both lay and clergy, may be born with certain "natural" leadership qualities. Nevertheless, it is a series of transformative experiences, which happen from birth and last over a lifetime, that mold us into the spiritual leaders we become. It is not one event or one seminar or one pivotal moment; instead, it is a lifetime of moments that find expression perhaps at a specific time or over a long period of time. The sum total of these transformative experiences both shapes us and drives us to do ministry in a particular context, at a particular time. These transformative experiences fall into four categories: passion, purpose, power, and partnerships. They are not linear. They are circular. They flow. There is a rhythm like a jazz musician playing improvisation. We learn the basics of the craft, and in concert with others we make music. Allow me to express a few thoughts about the four categories.

Passion

Passion is more than zeal. Passion is more than a deep interest in an activity or a perspective. Passion is more than an overly stated investment in a cause, a conversation, a creature, or an event. Passion is more than a romantic expression. Passion generates energy. Passion influences our choices. Passion colors our concerns over the consequences of our choices. Passion is the sum total of the life experiences that shape us and move us to act, think, and respond to situations in certain ways. Passion is our life history speaking through our actions. Passion is the system that formed us playing a symphony in harmony with our deepest emotions and most precious thoughts. Passion is the outcome of a lifetime of experiences waiting to explode once given the right set of conditions and circumstances. Passion attracts others. Passion polarizes. Passion by its very nature cannot be neutral or ho-hum. For this editor, learning to lead begins with passion. Dig deep into the life of any spiritual leader, and you will find a series of life events that led to his or her passion. Explore a leader's genogram (a map of one's genealogy) to realize that the passion was in his or her DNA.

Look at your own life history. What were the events and life experiences that drove you to do what you are doing or hope to do? Study the histories of leaders you admire. Read their biographies and autobiographies. Passion is the engine that drives us to act.

People follow spiritual leaders who express passion (ours and theirs) in either word or deed. Spiritual leaders with charisma or charm find their rootedness in passion. Passion is where we find our peace. Passion fuels our purpose.

Be it through teaching the Torah, leading morning prayers, helping domestic violence survivors, leading retreats, handling congregational finances, or preaching a sermon, we are driven by passion. Our spirit will not allow our passion to be hidden. It must find voice and be heard.

Purpose

The sales of Rick Warren's book *The Purpose Driven Life* made it clear that people are searching for their purpose. Armed with our passions, we seek avenues for our passions to be expressed. The end result is our passions find a cause, a situation, an organization, an institution, or people that provide us with a platform. As we express our passions, we find our purpose. We teach. We sing. We organize. We coach. We care for others.

We find our purpose and in so doing create sacred spaces to express our passions. Purpose also comes out of community. We seek and find others with similar passions. We analyze, evaluate, plan, and act out of our sense of purpose. Purpose is about doing.

Power

Imagine being in touch with your passions, thus forming your purpose, only to realize that you are void of any power to turn your passions and purpose into reality. We need power. Our contributors will give examples of the need for power to effect change, to lead people, and to make a difference. Power need not be abusive power over others, but power to do, accomplish, and be rooted in positive purposes to help others. Power gives permission to our purposes.

Power provides both the inner and the outer strength for spiritual leaders to fight evil in its various forms, systemic and individual. Power gives spiritual leaders the will to resist forces that are abusive, harmful, greedy, exploitive, manipulative, retaliatory, and intimidating. Power comes from prayer, meditation, fasting, and spiritual disciplines that bring us to a closer relationship with our higher being. Power comes from organized people with organized money. Power is the engine that helps spiritual leaders realize their goals, sometimes against great odds. Spiritual leaders are not against power. Spiritual leaders are against abusive power that harms others and destroys lives. Spiritual leaders must understand the effective use of power.

Partnerships

Disasters and community tragedies have forced many spiritual leaders to the realization that we must work together across faith traditions. Friday through Sunday we may find ourselves in different houses of worship; however, our real-time lived experiences throughout the week cry for multifaith collaboration. We need each other to survive. We do an injustice to our partnerships if we do not take the time to learn about the traditions, values, histories, dreams, successes, and challenges that are faced by those with whom we form partnerships. Learning to lead must involve and be heavily invested in collaborative partnerships.

Final Words

This book will enhance your ministry. We will answer the questions set forth in the four sections. Think of this as a handbook, a ready reference when needed, or a guide through the uncharted waters of theological education for the twenty-first century. We will celebrate with you as you discover and act on your passion, purpose, power, and partnerships.

Finally, we welcome your feedback, stories, successes, and challenges, and any opportunity to be in dialogue, be it written, verbal, or face-to-face. Read this book in good health. Peace!

PART I

What Are the Foundations of Spiritual Leadership?

1

Singing the Creator's Song in a Strange Land

Lisa Sharon Harper, MA, MFA

We sat in the office of New York Faith & Justice (NYFJ), an ecumenical antipoverty network in New York City. Flip-chart paper lined the walls. For the past hour NYFJ staff and volunteers had gleaned God's lessons on leadership at the end of a heavy year of organizing. At the top of the list, written in bold print and all caps: "Leadership is not about the leader." This was a striking lesson for my twenty-something and thirty-something staff, who grew up in the era of reality TV, watching shows like *The Apprentice*, *The Kardashians*, and *Dancing with the Stars*. In today's personality-driven world where celebrity is celebrated over substance, and money, fame, and power are desired more than character, it is easy to mistake the force of charisma for leadership.

These days even our governing bodies can feel more like reality TV stars rather than men and women engaged in the art of the possible. Across the nation, governors, state legislators, and members of the United States Congress are becoming famous for legislation less motivated by the desire to govern than by the desire to win ideological battles. These high-stakes battles are fought through the spin of twenty-four-hour cable news cycles with what seems to be little regard for how their rhetoric and policies will affect the actual lives of real people. State capitals across the country have witnessed shutdowns, sit-ins, and backroom deals that, in my opinion, have circumvented

3

the common good in order to press forward an ideological self-serving agenda. In 2011, Wisconsin governor Scott Walker pulled political pranks to pass legislation that effectively plundered Wisconsin's workers of their constitutional right to organize—a provision that protects the interests of citizens against exploitation. In Arizona and Alabama, in 2010 and 2011, respectively, the legislatures passed two of the most controversial immigration laws our nation has ever seen. It appeared as though it did not matter to these leaders that the majority of their electorate did not support their laws. Nor did it seem to matter that people made in the image of God were being played like pawns in an ideological game.

Likewise, the 2011 Arab Spring brought the ousters of Middle Eastern dictators, the likes of which the world has never seen before. These despots—placed and propped up by Western geopolitical powers—controlled their masses by military might and censored media. They played their own people like pawns in a high-stakes game of economic manipulation and exploitation. Ultimately, the autocrats lost.

What, then, is leadership? If not celebrity, if not the ability to guide the masses by the force of personality, might, or money, then what is godly leadership?

The biblical creation stories lay a valuable foundation of the concept of godly leadership. The creation story of Genesis chapter 1, written in the form of an epic poem, offers higher truths about the nature of our relationships with God, each other, the rest of creation, and the systems that govern us. The second creation story, found in Genesis chapter 2, offers a more intimate picture of the relationship between God and humanity and our role as ones exercising co-dominion with God.

Genesis 1 is written in the classic Hebraic seven-day structure of an epic poem. In the beginning, before anything or anyone is created, there is God—the ultimate leader—the one who creates all things and weaves all creation into an interdependent web of relationships. On the first three days, God creates order from chaos by separating light from darkness, day from night, and land from sea and sky. On the second three days, God fills each domain. God places the sun, moon, stars, and birds in the sky; fish and sea monsters in the deep; and plants and animals upon the earth.

To grasp the nature of godly leadership in Genesis, it is crucial to understand three words and phrases—image (*tzelem*), dominion (*radah*), and very good (*tov me'od*)—as they are used in the text itself. These words open windows through which we might see key goals and principles of leadership as well as vital biblical roles of leaders.

Early on the sixth day the Creator creates humanity in the image (*tzelem*) of God (Genesis 1:26). The word *tzelem* means "representative figure" and is the Hebrew equivalent of the Greek word *eikon*. In the Roman era, *eikon* was used to describe the image of the Caesars on coins or in the forms of statues or symbols at the entrances to cities. Wherever the coins were exchanged and wherever the statues stood, people understood, "Caesar rules here." In like manner, all humanity was made in the *tzelem* of God to be representative figures of Creator God. We were created such that wherever we stand, all creation would know, "God rules here."

This is a revolutionary claim! The original hearers of Genesis lived in an agrarian society where the elements were believed to be gods. Humans were at their mercy. And they played people like pawns in their self-serving games and ritual sacrifices. Similarly, kings were thought to be the only representative figures of the gods. Yet, the writer of Genesis 1 turns the world on its ear. The elements are *not* gods! Rather, they were created *by* God. And every single human is a representative figure of that very same God! Every single human is worthy of the dignity, respect, honor, and protection usually bestowed upon kings! Every life is sacred.

Then, in the same sentence, the writer reveals what it means to be made in God's image: "and let them have dominion." Thus, in the text, the ability to exercise dominion is intricately linked with what it means to be made in the image of God—what it means to be human. The converse is also true; if someone's ability to exercise dominion is hindered or denied, then the image of God in the person is diminished.

Controversy abounds in the quest to discern the meaning of the Genesis 1 word "dominion." Typically translated to mean "to rule over," as a king rules a kingdom, the biblical concept of dominion has been widely interpreted through the modern-era lens of Western imperialism, colonization, and domination of one individual, thought, or nation over another. "Dominion" has been misused and abused to justify all sorts of evil against fellow human beings and the land. The word does not have to be interpreted in this way and, I dare say, should not be interpreted this way if understood in context. Several things must be considered about God's call for humanity to exercise dominion to begin to understand the writer's use of the word. First, what did God's dominion look like? Second, what does the actual Hebrew word for "dominion" used in the text mean? Third, how are the parameters of human dominion different from those of God's?

If humanity is made in God's image, then our human dominion should also be in God's image. Our dominion should be a representation of God's kind of dominion. Throughout Genesis 1, Creator God (Elohim, which means "ruler," "Divine," or "true God") exercises dominion: Elohim speaks the world into being (Genesis 1:1). Genesis 1:2 says the earth was formless. The Hebrew word for "formless" is *tohu*. It means "confusion, emptiness, chaos." Elohim takes chaos and confusion and creates order. Elohim creates all things in relationship with each other. All of creation is provided for. The sun and moon let humans know when it is time to sleep and time to wake. The stars tell these agrarian people when to sow and when to reap the harvest. The light provides nutrients for vegetation. The vegetation provides food for animals. And the humans provide stewardship for all the rest of creation. They are not given dominion over each other, for only Elohim has that privilege in Genesis 1 and 2, before the Fall in Genesis 3. To boot, Elohim's kind of dominion is one that provides for all. Elohim's kind of dominion includes every created being in the act and responsibility to provide for the others. Elohim's kind of dominion does not exploit, does not pull power plays, does not seek its own good at the expense of others, and provides for the smallest creature as well as it provides for the most grand.

Also, Creator God's dominion is characterized by integrity. The Creator calls forth created beings to thrive on earth as they were created—not trying to be something they are not. The repeated phrase "after their own kind" offers a window into Elohim's value for integrity. The phrase is repeated each time God creates a new creature and commands it to multiply and fill the earth. The phrase is *not* a basis for racial, ethnic, or national separatism, as some have argued.[1] Rather, it is a charge for each created species to embrace itself as it was created, to agree with God that it was made well, and ultimately to thrive as itself. If human dominion is to be a representative likeness of God's, then it must be one characterized by love, care, equity, and integrity.

The Hebrew word used in this text for dominion is *radah*, which means "to tread down," but not to annihilation. In the context of this epic poem, it is helpful to imagine the picture. God has just spoken the land, trees, and vegetation into life and filled the planet with creatures, each species testing the boundaries of its territory, its power, its existence. The call to *radah* in this context is a charge to maintain the boundaries that God established for creation in the beginning. In the cultural context, the original hearers lived in an agrarian society that had great connection to land and place. They would likely have interpreted *radah* as a call to steward and care for the land—to maintain the well-being of the relationship between humanity and all the rest of creation. Thus, humanity—the last born in the family of God's creatures—is charged with the task to steward, to shepherd, to lead its older created siblings.

Thus, in a fundamental way, we were all created to lead. The writer of Genesis is so overcome by this truth that the poetic text breaks into song! "So God created humankind in God's *tzelem*; in the *tzelem* of God, God created them; male and female God created them" (Genesis 1:27). Men and women, all of us, were created in God's *tzelem*! All of us were created to exercise dominion—not just kings and not just men. For this is what it means to be made in God's *tzelem*. This is what it means to be human.

Finally, at the end of the sixth day, the author declares, "God saw everything that God had made, and indeed, it was very good" (Genesis 1:31). The Hebrew words for "very good" are *tov me'od*. The word *me'od* means "exceeding, might, forceful." The word *tov* means "good," but in Hebrew culture goodness was understood to reside in the ties between things, not in the objects themselves. Thus, the author of Genesis 1 was communicating to the original hearer that all relationships in creation were forcefully good. The relationship between God and humanity was forcefully good. The relationship between men and women was forcefully good. The relationship between humanity and itself was forcefully good. The relationship between humanity and the rest of creation was forcefully good, and the relationship between humans and the systems that govern us were forcefully good. Human leadership reflected God's kind of leadership, and love was the tie that bound all creation together and to its Creator. At its essence, this is a description of what the dominion of God looks like, what it smells like. At its core, this is a description of the biblical concept of *shalom*—holistic peace.

So, what can we glean about godly leadership from Genesis 1? Humans were created to lead. We are charged by God to lead in a way that reflects God's kind of dominion. God's dominion is characterized by integrity, reciprocity, provision for all, provision by all, and the establishment of systems that maintain the forceful goodness of all relationships. God's dominion results in the wellness of all relationships, including the relationship between humanity and its governing systems. God's kind of dominion is ever seeking *shalom*.

Genesis 2 presents a much more intimate picture of the creation story, the relationship between humanity and God, and a more detailed picture of human dominion. Rather than writing a sweeping epic poem, the author of Genesis 2 tells a story with central characters and a choice. The Genesis 2 writer paints the picture of an extravagant garden and YHVH (proper name of God) in the muck—the personal, named ruler who is the true God, with hands in the mud molding humanity. God's hands mold the human into being. God's kiss breathes the breath of life into the human's body. This is paradise. It is not a modern vision where humanity is bound by no constraints, experiences no want, has no needs or responsibilities. No, this is a different kind of paradise. God places the beloved human in the middle of Eden, and immediately God sets a boundary and gives humans work to do (or, using the language of Genesis 1, dominion to exercise)—in paradise.

God plants two trees in the middle of this vast garden: the tree of life and the tree of the knowledge of good and evil (Genesis 2:9). One tree in the entire garden holds a special distinction. There is a command attached to it: "You may freely eat of every tree of the garden; but of the tree of the knowledge of good and evil you shall not eat, for in the day that you eat of it you shall die" (Genesis 2:16–17). Humanity may eat of any tree in the garden, but not from the tree of the knowledge of good and evil. There are many theories about the nature of the tree of the knowledge of good and evil. Some believe the fruit of the tree itself was evil. Others believe the tree is a metaphor for sin. I do not. In the text, the only distinction of this tree is the fact that it has a command attached to it. The tree itself establishes the only "do not" in paradise. Why would a loving God place something in paradise that could ruin it all? Precisely because God is a loving God. I believe God placed this boundary in paradise because it was not enough that God loved humanity. We were created for a reciprocal love relationship with God. That kind of love requires the opportunity to trust and to choose in or out of a relationship with God. The tree of the knowledge of good and evil offered the opportunity for humanity to trust God or not. It offered the opportunity to choose God's way to wholeness, peace, and *shalom*, or not. It also reminded humanity that it was not the Creator. Humans are creatures in need of God—even in paradise. At its heart, humanity's response to God's command was the one thing in paradise with the potential to reveal the measure of the created's love for the Creator and to remind the creature of its desire for God.

What can we learn about God's kind of dominion from this intimate narrative of creation offered in Genesis 2? God is not a dictator or an authoritarian. God does not demand love or allegiance. Rather, in God's domain, deep, personal, reciprocal love is the tie that binds. That love requires trust and choice. Anything less will forfeit the umbrella of *shalom* provided for under God's dominion.

Genesis 2 also provides a richer view of human dominion. "YHVH God took the man and put him in the garden of Eden to till [*avad*] it and keep [*shamar*] it" (Genesis 2:15). Genesis 1 introduced us to *radah*, "dominion." The writer of Genesis 2 fleshes out what *radah* looks like. Human dominion over the land looks like *avad*, which means "to labor" or "to serve as subjects," and *shamar*, which means "to guard" or "to protect." So, dominion over the land in Genesis 2 is to serve and protect. What's more? *Avad* requires that the one exercising dominion sees the land not as subject to the leader, but rather as something sacred that the leader is subject to. For, in Genesis 2, to lead is to serve.

Likewise, when God creates the animals from the ground, God gives the job of naming them to the human: "So out of the ground YHVH God formed every animal of the field and every bird of the air, and brought them to the man to see what he would call [*kara*] them;

and whatever the man called [*kara*] each living creature, that was its name" (Genesis 2:19). *Kara* means "to call out," "to summon," or "to appoint." In this text, the writer is communicating that the work of naming was an act of service and care for the human, not subjugation or domination. Picture it: the human watches the parade of newly formed creatures pass by, and with each name the human summons the essence of the animal to live into its ordained identity. There is care and discernment in the act of calling out the identity of the animals.

What implications can we draw about the nature of human dominion from the intimate picture of creation drawn in Genesis 2? Leadership is not about the leader. Human dominion is about serving and protecting the common good. It is about calling forth the sacred purposes of God in our world and in each follower. Conversely, self-serving acts of leadership are not from God. Nor are acts or systems devised by leaders that deny followers the ability to realize and embrace their callings acts of ungodly dominion. As well, acts or systems that cause followers themselves to squash their own identities or callings to increase the perceived power or stature of the leader are examples of ungodly dominion. They break *shalom* and thus hinder the advancement of the dominion of God.

The man and woman of Genesis 2 encounter their own moment of truth when they choose to ignore YHVH's command not to eat from the tree of the knowledge of good and evil. They choose their own way to peace, their own way to fulfillment. They want to be like God through the acquisition of knowledge (Genesis 3:5). So, they eat. Immediately, one by one every relationship the writer of Genesis 1 declared very good only one chapter and one verse before, crashes to the ground. The man and woman decide to rule themselves. They come out from under the umbrella of God's dominion. *Shalom* is shattered, and what follows is the result.

The first relationship to fall is humanity's relationship with self. Shame enters the world on that day (Genesis 3:7). The next relationship to sour is humanity's relationship with God. They run and hide from God, for fear of God's intent toward them (Genesis 3:8–10). Next, the relationship between men and women is turned on its ear. Previously men and women exercised co-dominion over the rest of creation; now men will rule over women as a result of stepping out from under the umbrella of God's dominion (Genesis 3:16). In fact, for the first time in the book of Genesis we see a human ruling over another human. Next, the relationship between humanity and the rest of creation is shattered when the serpent and the land are cursed (Genesis 3:14, 3:17–18). Finally, humanity's relationship with life itself is broken. Death enters the world, as promised (Genesis 3:22–24). And that is not the end of it. Genesis 4 brings the break in families as Cain rises up against Abel and Lamech subjugates his two wives, named Adah, which means "ornament," and Zillah, which can be translated "shadow." Genesis 11 brings the break in lingual groups that precipitates the break in ethnic groups at the Tower of Babel. And finally, Genesis 14 brings the first wars—the systematic subjugation and annihilation of whole groups of people by force.

What can we learn about leadership and dominion from Genesis 3–14? The choices that leaders make have far-reaching repercussions beyond themselves. How we exercise dominion matters. If we choose God's way to peace, if we exercise dominion in the likeness of God, then we will reap the benefits: the wellness and healing of broken relationships. If we come out from under the cover of God's kind of dominion, then we are left with ourselves. Biblical scholar Walter Brueggemann reminds us that God is the author of *shalom*, not humanity. The best that human dominion without God can do is to piece together a partial peace.

Notes

1. See John Birch Society and other hate groups that claim a biblical basis for their racist beliefs. In the January 2011 article "Fulfilling Father's Campaign to Segregate Public Schools, Koch Groups End Successful Integration Program in NC," Think Progress reported these racial attitudes were still actively at work in American political life today. http://thinkprogress.org/politics/2011/01/12/138501/koch-segregation.

About the Contributor

Lisa Sharon Harper, MA, MFA, is a speaker, an activist, an author, an award-winning playwright, and a poet. Currently she is director of mobilizing for Sojourners, a national Christian organization committed to faith in action for social justice. Harper was the founding executive director of New York Faith & Justice, an organization at the hub of a new ecumenical movement to end poverty in New York City. Her writing has been featured in the *National Civic Review*, *God's Politics* blog, the *Huffington Post*, *Patheos*, *Urban Faith*, *Prism*, and *Slant33*, where she has written extensively on the role of government, tax reform, comprehensive immigration reform, health care reform, poverty, racial justice, and transformational civic engagement. Harper's faith-rooted approach to advocacy and organizing has activated people of faith across the United States and around the world to address structural and political injustice as an outward demonstration of their personal faith. She earned her master's degree in human rights from Columbia University in New York City. Her book *Left, Right, and Christ: Evangelical Faith in Politics* is coauthored by D. C. Innes (an evangelical Republican who is also a Tea Partier). In it, Harper and Innes explore their philosophies of government and business as well as six major issues the next generations of evangelicals must wrestle with to be faithful witnesses in the public square.

2

The Psychology of Learning to Lead

Jeffrey R. Gardere, PhD

Many of the chapters of this book examine how we prepare clergy individuals to become effective leaders from a spiritual or religious point of view. This chapter will provide a different take; it will give a psychological framework on the character traits, qualities, and skills that are essential to the learning process of becoming an effective and outstanding leader, not only in the secular world but also most importantly and specifically in the religious community. This is an important topic given that many people buy into the myths that only certain individuals are born to lead or that anyone can easily learn leadership skills by experience alone. Because of these misconceptions, individuals are assigned to or take on positions of leadership with no preparation or a theoretical framework. The result is absent, nondescript, or even disastrous leadership, with the collateral damage being uninspired, confused, or disillusioned workers, followers, or group members. The reality is that good leadership may come more naturally to some because of their attributes or personalities. But whether someone has a natural talent for it or not, anyone can become a good leader if he or she is willing to learn, earn, and practice the traits and principles of effective leadership.

The clergyperson who is an emerging leader or placed in a position of authority should not leave it up to chance or improvisation to reach the goal of competent, good, or even great leadership. If the leadership fails, the cost to the members or congregation may be too heavy. It may compromise their faith in their spirituality and in God. At the very least, we have witnessed that ministries with weak leadership do not grow in membership, struggle financially and spiritually, and eventually fail. Given the incredible responsibility of being a representative of God and caring for the souls of the members of the congregation, it is incumbent upon clergy to take their ministry and the development of their leadership skills very seriously. They must make a conscious, dedicated, and active effort to learn, study, and develop character traits that lead to effective and great leadership. Furthermore, they must continue to actively evolve and enhance those leadership skills throughout their lifetime as the spiritual leader of their flock.

Although secular and religious leaders share many of the same duties regarding those who are in their charge, there are also significant differences in their responsibilities and therefore how they lead. Secular leaders are often responsible for some but not all aspects of the welfare of their employees, members, stakeholders, or subordinates. For example, when employees leave the worksite and go home, their bosses are not responsible, nor do they concern themselves with their behavior. The clergy's responsibilities, on the other hand, are far more comprehensive. They must not only attend to the general welfare of their followers or congregation, but they must also do so within and outside the house of worship. This means they also have the ultimate responsibility of caring for the spirituality and souls of these individuals. In essence, clergy help them live righteously in this life on Earth and also help them maintain and strengthen their spirituality to better prepare for the afterlife with the Creator. Now that's a lot of responsibility! Therefore, given these differences, clergy should learn the basic character traits and skills that apply to both secular and clergy leadership. However, because of their additional and complex responsibilities, they must also acquire another set of character traits and skills that may be optional to secular leadership but are absolutely necessary and essential to spiritual/clergy leadership.

Given these distinctions, the character traits and skills needed to become an effective clergy leader are divided into two sections. The first section will provide the traits and skills essential to basic and effective leadership. They include the following:

- Positive mental attitude
- Inspirational

- Future oriented
- Fair and open-minded
- Imaginative
- Dependability
- Decisiveness
- Intelligence
- Commitment
- Energy and enthusiasm
- Motivational
- Flexible
- Competence
- Confidence
- Courage
- Charisma

In essence, these traits address essential leadership and management skills that should and can be utilized by both secular and clergy leaders to maintain a healthy and dynamic organization.

The second section will address traits and skills essential and specific to effective clergy leadership. Truth be told, these traits should be at the foundation of effective leadership for secular leaders as well. The reality is, they are demonstrated by some good or great secular leaders, but not all, especially political and financial leaders who have been discovered to be mired in official misconduct. However, these same traits should not be omitted or compromised by clergy (although they too have sometimes fallen short and found themselves involved in public scandal). They are at the foundation of the faith-based leadership skills that clergy must utilize to be successful leaders who effectively minister to their congregations and help them maintain and grow their spirituality. They include the following:

- Honesty
- Integrity
- Humility
- Unselfishness
- Empathy and compassion

- Love and forgiveness
- Self-actualization

Both sets of traits and skills come from Santa Clara University and the Tom Peters Group and were part of the "Character and Traits in Leadership" articles on Donald R. Clark's *The Art and Science of Leadership* website; however, I have further defined and refined them for this chapter. In addition, I have placed them in a framework that can be utilized specifically by clergy to effectively lead and carry out their comprehensive duties and responsibilities.

Traits and Skills Essential to Basic and Effective Leadership

Positive Mental Attitude

Group members want leaders who can look at any negative situation and reframe it into a positive one. These leaders will see the silver lining in any dark cloud and view any situation as the glass being half full instead of half empty. This is called a positive mental attitude. Having that positive mental attitude allows leaders to keep almost any situation, especially a difficult one, from spiraling out of control. This positive mental attitude will be infectious. Over time, leaders' positive outlook will begin to shape or even reshape the attitude of the company, team, or congregation. They will become more of a light in the dark, and the members will be more empowered and inspired to stay positive in the face of any negative situation. This positive mental attitude will also make clergy leaders less tentative and more hopeful and effective in ministering to those who face extreme adversities such as emotional or personal poverty or illness.

Inspirational

Strong leaders can inspire the members of their group by consistently demonstrating good works, even in the face of some of the most difficult situations. But as part of this leadership they must be willing to serve as a living example of positivity and a can-do attitude. They must also continue to aspire to new heights and take on new challenges in order to remain an inspiration to their followers.

Clergy leaders should be viewed as being inspirational to their congregations by having an active ministry that takes on the many different challenges of the religious and secular community. By applying their leadership skills, religious faith, and moral convictions to address any kind of adversity, they will inspire their congregations to do the same. Finally, actively demonstrating this quality in word and behavior will inspire the congregation to strengthen its faith in God.

Future Oriented

Good, progressive, and action-oriented leaders not only think about present tasks and goals, but they also adjust their goals and those of the group to meet emerging trends. Even further, they will have a vision of the future where both the leader and the organization can become dynamic trendsetters in their own right. It should not be forgotten, however, that the future thinking, trends, and goals must be a shared vision between the leader and the group or religious membership. In other words, the group must be able to buy into and contribute to the vision.

The Reverend Billy Graham is an example of a future-oriented leader who used radio to spread his ministry. Some of today's mega-churches and superstar pastors were future oriented in terms of their use of television and even the Internet to recruit and minister to their congregations.

Fair and Open-Minded

We are presently in a tumultuous era in our history where purely authoritarian leaders are being overthrown by their formerly loyal subjects, citizens, and followers. There are many reasons this is happening, including financial inequities, religious and political unrest, and human rights violations. In essence, these leaders did not listen to the people and fell out of step with the trends and direction of their nations. The lesson that can be learned here is that effective and *enduring* leadership utilizes the traits and principles of being democratic, fair, and open-minded. These traits will help leaders be more open and sensitive to the views, opinions, values, and ideas of all group members. Being fair and open-minded will allow leaders to understand the needs and concerns of the group or congregation, as well as develop a more participatory style. In turn, this will allow leaders and their organizations to continue to grow, change, and prosper.

Imaginative

Leaders and their groups often find themselves in difficult situations that require good, if not great, problem-solving skills. Effective leaders cannot yield or give up on what may seem to be a daunting or impossible situation. As the leaders of the group, they must and are depended upon to act and do the best they can to solve the problem. They must use their initiative and challenge themselves to reach into their imagination, think outside of the box, and figure out a solution that may have evaded the organization or group. They must also use their leadership skills to inspire their team to also tap into their own imaginations or creative thinking and craft solutions together. This will make for a stronger, more dynamic group. For the clergy leader, imagination is often spurred by meditation, prayer, and the reading of scripture.

Dependability

Group members or congregants may come and go. They may not live up to their responsibilities or even go off task. But if nothing else, it is the responsibility of a leader to be consistent and dependable. For clergy, this dependability takes many forms, including fulfilling all leadership duties, and being present to help with any crisis, especially a spiritual one. Congregants should be able to count on their spiritual leaders even if they cannot count on friends or family members. The house of worship should be the first and last refuge.

Decisiveness

The leader must be the catalyst of the group or congregation, the one who decisively makes things happen and spurs the members into action. Leaders must be willing to make well-informed but definitive decisions when others are mired in indecision. But again, by taking the initiative and making the tough decisions, leaders will also inspire and teach the group to take the initiative to be more decisive in their own lives.

Intelligence

This does not mean that leaders have to have the highest academic credentials, but it does mean that they should be a "thinker" who stays informed about the community and world events. By actively increasing their awareness, they should increase their powers of discernment to be able to see the big picture, while those around them may be shortsighted or stuck on petty details. Religious leaders who stay informed and consider the political, financial, emotional, and spiritual issues of the day, are better able to improve the culture and welfare of the group or congregation.

Commitment

Good leaders should be completely committed to the mission of leading and taking on tasks as they occur. And, of course, they should also be completely invested in the time and commitment it will take to successfully fulfill these activities. But just as important, they should be completely committed to the members, especially if they expect the members to be committed to the ministry.

Unlike secular leaders who may show commitment to a "job," clergy leaders must show commitment to their avocation, spirituality, and religion. In other words, it's not about a job; it's about a lifelong and spiritual commitment to their mission, congregation, and God.

Take note: A leader should never take on a position of authority while eyeing another job in the distance. Those in the group will see themselves as nothing more than a stepping-stone for the leader. Certainly this will not engender any trust or even commitment from the group toward the leader and the leader's mission.

Energy and Enthusiasm

Having enthusiasm and energy is a vital part of being a "dynamic" and inspirational leader. These two qualities reflect and enhance many other leadership qualities, including commitment, creativity, decisiveness, positive mental attitude, courage, and charisma. Enthusiasm and energy demonstrate that the leader is primed and ready to take on any challenge and has the physical and emotional stamina to see it through. These qualities in clergy indicate that they are excited about leading, caring for, and working with their followers, but most of all that they are excited about worshipping with and being in the "faith" with them.

Motivational

The best leaders are motivational leaders. Still, there are some effective leaders who are not necessarily motivational. Often their achievements are not trumpeted or exciting, but are simply effective. Thus, they may be competent but not motivational. The good clergy leader should make every effort to be motivational by demonstrating positive initiatives and behaviors that will spur the congregation to their own positive actions. As well, believing in something that some may consider to be esoteric, such as God and spirituality, requires faith. The good clergy leader can be more effective in spurring the members of the congregation to increase their faith by motivating them to pray and worship, instead of commanding them to do so.

Flexible

There are three forms of leadership: authoritarian, participatory, and delegative. The authoritarian leader rules absolutely, with no real input from the group. The participatory leader is very involved with the group and believes in a team approach. The delegatory leader will take a more hands-off approach and allow the group more independence and autonomy in doing the work. Research has shown time and again that the most effective leaders will be flexible enough to move through and incorporate all three aspects of these leadership styles given the needs of the organization or the task at hand. As part of this flexibility, effective leaders will also be open to compromise and cooperation in their approach in order to be more participatory with the group or congregation and be inclusive of their ideas. In turn, this will result in a harder working and more empowered group. The remaining traits are what I call "The Four Cs of Effective Leadership."

The Four Cs of Effective Leadership

Competence

Effective leaders must have a command over whatever subject they are discussing, tackling, or making a decision on. Otherwise, their incompetence will cause members of the group to lose confidence in their abilities and leadership and eventually stop following or listening.

Confidence

Strong leaders must believe in their abilities, actions, and decisions. Without this confidence they will not be able to assert their positions or push through their ideas to accomplish or resolve a task, which may result in their being ineffective and weak leaders.

Courage

There are many things in life that may cause anxiety or fear. However, leaders must be willing to step into that arena and experience anxiety, especially when they are stepping out of their comfort zone. If they cannot muster the courage to take on the unknown, then both they and their members will soon become stagnant.

Charisma

Many people believe that you can only be born with charisma, that chemistry that causes others to be attracted to your qualities, in this case your standing as a leader. I firmly believe, however, that charisma can be developed by constantly working on and exhibiting many of the principles, traits, and qualities that are a part of dynamic leadership. For example, leaders who can *confidently* and *courageously* step in and take charge, providing the right direction with *competent* advice, based on intelligence and ethics, are leaders who are *charismatic*.

I believe that charisma is especially important for clergy leaders who want to attract, grow, and retain their congregations. Sadly, the competition for souls is not just between the devil and God but also between religions, denominations, and houses of worship! The clergy who have developed charisma as part of their leadership skills are the ones who appear to have the larger and more successful ministries. Because of their charismatic leadership, they are able to command more attention from congregants and potential congregants, and generate more publicity.

Traits and Skills Essential and Specific to Effective Clergy Leadership

Honesty

Honesty is perhaps one of the most essential qualities of a good leader. Honest leaders must not be deceptive but must strive to be truthful in actions and words. Honest leaders must be sincere, and their motivations must never be deceitful, exploitive, or self-serving.

For spiritual leaders, honesty is not an option; it is mandatory, given that they are considered to be an earthly representative of God.

Therefore, they must follow both secular and spiritual laws and be honest not only in the eyes of all people but also in the eyes of God.

The end result of these different aspects of honesty is that people will follow and believe in a leader they can trust.

Integrity

The perfect partner trait to honesty is integrity. Here the leader must consistently live by and display sound moral character and ethical principles. Again, it goes back to the issue of trust. People will follow and work for a leader and be invested in the mission if they believe the leader operates from the highest heights of personal and professional integrity and is not corrupted or corruptible.

Honesty and integrity may be excused or overlooked for some secular and political leaders as long as they are extremely effective or powerful and benefit some of those they lead, especially the special interest groups. The spiritual community is much less tolerant of dishonest or immoral clergy leaders, primarily because religions hold, at their foundation, the earnest avoidance of sinful behaviors and immorality. But just as important, they do not want their trust violated by clergy leaders whom they often hold in the highest esteem.

For clergy leaders, having integrity will cement the trust of their members and will allow them to be a powerful role model who can inspire morality and spirituality.

Humility

Good clergy leaders clearly understand that to be true to their calling, they must not only "serve" God, but also must balance their authoritative status with the humility of "serving" their congregation and the community.

Secular law enforces the idea that we are all created equal and therefore are equal by law. However, the contradiction in many workplaces is that the CEO and others in positions of management and leadership are superior to their subordinates and are accorded much more money and privilege. That is part of the reason that we are seeing class wars not just around the world but also in the United States. Religion/spirituality, on the other hand, reinforces the idea that we are all created equal and are equal in the sight of God. But unlike in the secular world, this message remains consistent in that clergy leaders must remain humble and constantly remind themselves and the congregation that despite their exalted position, they should not exalt themselves above God or their own congregation. They may be the spiritual leaders, but just like the members of the congregation, they are only human and have the same temptations, weaknesses, sins, and failings. They understand the struggle to stay strong in the faith and do what is right. Clergy and congregants are in a struggle *together* to increase their faith and do right by God. Although clergy have the position of authority over the group, they understand that they must be role models and humbly serve the congregation, so that they in turn can learn to serve others in the name of God. Humility and service not only keep religious leaders grounded and more accessible to the group, but they also keep them more focused on service and obedience to God.

Unselfishness

Effective clergy leaders must continually demonstrate the quality of unselfishness in their actions and duties, for many reasons. First and foremost, most religions believe that the path to God is by giving of yourself unselfishly through caring and ministering to those who are less fortunate. These acts will increase your spirituality and bring you closer to God. Therefore, spiritual leaders must dedicate much of their time to ministering to the less fortunate in the congregation and community. The congregants will do the same because they will follow the examples of the clergy leader.

Secondly, leaders who visibly put the needs of their members before their own will always have the trust and love of their congregation.

Finally, many religions and especially the houses of worship believe in and survive through tithing. The principle of tithing is that in order to be blessed by God with financial and other types of prosperity, you must prove your love to God by tithing and giving your time and effort to the religious organization or house of worship. Thus, it only makes sense that if spiritual leaders expect the congregation to tithe to the house of worship, they must be willing to do the same, in time, effort, and giving money back to the organization.

Empathy and Compassion

Good clergy leaders must demonstrate empathy and compassion in dealing with congregants who may have all sorts of emotional, financial, medical, chemical abuse, and of course spiritual problems or issues. To be most effective and responsive to their followers, clergy leaders must substitute value judgments and frustration with empathy and compassion, no matter how disappointed they may be with congregants' issues, problems, and weaknesses. In fact, by treating people as adults who need help, instead of as children who should be punished, clergy empower congregants not to blame or condemn themselves, giving them more psychological and spiritual energy to do better and assist in their own intervention.

Love and Forgiveness

Up to this point I have not encountered any religion/spirituality that does not emphasize the importance of love and forgiveness, despite whatever failings a person may have. Effective clergy leaders never forget this tenent, and whether soft or strict with a congregant, they should always demonstrate the principle of love and forgiveness. In turn, that congregant will do the same for someone else. By the way, this is not only a religious tenent but a psychological one as well. Study upon study has shown that love and forgiveness emotionally benefits not just those who receive it, but even more so those who practice it.

Self-Actualization

The process of self-actualization is necessary for human beings to evolve in a positive and productive direction. Some people simply call it maturation; others call it personal evolution. I see it as climbing another emotional or psychological step toward reaching our personal and spiritual potential for greatness. The process of self-actualization—knowing oneself, knowing where one is going, and striving for personal and spiritual excellence—is a necessary process toward becoming a great clergy leader. Part of the clergy leader's mission is to help the membership reach personal and spiritual self-actualization, in order to live a more righteous and religious life and grow closer to God. It will be almost impossible for clergy leaders to accomplish this noble task, as well as effectively lead and minister, if they are not actively and continually attempting their own psychological and spiritual self-actualization.

How Can Clergy Develop Leadership Qualities, Traits, and Skills?

Clergypersons can learn the general traits and skills essential to effective leadership through reading and attending workshops, conferences, classes, and institutions of higher learning specializing in management degrees. They can also learn the traits and skills essential and specific to effective clergy leadership, in the same manner, as well as by attending religious institutions and seminaries. However, the traits that are specific to clergy leadership—honesty, integrity, humility, unselfishness, self-discipline, empathy, compassion, love, forgiveness, and self-actualization—also develop and become more meaningful and powerful over time. This process develops by learning, maturing, and self-actualizing from life and spiritual experiences that come from conflict, triumphs, mistakes, and failures. Thus, clergy must continually self-analyze and find positive emotional and spiritual meaning through day-to-day personal and professional experiences—the good, the bad, and the ugly. These life lessons will help them grow emotionally and spiritually, in order to develop and utilize these leadership traits and skills that help them survive and thrive, now and in the future. In addition to being more mature and self-actualized, they will be wiser and more spiritual in utilizing these same traits to minister to their members and become more effective and inspirational leaders. As a natural consequence, they will encourage their religious members also to self-actualize and grow in their faith to their organization and to God.

The Principles of Leadership

In addition to the study, acquisition, and execution of leadership traits and skills through self-growth and service to the followers and membership, there are the principles of leadership that clergy must incorporate into their leadership/management style to continue the process of becoming a more effective leader. The following are the "Principles of Leadership" that have been established by the US Army and that I have adapted to help clergy as they learn to lead:

Principles of Leadership for Clergy

- **Know yourself and seek self-improvement:** Of course you can seek self-improvement through all the methods I have discussed in the chapter, including continual study, training, and service. But you can also avail yourself of psychotherapy if you want to truly know yourself and how your life experiences have impacted your perceptions, work, relationships, spirituality, and leadership style. This knowledge can help you be more effective in working toward positive outcomes in your personal and professional life. As well, if you are more emotionally stable, it will be easier for you to develop and grow into being a more effective leader.

- **Know human nature and know your congregants:** Learn and study as much as you can about the nature and psychology of individuals and the dynamics of groups. Know the likes and dislikes of your congregants as well as some general aspects about their overall personalities. This will not only make it easier to minister to their needs, but knowing that you have taken the time to care about them in this way will also bring the group or membership closer to you and to one another.

- **Keep your group members informed:** With any kind of leadership, whether secular or religious, it is important to have effective and open communications with your group members. The leader who has good communication skills will always be up-to-date with whatever may be happening with the group and can address it right away.

- **Develop a sense of responsibility in your members:** As a leader, you must make sure the group members understand that you cannot do the work alone. Although you may direct and certainly should delegate, you expect a group effort. It is important that you hold every single member of the group responsible for their own actions and assigned tasks. Eventually, this will develop the sense of responsibility of the group members, resulting in a stronger and more independent congregation.

- **Ensure that tasks are understood, supervised, and accomplished:** To make sure tasks are accomplished, you must (1) be very clear in your communications as to what must be done and the specific result you expect, (2) provide supervision without being controlling or overbearing, and (3) set timelines for completed tasks.

- **Provide praise and positive reinforcement:** As an effective and energetic leader, provide as much praise and positive reinforcement as possible to your group members as they achieve individual successes and complete assigned tasks. Following this leadership principle will help you develop a reputation of being a positive and loving leader instead of a difficult or sour disciplinarian.

- **Train as a team:** Not only should you be going to workshops and classes to become a better leader, but you should also arrange for group workshops or classes for your members so that they can be trained in topics or areas that would enhance their competence and education, personal happiness, and spirituality. Training as a team will result in more group cohesiveness and a cooperative atmosphere and culture.

- **Use the full capabilities of your members and organization:** Establish that constant effort to discover and understand the overt and hidden talents of your group members. Then utilize those talents for the greater good of the group. This will result in your organization being more effective, more fluid, and certainly much more creative. Your individual members will feel recognized, valued, and more essential to the group.

Faith and Prayer: The Glue That Binds the Character Skills of Effective Leadership

In closing, if I have not stressed it enough, then let me stress this now: though this chapter is written from primarily a psychological knowledge base and point of view and utilizes general/secular leadership principles, the indisputable fact remains that an essential component of being an effective clergy leader is the spiritual bread and butter—faith and prayer!

Faith and prayer are not only the direct connection to God, but they are also the glue, the *force majeure* that can help the clergyperson develop, practice, understand, and stay true to the character skills and principles needed to make the lifelong transformation to being an effective and dynamic spiritual leader, a living embodiment of the Word of God.

Further Reading

Ngaro, Vaka. *To Know Christ, and to Make Him Known*. Rarotonga, Cook Islands: Takamoa Theological College, 2011.

Ridley, Matt. *Nature via Nurture: Genes, Experience and What Makes Us Human*. New York: HarperCollins, 2003.

Santa Clara University and the Tom Peters Group, "Traits of a Good Leader." Character and Traits in Leadership." In *Donald R. Clark, The Art and Science of Leadership* (2004). www.nwlink.com/~donclark/leader/leadchr.html.

US Army Handbook. *Military Leadership*. June 1973.

About the Contributor

Jeffrey R. Gardere, PhD, better known as America's psychologist, is one of the most widely sought-after experts in the field of mental health. In addition to having a private practice in Manhattan, he has garnered a reputation as being a top motivational and keynote speaker and empowerment and media coach. Dr. Gardere is an assistant clinical professor at Touro College of Osteopathic Medicine in New York City. He is also the host of *Dad Camp* (formerly on VH1), now on Twist TV in Canada, the chief contributor to HealthGuru.com, and is the wellness director for the Philip Stein Company. He is a contributor to NBC's *Today Show*, MSNBC, and the FOX Network. Dr. Gardere is the author of *Love Prescription* and the coauthor of *Practical Parenting* with Montel Williams, the Emmy award–winning TV talk show host. His first book, *Smart Parenting for African-Americans: Helping Your Kids Thrive in a Difficult World,* has been lauded as being "necessary for raising African-American children in today's society" (*Black Issues Book Review*).

3

The Universal Tools of Effective Leadership

Michael Gecan, BA

Although thousands of articles and books have been written about leadership—both in the broader public arena and in religious institutions—there is still a great deal of confusion and much misunderstanding about what leaders really *do*. The most practical way to test this out is to ask clergy and other leaders in religious institutions to look at their calendars and honestly report on what is written in them.

If the calendar is filled with group meetings, committee meetings, administrative work, and hours spent sending and responding to e-mails and other electronic messages, then we ask people how in the world they can operate with focus and impact in an increasingly chaotic and volatile world when they are not using any of the four tools of effective leadership that we believe are critical.

This challenge is issued in a context. And part of that context is contrasting what we call bureaucratic or maintenance organizations with relational organizing.

The bureaucratic organization has many physical structures (buildings, facilities, offices, and the like), many programmatic or procedural structures (committees, programs, services, meetings), and plenty of paper. It is not that any one of these characteristics is, in and of itself, negative. What is negative is when these characteristics represent what people consider to be the core of the organization, while ignoring other important qualities.

The relational organizing culture is very different. First and foremost, it is grounded in a fierce commitment to leadership—finding, engaging, training, mentoring, challenging, and supporting new and existing leaders. Leaders are defined, most basically, as people who are able to attract followers and produce those followers consistently—not talkers, not charismatic activists, not those with advanced degrees from prestigious institutions, not media darlings. Second, this culture regularly asks the radical questions: What is our business or mission? And who are our customers or constituents? Third, this culture tries out and tests partial or preliminary answers to these questions. It is not afraid of a rhythm of trial and error, using these experiences to arrive at good answers and new avenues of ministry and mission.

In a relational culture, the leaders are constantly using four tools:

- **Individual meetings**: which is by far the most important tool and the least used
- **Power (relational) analysis**: of both the institution and the broader community
- **Teaching and training**: which is used somewhat, but too narrowly
- **Action and evaluation**: which is also used, as in liturgy, but also narrowly

Individual Meetings

An individual meeting is a face-to-face, one-to-one meeting, in someone's home or apartment or workplace or local coffee shop, that takes about thirty minutes. The purpose of the meeting is not chitchat, whining, selling, gossip, sports talk, data collection, or therapy. The aim of the meeting is to initiate a public relationship with another person. Now, this seems so basic and so old-fashioned that many of you are wondering what we are talking about here. We are suggesting an approach to others that Dietrich Bonhoeffer, the great Lutheran theologian, described in this way:

> The first service that one owes to others in the fellowship consists in listening to them.... Those who cannot listen long and patiently will always be talking past others, and finally will no longer even notice it.... The death of the spiritual life starts here.... Brotherly

pastoral care is distinguished from preaching ... by the obligation of listening.[1]

If the death of the spiritual life starts in talking past others so frequently that you "finally will no longer even notice it," then the birth of the spiritual life starts in the individual meeting—in listening to the other person.

This is the truly radical act of effective organizing—not a slogan or a demonstration. Not an e-mail blitz or PowerPoint presentation. The commitment to listening to others means that the leaders who initiate them operate on the basis of several important assumptions.

The first assumption is that the other person is well worth listening to. The late political philosopher Bernard Crick described this as having a belief in the affirmative individual—that most people, most of the time, will do the right thing, if given the opportunity. So the very act of calling someone up and setting up an individual meeting with them, of going to their home and listening to them, of asking them what they think about the community or congregation or country, how they see the future, what hopes and dreams they have, where they've come from and how they see themselves five years in the future, is an act of recognition. You are saying to that person: you have value, ideas, dreams, plans, lessons, and insights that are well worth listening to.

The second assumption is that the person initiating the individual meeting—organizer, pastor, rabbi, imam, veteran leader—understands that the time devoted to individual meetings is more important than time spent in more conventional activities. "All real living," the great philosopher Martin Buber said, "is meeting." The initiator knows that the new dynamic created by meeting and relating to another person is rich with opportunity and possibility. The congregation isn't mostly in the building or staff or programs already in place. The congregation isn't in the head of the leader or in the mannerisms of the hierarchy. The congregation lives and grows in the interaction between existing and new leaders and members—in the very act of doing the individual meeting.

When a young assistant rabbi arrived in his new congregation recently, he started his ministry by doing nearly one hundred individual meetings. He sat in on other meetings and activities. He got a feel for the life of the synagogue. But the action that told him the most about the congregation—and told the congregation a great deal about him—was the fact that he spent many evenings in their homes and apartments, meeting face-to-face and one-to-one. He knew his congregants, and they knew him, much better after three months than many congregations know their new staff after several years. His sermons were spoken *to* specific people and their specific struggles and concerns, not to some generic congregation in some generic place. It's not that he used anyone's name. He didn't need to. People heard him talking directly to them, based on what he had absorbed in his initial round of individual meetings. He wasn't talking *past* others. He was talking to them and with them.

The third assumption, hinted at in the act of doing individual meetings but only proved over time, is that the corporate identity of the congregation remains in formation, that the newest member, the most recent arrival, is invited to join in the ongoing creation of the evolving local community. The relationship is not one-way, unilateral, provider to customer or client, but two-way, reciprocal, and mutual. This assumption is easier to convey when the congregation *is* relatively new, when it is in the first thirty or more years of its existence. The explosion of new evangelical churches in the past three decades is in part a product of the "burst of energy" that sometimes occurs when an institution is born and begins to grow at a rapid rate. More than 1,250 such churches, some as large as small American cities, have formed and developed during this period. The challenge to them now will be to maintain the sense of experimentation and outreach that characterized their early years. The tendency to mature, to become more bureaucratic and programmatic, to become formed, fixed, and no longer in need of large numbers of new members will tempt these congregations as it did more mainline religious bodies.

These three assumptions are what ideologues, advocates, and bureaucrats have long forgotten, if they ever considered them. The ideologue, left or right, knows all the answers and just wants the rest of the world to realize that, to fall in line, to swallow whole the analysis or platform or doctrine and parrot back the party line. The advocate knows all the answers too, and wants to speak for others, not listen to others, not wait for others to develop the ability and the skill to voice their own concerns. And the program director wants to deliver the service—the food or clothing or housing voucher—without getting to know the person who walks in the door, without asking what other aspects of their lives are working or have worked, without challenging the person to do as much for themselves as humanly possible before asking for help.

While the thirty-minute, face-to-face individual meeting is by far the most effective way to initiate and deepen a public relationship, there is a growing body of evidence supporting even more basic, more limited forms of person-to-person contact. Two Yale professors, Donald P. Green and Alan S. Gerber, have been analyzing different methods of engaging new voters. Their book *Get Out the Vote! How to Increase Voter Turnout* (Washington, DC: Brookings Institution Press, 2004) shows that two of the most heavily used approaches— persistent e-mail blitzes and computerized robo-calls—are infinitely expensive. That means there is no proof that an unlimited amount of money spent on these strategies yields the desired result: more voters. A call from a paid stranger (often from another part of the country, with a different accent than the person called) yields one new vote for every $200 spent. A call from a person in the same area as the person called costs approximately $35 per new vote. And a series of three visits from an area resident to a potential voter's home, where there is a direct, face-to-face interaction between the voter worker and the potential voter, is by far the most effective method—costing $19 per additional voter. We are not recommending this as an alternative or substitute for the in-depth individual meeting and long-term relationship building described earlier. But there are lessons here for a typical congregation.

Instead of sending out e-mails or relying on announcements in bulletins or remarks from the pulpit, it would be far better to put together a team of people interested in an event or an activity who would commit to contact ten or fifteen congregants each and then, before or after a service or other meeting, would take the time to greet each congregant, to describe the event that is coming up, and to invite them personally. It would also be helpful and respectful to thank each person directly who attends the event and to ask them for their thoughts and reflections about it. This is basic, minimal, but rarely done. Most institutions rely on indirect, wholesale, and often technological approaches, rather than the old-fashioned, person-to-person direct request.

Power (Relational) Analysis

Many leaders wander around their congregations, their communities, and their cities without any clear picture of the relational terrain. A basic understanding of which leaders have followings and influence, how they relate to one another, and who determines which decisions are made and how money is spent is called a power analysis. At bottom, it is an understanding of the way key leaders in institutions relate and how those institutions function in the real world.

Not to have this map—objective, visible, changing as relationships change—is an invitation to get lost and stay lost. For example, in some mosques, the imam is both the spiritual and the operational leader. There may be a board, and the imam may relate to it in various ways, but he's clearly in charge. If you want to work well with this particular mosque, you had better understand this and figure out how to respect him and relate to and through him. In another mosque, the imam may be the spiritual leader, but the president of the board may be the operational leader, and three or four key members of the board may be key supporters of the president. In that case, obviously, a relationship with the president is critical, while showing respect for the spiritual role of the imam would be important. In black church settings, some congregations are pastors' churches, some are deacons' churches, while still others are steered by several families with deep followings in the community.

Unfortunately, instead of a power analysis, many people operate through their own preconceptions of how institutions *should* function, or they engage in wishful thinking, or they accept the stereotypes or abstractions peddled by others. In organizing parlance, people remain in the world as they think it should be, rather than taking the time and investing the energy to decipher how a congregation operates at this particular time, in this particular place, in the world as it is.

It's also important to understand how each city and region developed, how its culture was created and evolved. For example, in the Midwest, clergy or organizers should read a few key books: *Nature's Metropolis*, by William Cronon; *Caught in the Middle*, by Richard Longworth; *Boss*, by the late Mike Royko; and *The New Chicago*, by a group of DePaul University professors. Of course, one could think of many more excellent accounts of the history, politics, and economics of the region, but just these four books would help someone *locate* himself or herself in a city. In New York City, you might read *The Island at the Center of the World*, by Russell Shorto; chapters from *Gotham*, by Wallace and Burroughs; chapters from *The Power Broker*, by Robert Caro; and *City for Sale*, by Barrett and Newfield. The point is that the people walking into any church, synagogue, or mosque all live in time and in space—in places and periods shaped by events and geography. A working timeline and a practical social and political map are critical to anyone who wants to understand them and who hopes to move with them into the future.

Teaching and Training

Almost every religious institution takes seriously the task of teaching its members about doctrines and traditions. But very few institutions take the time to instruct members about how to master the basic tools of leadership in the institution. In the Roman Catholic setting, there is a Rite of Christian Initiation, which prepares someone seeking to join the church with an understanding of basic tenets and beliefs, but there is no rite of leadership initiation. What should a leader learn to operate as effectively as possible in the congregation?

A curriculum of leadership initiation and development would include the following:

- How to start and build public relationships
  - How to do effective individual meetings
  - How to remain public and avoid private-type issues
  - How to probe other leaders and avoid prying

- How to run effective public meetings
  - Why one hour is plenty of time for an excellent meeting
  - Why the meeting is not an end in itself—which means that the work before and after the meeting are more important

- How to design actions and reduce "groups"
  - How to break down problems into issues that can be addressed
  - How to design actions that get reactions
  - How to end what isn't working and go back to the drawing board

- How to create a set of focused campaigns and avoid scores of de-energizing activities
- How to do a power analysis of a social or institutional environment before acting
- How to identify and align new allies
- How to create and sustain a relational organization and limit the bureaucratic demands on leaders

The time and energy of leaders are a congregation's most precious commodities. But most voluntary organizations don't equip their leaders to use their time and energy effectively. Many savvy leaders sense this and either stop leading or limit their leading after a while. It is no small miracle that many people have remained as engaged as they have. With some basic and early preparation, they could—and will—become much more effective and satisfied leaders. And their institutions will begin to reap the full benefit of the insights and initiative that they bring to the public arena.

Action and Evaluation

While there may be a great deal of activity in a congregation—many committees with full schedules of meetings, events, luncheons, and the like—there is often very little focused *action*. The weekly liturgy may be the exception—perhaps the only exception—in a large majority of institutions. But even that action may take place at two or three or even more times, so that the members of the congregation do not even do that together. As a result, most congregations never become more than the sum of their parts. Or, in the worst cases, the parts become more important to people than the whole. The committee, the clique, the service that you and your friends attend become the first priority. Any threat to that from other parts of the congregation can be met with fierce resistance and can create resentments. The challenge for all institutions is how to act together at times, so that all leaders and staff are focused on the same goal, are pulling in the same direction, and are learning from the same experience. Designing meaningful action—with leaders, based on the stories heard in individual meetings, firmly grounded in an analysis of

the power dynamics of a community or city, and preceded by training that equips leaders to succeed and learn—is the fourth and final
tool of effective leadership.

Healthy congregations use these tools creatively, not sequentially,
and adapt them to their own context. They stop setting up more and
more committees and having more and more meetings. They relate,
learn, act, and reflect on their actions.

Notes

1. Dietrich Bonhoeffer, *Life Together: A Discussion of Christian Fellowship* (New
York: HarperCollins, 1954), 97–98.

About the Contributor

Michael Gecan, BA, is codirector of the Industrial Areas Foundation
(IAF) and a community organizer. He was trained in part by Saul
Alinsky. Gecan is lead organizer for East Brooklyn Congregations and
other New York–based organizations as well as the executive director
of United Power for Action and Justice, a Chicago-based IAF affiliate.
Gecan spent two decades wrestling with New York politicians in an
impassioned effort against all odds to build three thousand new homes.
His book, *Going Public: An Organizer's Guide to Citizen Action*, tells
how organized citizens can, with discipline and dignity, outmaneuver
bureaucracies and generate change. Gecan's vision of the richness of
community life and the value of public action has roots in the rough
Chicago neighborhood where he was raised.

4

Healthy Clergy, Healthy Congregations, and Healthy Communities

Tanya Pagán Raggio-Ashley, MD, MPH, FAAP

Physical, emotional, and spiritual well-being is profoundly impacted by the manner in which clergy, congregations, and the greater community interact and care for one another, as well as the environment in which they live, work, play, and pray. Healthy clergy, healthy congregations, and healthy communities are achievable by collaborating to improve our environmental, social, and living conditions.

Defining Healthy Clergy, Healthy Congregations, and Healthy Communities

How do you define health, healthy clergy, healthy congregations, and healthy communities? Where is health addressed in your spiritual text? Take a moment and write down your thoughts. If you are in a group, consider sharing them with one another.

There is no secret to becoming healthy. Some call it the rhythm of life. Others refer to it as yin and yang, and many feel it is rooted in balance. The challenge is to gather what most of us have learned from our elders and then both apply and practice this wisdom in the very fast, very busy world we live in, where one can be virtually accessible 24/7 via cell phones, texting, and the Internet.

We will discuss a few ways to achieve health addressed in our spiritual texts as well as by the World Health Organization's definition:

"Health is a state of complete physical, mental, and social well-being and not merely the absence of disease or infirmity."[1]

Like individuals, the attainment of health at the community or population base level may differ due to regional and cultural variations. Yet the elements of what will enable us to build a healthy congregation and community should be constant. These may be referred to as social determinants of health, defined as "the conditions in which people are born, grow, live, work and age, including the health system. These circumstances are shaped by the distribution of money, power and resources at global, national and local levels, which are themselves influenced by policy choices. The social determinants of health are mostly responsible for health inequities—the unfair and avoidable differences in health status seen within and between countries."[2]

One way healthy clergy can be defined is as individuals who have learned to become resilient enough to deal with life's stressors, eustress as well as distress, to have fulfilling personal as well as professional lives. This definition can also apply to healthy congregations and communities reaching their maximal potential, by creating an inclusive, nurturing environment where all persons have the opportunity to thrive and lead fulfilling lives.

Clergy Health and Its Impact on Congregational and Community Health

Clergy are usually attempting to balance a combination of commitments to their higher power followed by spouses or partners, children, other family members such as maturing parents, work, community occasionally, and lastly themselves! Clergy frequently share that their occupation "is a calling," but it is also a job with many responsibilities, including but not limited to leader of a house of worship, where they may also serve as chief financial officer, cook, cleaner, and repair person; chaplain; counselor; seminary professor; and so on. Some are fortunate enough to have lay leaders in their congregations as well as a few members with whom to share these responsibilities. Yet clergy, like many others, may need a secular job to sufficiently care for themselves as well as their families. Clergy are increasingly bi-vocational by necessity as well as by education and training, especially those for whom it is a second career.

So where does it state in your holy book, your Bible, Torah, Qur'an, or other spiritual texts, that clergy should care for themselves last? Most indicate the importance of balance, nutrition, not overindulging, viewing our body as a temple to be cared for and honored.[3] In addition, the stated attributes of a good leader, such as wisdom, include delegating and seeking help and assistance from others.[4] Effective delegation is essential, because sometimes the needs and care of the congregation and the community may eclipse those of the clergy as well as family members, which can adversely impact the health of all. When clergy are too overworked and overwhelmed, they may begin to burn out and shut down, losing their vitality, becoming emotionally as well as physically ill. So how do the ultimate caregivers administer self-care before they get to this point?

Let's refer to a case example. Please note that this is a compilation of many real scenarios. Clergy Eternal (CE) is forty-eight years old and has a significant other (SO) and three children—a young adult at home, one in college, and the youngest in high school. CE has always enjoyed the day-to-day responsibilities of being a clergyperson, such as interacting with the congregation and the community; celebrating life-cycle events, including marriages, births, baptisms, and rites of passage; leading worship; and participating in the activities and missions of the house of worship as well as in the community.

Please take some time to consider and answer the following questions:

- Where are you in your ministry?
- Where are you in your spiritual journey?
- How would you rate your job satisfaction? How do you feel following worship?
- How do you feel following meetings with the leadership of your congregation?
- How do you know when it is time to shut down for the day?

However, of late, CE is exercising less, has gained a little weight, and is drinking more than usual. CE has also had some sleepless nights worrying about home and church finances. With the downturn of the economy, many more people are coming to the house of worship, which CE considers a blessing, but giving and donations are really down. The congregation is having trouble paying the bills and maintaining the building's aging structure. Many in the community as well as the congregation are hungry and homeless, so they are very reliant on the house of worship. CE is working harder than ever and has little opportunity for family time.

- What might you suggest to CE?
- What do you do to relax?
- How is your nutrition?
- Do you exercise, and if so, what do you do and how often?
- When was the last time you had a checkup?
- Do you or have you ever considered seeing a therapist?

Perhaps CE could consider getting together with other clergy, preferably in person but even by phone or online for support. A discussion addressing that self-care is not selfish, but selfless and self-preserving, might be helpful. CE might want to return to exercising, especially aerobic activities such as walking or running, building up to at least thirty minutes five days a week, which has been shown to elevate mood, decrease some anxiety and depression, and perhaps even help with sleep. CE might consider exploring the local Y or a similar type of community organization for other activities such as swimming, stretching, yoga, salsa, two-step, swing dancing, and so on. If CE hasn't been exercising in a while, a visit to a health care provider would be prudent.

In addition, CE might consider seeing a therapist, primary care physician or other provider, and a dentist for further assessment and evaluation. If CE does not have insurance or inadequate insurance, this should not be a barrier to accessing care. CE may not be aware of insurance coverage under the Affordable Care Act (ACA).[5] A very important aspect of ACA is that many who were formerly uninsured or uninsurable are eligible for coverage. For those who are insured, most co-pays for preventive services are waived. Some state and local county health departments provide health and public health services, such as immunizations, screening, and treatment for tuberculosis, hepatitis, sexually transmitted infections, and so on. There are Federally Qualified Health Centers (FQHCs)[6] in most states and US territories providing health care, including mental and dental health services. Many of these centers were started during the early 1960s by clergy and their congregations. If any problems are identified in CE such as elevated blood pressure, high cholesterol, or diabetes requiring medications, the

FQHCs as well as many local pharmacies have programs where CE can receive medications at low cost and sometimes for free. There are also many faith-based entities, health care providers, hospitals, and others that provide volunteer health care as well. Please take a moment to ask yourself the following questions:

- Do I take time to pray and meditate?
- Do I have a day of rest?
- When was the last time I took a vacation?
- What do I do for fun and how often?
- What gives me joy or pleasure?

CE sometimes feels too busy to pray, let alone meditate. Many in the medical and public health community have come full circle, acknowledging that spirituality and praying for others (aka intercessory prayer) can actually help improve health outcomes! Perhaps CE can request a Sabbath day other than the one recognized by the denomination, as the latter is really a workday for CE and the SO. CE might also want to consider having a date night with the SO and taking a vacation, even if it is a local one, with their children. Some foundations, such as the Lilly Endowment National Clergy Renewal Program, even support clergy and their houses of worship to allow brief sabbaticals.[7]

Certainly it would be very helpful to assess CE's nutritional status. What does CE eat, where, and when, and is CE taking any supplements? CE might benefit from being evaluated by a registered dietitian. We would like CE to have a balanced diet that includes fresh fruit and vegetables, is high in fiber, and is low in saturated fats and refined sugar. If CE is eating out a lot, especially fast foods, CE should consider preparing food at home and eating there more often. This would not only improve CE's health but also enable CE to spend more quality time with family and save a lot of money. For a more thorough discussion on individual health, wellness, prevention, screening, and treatment, see *The Right Road Life: Choices for Clergy,* by Gwen Wagstrom Halaas, MD;[8] the chapter "Self Care—Not an Option," in *Disaster Spiritual Care,* edited by Rev. Dr. Willard W. C. Ashley Sr. and Rabbi Stephen Roberts;[9] and *You—The Owners Manual: An Insider's Guide to Your Body That Will Make You Healthier and Younger,* by Drs. Mehmet C. Oz and Michael F. Roizen.[10]

women to conduct self-breast examinations, obtain genetic testing, and have early and more aggressive screening as appropriate.

Some male clergy who have accompanied their congregational and community members for prostate screening have tested positive for cancer. They have encouraged others by sharing their treatment journey. Many clergy openly discuss HIV, cardiovascular diseases, cancer (e.g., skin, oral, colon, breast, cervical), mental health, autism, influenza, pneumonia, and so on. The Lott Carey Baptist Foreign Mission Society has encouraged African Americans and other communities to participate in a National Week of Prayer for the Healing of AIDS, providing education and encouraging prevention, screening, and treatment as well as compassion and healing. In another congregation, one of the deacons, who is also a licensed clinical social worker, collaborated with clergy to develop a partnership and program to address education, prevention, and treatment of mental illness titled PEWS, Promoting Emotional Wellness and Spirituality Programs.[23]

Clergy leaders are powerful in that they can dispel myths and encourage intervention, screening, and treatment (see part IV). Religious leaders can communicate whether or not it is "safe" for community members to interact with representatives of the medical and public health communities (MPHC). Imams, rabbis, pastors, and other spiritual leaders play a critical role in educating the MPHC regarding religious and cultural norms impacting health and health care needs, creating an atmosphere of respect and trust between the MPHC and members of the house of worship and sometimes the community at large. The role of cultural broker is a very important one, especially for many congregations that are serving diverse immigrant communities. Some of the members may be dealing with the challenges of recent immigration, language barriers, and issues of trust as well as acculturation, especially among younger family members (see chapters 12 and 17).

Congregations can benefit from one another regarding having a healthier lifestyle. Some diets are based on spiritual texts such as the Levitical dietary laws and the Qur'an, while others are rooted in our rich diverse cultures. In addition to the Levitical dietary laws, the Seventh-Day Adventist Church encourages a lacto-ovo-vegetarian diet. In Ayurveda, originating in India, herbs and spices are used in a curative manner. Acupuncture, originating in China, is recognized for improving chronic back pain so dramatically that it is also reimbursed by many US health insurers. Many individuals utilize both Western and indigenous healers from all over the world. Many forms of complementary and alternative medicine (CAM) are used by people in the United States and around the world.[24]

Clergy health ministries may provide direct health care, develop health care partnerships, and provide health fairs for the congregation and community to address wellness and prevention initiatives and improve access to health care. Such partnerships can also apply to working with police on increasing community safety while decreasing violence and providing recreational activities for our youth. Other relationships might include collaborating with local schools, community colleges, and others on improving the quality of the educational system while increasing the health career pipeline and expanding health care services.

In addition, for almost every major chronic disease one can think of, there are public resources from the federal, state, county, and local governments as well as from local hospitals and foundations to raise awareness and provide screening and links to potentially free or low-cost services. The Department of Health and Human Services Center for Faith-Based and Neighborhood Partnerships serves to develop congregational and community partnerships and functions as a portal to disseminate information about other federal resources.[25] The US Department of Agriculture has replaced the Food Pyramid with Choose My Plate, which recommends that a meal should be composed of one-half vegetables and fruits, one-quarter grains, and one-quarter protein.[26] The Let's Move campaign encourages increased physical activity and better eating habits in order to solve the challenge of childhood obesity within one generation.[27] Other faith-based activities include encouraging bone marrow screening, organ donation, and cancer screening, among many others. Many of these resources are accessible on the Internet and can be downloaded.

Regarding mental wellness and mental health, in *Creating a Healthier Church*,[28] Rev. Dr. Ronald W. Richardson examines the clergy and the congregation through the lens of Bowenian family systems theory.[29] This theory includes understanding the impact and influence of the congregation as a family with a history as well as roles and relationships.

Developing a congregational genogram might be helpful in further understanding these dynamics. By doing so, clergy can better appreciate their role as a new member of the congregation's family system and differentiate between supportive congregational-clergy relationships and those that may create anxiety and stress. Clergy self-differentiation from the congregation is essential to healthy and effective development. It is also important for clergy to delegate and engage the skills of others in behavioral health, such as licensed clinical social workers, psychotherapists psychologists, and psychiatrists, to assist them as well as the congregation.

The importance of clergy leaders delegating and engaging the support, wisdom, and skills of others, especially congregational leaders and members, should not be underestimated. Many congregations have lay leaders who, in addition to providing fiduciary responsibility, provide "care" to individuals and families, making phone calls and home and hospital visits. Most congregations have health ministries, with people who desire to help. If the skills are not available within your congregation, go to the community. There are many people in practice, in school, or in training who desire or are required to provide community service or need to complete an internship who would enjoy collaborating with clergy, congregations, and the community to achieve their health and wellness goals. Some of the most effective persons to recruit are the behavioral health specialists already mentioned, nurses, nursing assistants, physicians, dentists, medical and dental assistants, dental hygienists, physical therapists, trainers, nutritionists, acupuncturists, teachers, gardeners, and many others. It is also important to recognize, respect, and remember the importance and requirement for the confidentiality and safety of congregational members. Many congregations require clearances and background checks for people to provide such services, which is not only understandable but also legally advisable.

Creating Healthy Congregations and Communities: Improving the Social Determinants of Health

Healthy communities is a fascinating concept because historically we lived, worked, prayed, and played in the same community. Yet increasingly people are traveling great distances to attend their houses of worship; some even do so virtually and globally via the Internet. Most of us take our living conditions for granted—clean air, clean water, the availability of a fresh, safe food supply, and the ability to eliminate sewage. Yet for the majority of the world, these are the leading contributory factors to death and disability and the foundation of Maslow's Hierarchy of Needs.[30] Many congregations provide funds for overseas missions to improve such conditions. There are also many US communities where the air is so polluted from garbage burning, factories, secondhand smoke, and so on that many populations suffer very high rates of asthma and other respiratory conditions. In other communities, contaminants from landfills and dumping of products from a wide range of businesses, some which have been closed for many years, can be associated with cancers and other illnesses.[31] These unhealthy conditions are usually located in low-income communities, urban as well as rural areas, creating health disparities and health inequities. Although the poor and minorities are disproportionately affected, these conditions impact all persons, especially with the gentrification of urban areas, renovation of old homes, and new construction on contaminated soil. Our places of work, especially those where windows are sealed or where there is no sunlight, may also create an unhealthy environment.

Improving the living conditions and environment within the community where houses of worship are located is possible and being done every day! This will have a positive cascading effect on the health of the community, congregations, clergy, and their families. Historically, clergy and congregations have improved their community conditions through working with local community members, leaders, and other organizations. Together they identify community concerns, develop plans, and implement interventions for issues such as the availability of clean water, sewage elimination, improved and affordable housing, schools, health care services, elimination of activities leading to increased violence such as illicit drugs and gangs, environmental cleanup, community gardens, the availability of high-quality food including fresh fruits and vegetables, and so on. Congregational leaders have also functioned as lay epidemiologists, noticing and sharing with other clergy the unusually high numbers of members with cancer or other illnesses and realizing their rates are far higher than those in surrounding communities, while also recognizing that the cause needs to be identified and action taken. Some recent community innovations include "going green" and utilizing solar energy, like the Florida Avenue Baptist Church in Washington DC.[32] Other congregations focus on improving the financial health or wellness of their members, which has a significant impact on decreasing their anxiety and improving their health and standard of living.

Bringing the community into the house of worship, and the congregation into the community, is another way to raise the overall health for all. Frequently we speak of helping the least of our brethren by providing food, clothing, and sometimes shelter. Congregations can also address the needs and health of all age cohorts by converting their house of worship for multipurpose use, such as hosting AARP, youth groups, recovery meetings, day care, after-school programs including physical recreation, and so on. Many communities have food banks or other resources to assist congregations with their mission.

In closing, clergy, congregational, and community health rely on treating one another with charity (love), kindness, and forgiveness. This involves understanding and appreciating each other's various roles and responsibilities and having mutually realistic expectations and, most important, respect. Clergy leaders can serve as role models through their own self-care while providing the theological foundation for health, including mental health, for the congregation as well as the community. This can also be done in an interfaith, multicultural, multilingual manner to benefit the entire community while building bridges and being cost-effective.

Notes

1. World Health Organization, "WHO Definition of Health," www.who.int/about/definition/en/print.html.

2. World Health Organization, www.who.int/social_determinants/en.

3. "Don't you realize that your body is the temple of the Holy Spirit, who lives in you and was given to you by God? You do not belong to yourself, for God bought you with a high price. So you must honor God with your body" (1 Corinthians 6:19–20). All scripture quotes are taken from the *New Living Translation Bible* (2012), which can be accessed at www.biblegateway.com/versions/New-Living-Translation-NLT-Bible.

4. "'This is not good!' Moses' father-in-law exclaimed. 'You're going to wear yourself out—and the people, too. This job is too heavy a burden for you to

handle all by yourself. Now listen to me, and let me give you a word of advice, and may God be with you.... But select from all the people some capable, honest men who fear God and hate bribes. Appoint them as leaders over groups of one thousand, one hundred, fifty, and ten. They should always be available to solve the people's common disputes, but have them bring the major cases to you. Let the leaders decide the smaller matters themselves. They will help you carry the load, making the task easier for you. If you follow this advice, and if God commands you to do so, then you will be able to endure the pressures, and all these people will go home in peace'" (Exodus 18:17–23).

5. Affordable Care Act (ACA), www.healthcare.gov/ACA, highlights: "On March 23, 2010, President Obama signed the Affordable Care Act ... a comprehensive health insurance reform that will roll out over four years and beyond, with most changes taking place by 2014.... Health plans cannot limit or deny benefits or deny coverage for a child younger than age 19 simply because the child has a pre-existing condition, that is, a health problem that developed before the child applied to join the plan.... A Pre-Existing Condition Insurance Plan (PCIP) provides new coverage options to individuals who have been uninsured for at least six months because of a pre-existing condition.... Starting in 2014, these protections will be extended to Americans of all ages.... [Many] young adults are allowed to stay on their parent's plan until they turn 26 years old.... [It will] cover certain preventive services such as mammograms and colonoscopies without charging a deductible, co-pay or coinsurance ... strengthens Medicare and provides access to preventive services and prescription drug discounts for seniors.... Women can receive preventive care without copays," and much more. See the ACA website to access implementation in your state.

6. Federally Qualified Health Centers, http://findahealthcenter.hrsa.gov/Search_HCC.aspx.

7. National Clergy Renewal Program, Lilly Endowment, www.clergyrenewal.org.

8. GwenWagstrom Halaas, *The Right Road: Life Choices for Clergy* (Minneapolis: Fortress Press, 2004).

9. Tanya Pagán Raggio-Ashley and Willard W. C. Ashley Sr., "Self-Care—Not an Option," in *Disaster Spiritual Care: Practical Clergy Responses to Community, Regional and National Tragedy*, ed. Stephen B. Roberts and Willard W. C. Ashley Sr. (Woodstock, VT: SkyLight Paths Publishing, 2008).

10. Mehmet C. Oz and Michael E. Roizen, *You—The Owners Manual: An Insider's Guide to Your Body That Will Make You Healthier and Younger* (New York: Harper, 2005).

11. Bureau of Labor Statistics, Department of Labor, *Occupational Outlook Handbook*, 2010–2011 ed., www.bls.gov/oes/current/oes212011.htm; O*NET Online, "Summary Report for Clergy," www.onetonline.org/link/summary/21-2011.00.

12. Mark Chaves, Shawna Anderson, and Jason Byassee, *National Congregations Study: Church Size and Clergy Age*, part I. http://oneinjesus.info/2009/01/changes-in-church-demographics-church-size-and-clergy-age.

13. Jacques Bertillon, "Influence of Occupation on Mortality," *Journal of the Royal Statistical Society 55*, no. 4 (1982), translated from *Journal de la Société de Statistique de Paris* (1892), www.jstor.org/pss/2979582.

14. Douglas J. Brenner, *Does Stress Damage the Brain? Understanding Trauma-Related Disorders from a Mind-Body Perspective* (New York: W.W. Norton and Company, 2005). Acute stress can create a fight-or-flight response, causing our bodies to release increased levels of adrenaline or epinephrine, increasing our heart rates and blood pressure but usually returning to normal. However, chronic stress results in the adrenal glands releasing increased levels of cortisol over a prolonged period of time, chronically elevating blood pressure; creating ulcers; impairing the immune system, predisposing us to infections, cancer, and increased abdominal girth (fat); and causing us to crave comfort foods high in fats, carbohydrates, and sugar, predisposing us to diabetes and cardiovascular disease.

15. H. T. Holmes and R. H. Rahe, "The Social Readjustments Rating Scales," *Journal of Psychosomatic Research* 111 (1967): 213–18.

16. R. M. Oswald, *Clergy Self-Care: Finding a Balance for Effective Ministry* (Herndon, VA: Alban Institute, 1991).

17. "Disparities Fast Facts," Robert Wood Johnson Foundation, www.rwjf.org/healthpolicy/disparities/fastfacts.jsp.

18. Martin Luther King autopsy, www.autopsyfiles.org/reports/Celebs/king%20jr,%20martin%20luther_report.pdf.

19. A. M. Mujahid, "25 Ways to Deal with Stress and Anxiety," Sound Vision, http://soundvision.com/info/peace/stresstips.asp.

20. "Anxiety in the heart of a person causes dejection, but a good word will turn it into joy" (Proverbs 12:25); Sarah Esther Crispe, "A Torah Approach to Anxiety Relief," *The Jewish Woman*, www.chabad.org/theJewishWoman/article_cdo/aid/514028/jewish/A-Torah-Approach-to-Anxiety-Relief.htm.

21. J. O. Prochaska, C. C. DiClemente, and C. Carlo, "Toward a Comprehensive Model of Change" in *Treating Addictive Behaviors: Processes of Change*, ed. W. R. Miller and N. Heather (New York: Plenum Press, 1986), 3–27.

22. Laurie Goodstein, "Serenity Prayer Skeptic Now Credits Nieburh," *New York Times*, November 27, 2009, www.nytimes.com/2009/11/28/us/28prayer.html.

23. L. Williams, "Promoting Emotional Wellness and Spirituality Programs," Mental Health Association of New Jersey (personal communication and unpublished curriculum).

24. National Center for Complementary and Alternative Medicine, http://nccam.nih.gov.

25. Department of Health and Human Services Center for Faith-Based and Neighborhood Partnerships, www.hhs.gov/partnerships.

26. Choose My Plate, www.choosemyplate.gov.

27. Let's Move, www.letsmove.gov.

28. R. W. Richardson, *Creating a Healthier Church: Family Systems Theory, Leadership, and Congregational Life* (Minneapolis: Fortress Press, 1996).

29. M. E. Kerr and M. Bowen, *Family Evaluation: An Approach Based on Bowen Theory* (New York: W.W. Norton, 1988).

30. A. H. Maslow, "A Theory of Human Motivation," *Psychological Review* 50 (1943): 370–96, http://psychclassics.yorku.ca/Maslow/motivation.htm.

31. "700,000-Ton Cleanup Settlement Reached in Jersey City Toxic Chromium Case: After 30 Years, Local Community Triumphs in Cancer-Causing Chemical Battle," National Resources Defense Council, www.nrdc.org/media/2011/110406.asp.

32. "This Little Light of Mine … Is Going Solar," *Politics 365*, http://politic365.com/2011/04/27/this-little-light-of-mine-is-going-solar.

Further Reading

HEALTH DISPARITIES AND SOCIAL DETERMINANTS OF HEALTH BY RACE AND ETHNICITY

Adams, M., W. Blumenfeld, R. Castañeda, H. W. Hackman, M. L. Peters, and X. Zuñiga, eds. *Readings for Diversity and Social Justice*. 2nd ed. New York: Routledge, 2010.

Aguirre-Molina, M., C. W. Molina, and R. E. Zambrana. *Health Issues in the Latino Community*. San Francisco: Jossey-Bass, 2001.

Delgado, J. L. *Latina Guide to Health*. New York: Newmarket Press, 2010.

Gaston, M., and G. K. Porter. *Prime Time: The African American Woman's Complete Guide to Midlife Health and Wellness*. New York: One World Press, 2001.

LaVeist, T. A. *Minority Populations and Health*. San Francisco: John Wiley & Sons, 2005.

Satcher, D., and R. Pamies. *Multicultural Medicine and Health Disparities*. New York: McGraw-Hill, 2005.

Trinh-Shevrin, C., N. S. Islam, and M. J. Rey, eds. *Asian American Communities and Health: Context, Research, Policy and Action*. San Francisco: John Wiley & Sons, 2009.

SPIRITUALITY, STRESS, HEALTH, AND BEHAVIORAL HEALTH (FAMILY THERAPY)

Bowen, M. *Family Therapy in Clinical Practice*. New York: Jason Aronson, 1978.

Figueroa, L. R., B. Davis, S. Baker, and J. B. Bunch. "The Influence of Spirituality on Health Care-Seeking Behaviors among African Americans." *ABNF Journal* 17, no. 2 (Spring 2006): 82–88.

Hager, W. D., and L. C. Hager. *Stress and a Women's Body*. Grand Rapids, MI: Fleming H. Revell, 1996.

McGoldrick, M., and K. V. Hardy, eds. *Re-Visioning Family Therapy: Race, Culture and Gender in Clinical Practice*. 2nd ed. New York: Guilford Press, 2008.

Puchalski, C. M. "The Role of Spirituality in Health Care." *Baylor University Medical Center Proceedings* 14, no. 4 (October 2001): 352–57.

FAITH-BASED HEALTH RESOURCES FOR
CLERGY AND CONGREGATIONS

American Muslim Health Care Professionals: www.amhp.us.

Duke Clergy Health Initiative: http://divinity.duke.edu/initiaties-centers/ clergy-health-initiative. The Duke Clergy Health Initiative is a $12 million, seven-year program intended to improve the health and well-being of United Methodist clergy in North Carolina.

Meeting the Health Care Needs of American Muslims: http://ispu.org/ GetReports/35/2110/Publications.aspx.

Program for Jewish Genetic Health, Yeshiva University and Einstein School of Medicine: http://home.yu.edu/genetichealth. The Program for Jewish Genetic Health represents an attempt to develop a centralized resource for the Jewish community.

Pulpit & Pew: http://pulpitandpew.org. A now-completed interdenominational research project funded by The Lilly Endowment to assess the state of the pastorate in the United States. Based at Duke Divinity School and active from 2001 to 2005, it conducted a nationwide pastor survey, in-depth interviews, and conferences and produced written reports and books.

Seventh-Day Adventist Health Message: www.sdada.org/sdahealth.htm.

United Methodist Committee on Relief: Congregational Health and Health Ministry; Parish Nurse/Faith Community Nurse, Health Advocate and Participatory Health Group, http://new.gbgm-umc.org/umcor/work/health/congregational.

RESOURCES ON HEALTH DISPARITIES AND SOCIAL
DETERMINANTS OF HEALTH BY RACE AND ETHNICITY

CDC Fast Facts: www.cdc.gov/nchs/fastats/default.htm.

NIH NLM Medline Health: www.nlm.nih.gov/medlineplus/hispanicamericanhealth. html; www.nlm.nih.gov/medlineplus/africanamericanhealth.html; www.nlm.nih.gov/medlineplus/asianamericanhealth.html.

Pew Hispanic Center: www.pewhispanic.org.

About the Contributor

Tanya Pagán Raggio-Ashley, MD, MPH, FAAP, has dedicated her professional life to improving social determinants of health to reduce racial and ethnic health disparities and ultimately create health equity for all. She has taught seminary students and clergy about primary care, public health, and the important role of clergy in health promotion and disease prevention. She was awarded the Dr. Helen Rodriquez-Trias Women in Medicine Award by the National Hispanic Medical Association for her efforts. She has collaborated with her husband, Rev. Dr. Willard W. C. Ashley Sr., to teach and host seminars for clergy, seminary students, congregational members, and the community at large. She has held the position of associate professor of medicine at several universities and is board certified in preventative medicine and pediatrics. She holds a bachelor's of science and a doctor of medicine from Rutgers University. She completed a master's in public health and a fellowship in cardio-vascular epidemiology at the University of Pittsburgh Graduate School of Public Health.

5

Friendships

Rev. Lee B. Spitzer, MDiv, DMin

During my bicoastal seminary experience, two extraordinary inter-generational friendships made a profound impact on my preparation for spiritual leadership as a congregational pastor and regional minister.

The first friendship was with Mr. William Williamson, who was a lay leader in an Episcopal church in Glendale, California. My field education assignment at St. Mark's focused on junior and senior high ministry, but Bill's friendship enabled me to explore the role of laity as servant-leaders and how evangelical outreach could be practiced in a mainline context according to honest relational principles and values. He passed away shortly after my time at the church concluded, but I have never forgotten his gentle personality that was balanced by a dogged determination to share Jesus with everyone he encountered. What else would one expect from a retired salesperson who loved both God and people?

After transferring to Gordon-Conwell Theological Seminary half-way through my master of divinity studies, I interviewed at three churches to obtain another youth ministry field education position. The first two interviews were less than memorable, but within ten minutes of meeting Rev. Dr. Howard Keeley, in his well-organized and tidy office, I knew I had found an exceptional mentor as well as a much-needed field education position. What I did not recognize immediately was that I also had gained a lifelong friend who would commit himself to helping me develop into an effective, well-rounded minister of the Gospel of Jesus.

Through Howard's friendship, I observed how a healthy and faithful pastor serves God's people, encourages them to embrace their call to authentic and risky discipleship, and prophetically addresses societal issues. As our trust and love for one another developed, I could plumb his wisdom, probe my own emerging spirituality with his support and guidance, and discover my unique voice as a spiritual leader. Howard gifted me with a safe yet challenging relationship in which I could apply seminary-based knowledge in a real-world church context.

To become effective pastoral leaders, seminarians and other candidates for pastoral leadership need to recognize and appreciate the role that relationships play in every form of ministry. Isolated and lonely leaders make vocational mistakes, are more prone to violate ethical boundaries and professional norms, and experience less satisfaction and joy in service.[1] In addition to theological and preaching skills, twenty-first-century clergy must possess a keen awareness of how to create and foster friendships—with mentors, congregational members, ministerial peers, and others who do not have a direct connection to their field of service.

Forming Future Leaders: The Challenge of Friendship in the Seminary Context

Paul's relationship with Timothy is often cited as a model for forming future pastoral leaders in an intergenerational context (2 Timothy 2:2). Paul's discipleship of Timothy was not merely intellectual and certainly not classroom-bound, but rather was personal enough to merit exclamations of affection. Timothy is Paul's "dear" (2 Timothy 1:2) and "true son in the faith" (1 Timothy 1:2; see also 1 Timothy 1:18). Their loving relationship helped shape Timothy's understanding and practice of ministry, as both letters illustrate.

L. Gregory Jones and Kevin R. Armstrong, authors of *Resurrecting Excellence*, speak of a troubling reality regarding seminarians: "The quality of those entering the ministry seems to have declined relative to other vocations."[2] Setting aside the question of how one would validate such a claim, I believe my experience working with other clergy and seminarians over the past three decades as a church pastor and regional minister resonates with the controversial criticism they make. The multifaceted quality decline they cite is clustered in one particular area—relational skills. A majority of seminarians who seek ordination in my regional judicatory come with a number of profound relational deficits, including the loss of one or more parents in their home of origin, one or more failed marriages in their own lives, difficulty in establishing and maintaining peer and intergenerational friendships, and the absence of long-term connections to a specific church community. They desire to experience deep and authentic relationships but are entering into leadership positions with a scarcity of positive personal experience. They are like Elie Wiesel's Gamaliel in *The Time of the Uprooted*, who is lonely and isolated while possessing a "romantic faith in friendship"—and they suffer from the same defect that Gamaliel sees in Moses and Socrates; even though these two leaders "had disciples and lieutenants, they had no friends."[3] Bruce Demarest, professor at Denver Seminary, remains sympathetic while issuing a similar judgment:

> Some future ministers and missionaries enter seminary with poor images of God and self. Others struggle with wounds from dysfunctional family environments. Still others cannot escape secret sins, and live imprisoned in guilt, anxiety, and depression. These idealistic students represent the best in our churches. They deeply long to succeed in the Christian life, but don't know how to pull it off.[4]

Once in positions of church leadership, the vocational aspirations of relationally challenged pastors often are dashed by fundamental mistakes they make. Rarely do doctrinal issues or theological controversies undermine a pastor's ministry or career. In the overwhelming number of cases where a rift has developed between clergy and congregations, pastors have contributed to the estrangement by:

- Failing to earn social capital and trust before initiating risky changes
- Neglecting social visits that could help establish relationships
- Avoiding opportunities for pastoral care during hospitalizations and other medical crises, giving the impression that they do not care about those in need

- Cutting off relationships and isolating themselves from members of the congregation
- Elevating projects and programs above personal feelings, which is often interpreted as a lack of pastoral sensitivity

Friendship with Mentors: Passing on Wisdom

In his classic book *Spiritual Care*, Dietrich Bonhoeffer asserts:

> Mutual help in ministry is taken for granted. But we need more; we need another to care for our soul. Everyone who cares for the soul needs a person to care for his or her soul. Only one who has been under spiritual care is able to exercise spiritual care.[5]

There are many people who seek to earn a living from mentoring both inexperienced and veteran clergy. Spiritual directors provide various forms of guidance to facilitate spiritual growth, mentors are willing to share knowledge and skills, psychologists are prepared to guide others into deeper psychological insight, and coaches seek to enhance vocational performance. All four forms of vocational support have their place and may be helpful, but all risk becoming, in Adin Steinsaltz's words, "commercial relationships" in which we "hire professionals as substitutes for friends."[6] In my opinion, emerging and experienced leaders need to develop and maintain authentic (noncommercial) friendships with people who have journeyed further down the path than we have. These relationships must exhibit all the deep characteristics of friendship: both people treat each other as equals, personal sharing is mutual and freely offered, both seek to help the other experience their potential as people made in the image of God, and love and trust permeate the relationship. In *Making Friends, Making Disciples*, I offer the following definition of friendship, which applies to friendships in general and the mentor pastor–younger pastor relationship in particular:

> A friend is a person I love who also loves me—through our linked journeys, bonds of devotion, affection, loyalty, trust and caring grow between us, so that we desire to share our hopes, dreams, joys and fears with each other. My friends exert influence over my heart; the deeper our friendship, the more vulnerable and self-revealing I am willing to be, and the more their

opinions and feelings about me affect me. Together with my friends, I hope to fulfill God's will and change the world for Christ.[7]

Mentor friends are willing to link their spiritual journeys to those who have less experience. They are motivated not by financial gain but by a personal affection for the one into whom they are pouring themselves. They give away their heart as well as their expertise. Mentor friends are open to being changed by the relationship, even as they seek to promote and support the ongoing growth of the younger pastor. They seek to influence others so that they might embrace and fulfill God's will. Ray Pahl, British sociologist, quotes the work of Graham Allan and Rebecca Adams, coeditors of *Placing Friendship in Context*, who note, "Our friends, in numerous ways, challenge our pretensions and evaluate our claims, all the while confirming our personal and structural identity."[8] This is the task and privilege of the mentor friend.

Bruce Demarest, based on his understanding of the spiritual direction model employed by Jesus with his disciples (whom he called "friends" in John 15:13–15), suggests that mentor friends should concentrate "on primary issues of knowing, being, and doing—constantly directing people to right beliefs, right relationships, and right conduct."[9] This is a positive and balanced agenda for a healthy mentor pastor–younger pastor friendship in which wisdom may be passed on from one generation to the next. Guidelines that may be useful in facilitating such relationships should be kept in mind by both sides of the friendship.

Mentor friends should:

1. Share as openly and vulnerably as possible, while maintaining an appropriate level of self-revelation so as to not overwhelm younger pastors.
2. Listen carefully to the soul of younger pastors (their needs, desires, hopes, dreams, and fears) and encourage them to discern the Spirit's responses to these yearnings.
3. Invite younger pastors to explore God's will for their personal life, relationships, and vocational service, so that they may appreciate on a deeper level their spiritual journeys in light of scripture and personal experience.

4. Model healthy friendships and encourage younger pastors to develop other friendships with a variety of people.

5. Exercise patience in encouraging growth and change, recognizing that younger pastors' experience level, depth of wisdom, and psychological maturity will not equal their own.

6. Balance affirmation with constructive criticism, to maximize growth in self-understanding while preserving a healthy sense of self.

7. Rejoice in the achievements of younger pastors without seeking to claim credit for the successes.

8. Encourage independence and discourage unhealthy moves toward codependency.

9. Recognize that younger pastors should discover their own voice as ministers, and should not become carbon copies of their mentors.

10. Never abuse their position of trust and authority as a soul guide to take advantage of or manipulate younger pastors.

Younger pastors who engage mentor friends should:

1. Respect mentors and commit themselves to opening their hearts and minds to the wisdom that mentors will seek to share.

2. Share their personal thoughts and feelings without seeking to impress mentor friends.

3. Ask as many questions as possible as the relationship progresses and different contexts for discussion naturally emerge. They should take advantage of every opportunity to seek wisdom!

4. Recognize and accept mentor friends' weaknesses as well as their strengths. Mentors should not be deified. Younger pastors can learn from all aspects of mentors' lives.

5. Receive criticism and correction from mentors, knowing that the criticism is intended to help younger pastors reach their potential as disciples and spiritual leaders.

6. Trust mentors' counsel, and when appropriate, question their perspectives with humility and out of a desire to learn.

7. Imitate mentors' spiritual outlook (1 Corinthians 11:1), as opposed to superficial mimicry of speaking style, mannerisms, and so on.

8. Seek for and maintain other relationships to avoid becoming too dependent on mentors, recognizing that they also deserve to enjoy additional friendships.

9. Take responsibility for initiating and contributing to conversations about their spiritual journeys and ministry experiences.

10. Express appreciation for the willingness of mentors to share their friendship, especially if the friendship continues to grow and deepen.

Not all friendships with mentors are meant to last a lifetime. There are a number of legitimate reasons why a mentor friendship may come to a conclusion:

- The relationship may cease because of a geographical relocation or a ministry reassignment.
- The friendship has achieved its purpose or goal, and one or both of the friends sense a need to move on to other relationships.
- Health or schedule no longer permits the relationship to continue.
- The younger pastor's journey requires seeking another mentor with a different skill set and perspective.

Sadly, there are times when a relationship should terminate for less positive reasons, such as when:

- An abuse of trust or power has taken place.
- The relationship ceases to produce spiritual fruit.
- The younger pastor becomes too dependent on the strength and support of the mentor friend.

- The mentor refuses or has ceased to give the younger pastor the psychological and spiritual space needed to develop his or her own style of leadership and ministerial practice.

The transition from seminarian to pastor impacts the mentor friendship in both subtle and obvious ways. If the transition entails a significant geographical relocation, the relationship may end without either party experiencing guilt. In many instances, graduation marks the end of the mentor journey, and neither party is expected to maintain more than a casual relationship thereafter.

In some cases, the relationship may transcend the conclusion of the educational journey and reconfigure itself into a less utilitarian collegial friendship. To be sure, spiritual formation may continue to take place, but the friendship now has the opportunity to be characterized by Aristotle's classical understanding of authentic friendship—a mutual appreciation for each other's virtue.[10] The mentor becomes a cherished colleague who continues to share as a fellow minister instead of as a teacher.

Clergy and Circles of Friendship

Once situated in a congregation or another vocational setting, clergy need to be intentional about developing healthy and vital circles of friendship. This is at least as critical as establishing credibility as a theological authority, an organizational leader, or a skillful practitioner—and perhaps more difficult!

Friendships are experienced in varying levels of intensity; some of our friends are extremely close to our heart and serve as best or special friends, while with others we are content simply to socialize and share at a more superficial level.[11] As clergy invite others to journey alongside them, the following considerations may be helpful to keep in mind:

1. **Maturity levels:** Clergy should maintain relationships with people of varying levels of spiritual and psychological maturity. Some of our friends should have more life experience and wisdom than we currently possess, while others may be at a maturity level closer to our own. As we age, we should cultivate friendships with younger people, so we can pass on our wisdom and gain fresh ideas from them.

2. **Vocational diversity:** Clergy should seek out friends from various professions to bring additional streams of thought and inspiration into our lives.

3. **Congregation and community:** Faith leaders should enjoy deep and satisfying relationships with selected members of their house of worship and also with those who have no connection to their congregation. A balance in this regard provides faith leaders with space to place our pastoral role aside and just "be human." In cases of congregational strife, friendships with community members can provide solace and perspective.

4. **Multifaith relationships:** Faith leaders should seek out friendships with people of integrity from various communities of faith. Such friendships may inform our own sense of spiritual identity while modeling tolerance and acceptance.

5. **Multicultural friendships:** Our friendships should embody the ideal of multiculturalism.

6. **Opposite-sex friendships:** Friendships with our spouse (if we are married) and other members of the opposite sex enrich us and can be nurtured without breaching ethical and moral boundaries.

The grand theme that runs through the six guidelines is *variety*. Our friendship circles are most satisfying when they are populated with people from many backgrounds and life experiences. Through our circles of friends, the Holy Spirit speaks to our souls, surprises us with new wisdom and insight, and manifests the presence and love of Jesus—who knows just how to be present in and through our friendships: "For where two or three come together in my name, there am I with them" (Matthew 18:20).

Notes

1. L. Gregory Jones and Kevin R. Armstrong, *Resurrecting Excellence: Shaping Faithful Christian Ministry* (Grand Rapids, MI: William B. Eerdmans, 2006), 24.
2. Ibid., 25.
3. Elie Wiesel, *The Time of the Uprooted*, trans. David Hapgood (New York: Alfred A. Knopf, 2005), 154.

4. Bruce Demarest, *Soulguide: Following Jesus as Spiritual Director* (Colorado Springs: NavPress, 2003), 24. See also Henri Nouwen, *Intimacy: Essays in Pastoral Psychology* (San Francisco: Harper and Row, 1969), 97: "Just as a man who wants to be aware of his breathing is in danger, and one who wants to control his heartbeat cannot live, a seminarian who speaks all the time about friendship, love and community might miss the opportunity to experience any of these realities. The lack of participation in life is usually related to an often unconscious anxiety."

5. Dietrich Bonhoeffer, *Spiritual Care*, trans. Jay C. Rochelle (Philadelphia: Fortress Press, 1985), 66.

6. Adin Steinsaltz, *Simple Words: Thinking About What Really Matters in Life* (New York: Simon and Schuster, 2008), 70.

7. Lee B. Spitzer, *Making Friends, Making Disciples: Growing Your Church through Authentic Relationships* (Valley Forge, PA: Judson Press, 2010), xii–xiii.

8. Ray Pahl, *On Friendship* (Cambridge, MA: Polity, 2000), 10.

9. Demarest, *Soulguide*, 5.

10. Aristotle, *The Nicomachean Ethics*, rev. ed., trans. J. A. K. Thompson (London: Penguin Books, 2006), books 8–9.

11. For a comprehensive treatment of friendship circles, see Spitzer, *Making Friends, Making Disciples*.

Further Reading

Adams, Rebecca G., and Graham Allan, eds. *Placing Friendship in Context.* Cambridge: Cambridge University Press, 1998.

Aelred, Rievaulx of. *Spiritual Friendship.* Translated by Mary Eugenia Laker. Kalamazoo, MI: Cistercian Publications, 1977.

Blieszner, Rosemary, and Rebecca G. Adams. *Adult Friendship.* Newbury Park, CA: Sage Publications, 1992.

Cacioppo, John T., and William Patrick. *Loneliness: Human Nature and the Need for Social Connection.* New York: W. W. Norton, 2008.

Fehr, Beverley. *Friendship Processes.* Thousand Oaks, CA: Sage Publications, 1996.

Monsour, Michael. *Women and Men as Friends: Relationships across the Life Span in the 21st Century.* Mahwah, NJ: Lawrence Earlbaum Associates, 2002.

Pangle, Lorraine Smith. *Aristotle and the Philosophy of Friendship.* Cambridge: Cambridge University Press, 2003.

Putnam, Robert D. *Bowling Alone: The Collapse and Revival of American Community.* New York: Simon and Schuster Paperbacks, 2000.

Rawlins, William K. *The Compass of Friendship: Narratives, Identities and Dialogues.* Los Angeles: Sage Publications, 2009.

Werking, Kathy. *We're Just Good Friends: Women and Men in Nonromantic Relationships.* New York: Guilford Press, 1997.

About the Contributor

Rev. Lee B. Spitzer, MDiv, DMin, is the executive minister and senior regional pastor of the American Baptist Churches of New Jersey. He has pastored American Baptist congregations in Rhode Island, New Jersey, and Nebraska. He is the author of several books on spirituality and relational theology, including *Making Friends, Making Disciples*, *Jesus Christ from Cover to Cover*, and *Endless Possibilities: Exploring the Journeys of Your Life*.

PART II

How Do You Evaluate
Spiritual Leadership?

6

Bi-vocational Clergy
(and Congregations)

Rev. Renee S. House, MDiv, PhD

Several months of reflection on the assigned topic of "bi-vocational clergy," sometimes called "tentmakers," has left me feeling as though I am waltzing with a two-hundred-pound octopus, one hand tied behind my back. When the editor of this book, my faculty colleague at New Brunswick Theological Seminary, invited me to write about bi-vocational clergy, he said something like, "It's a no-brainer; it's what we do at New Brunswick. It's a chance to tell our story." It is true. Many of the students at our mid-sized Protestant seminary are engaged in full-time "secular" vocations and anticipate, or already are, serving in congregations with regular, part-time ministerial responsibilities. They may be the sole pastor of the congregation or part of a ministerial staff. Some are paid, but many serve without any compensation. Despite my engagement with a growing number of students from multiple church traditions who are or will be bi-vocational clergy and my experience of the same phenomenon in the mainline denomination where I minister, I had not taken the time to fully grasp the implications of this reality for the church *and* for graduate theological education. I offer my reflections from within the Judeo-Christian framework, trusting that some aspects will resonate with other religious traditions.

The truth is, writing on the topic of bi-vocational ministries has seemed overwhelming because it is linked to other major shifts in church and society. Mainline Protestant Christian church membership has been in decline for nearly half a decade; local churches are shutting

their doors, denominational staff and financial resources are shrinking. This has forced many congregations to choose bi-vocational pastors as a default for the sake of survival. At the same time, new forms
of "church" are emerging locally and globally. There are "base communities" in Latin America, household churches in Philadelphia, and
"new monastic communities" where Christians are moving in groups
into abandoned urban communities to rebuild houses and live in them,
to work and worship as they seek the welfare of the city.[1] These emerging forms of church practice radical, embodied, embedded, prophetic,
communal Christianity and are often led by bi-vocational clergy, whose
central role is to enable the whole community to reflect with biblical
and theological depth on the full scope of human existence and to act
in ways that manifest the Lordship of Christ over creation and societies.

Social inequities increase daily, leaving disproportionate numbers
of racial-ethnic minority persons living in poverty or in prison in a sup-
posedly color-blind society. Young adults "occupy Wall Street," raising
critical questions about work, calling, and vocation and demanding
socioeconomic reforms that resist the destructive values of consumer
capitalism. The political process has stalled in the face of human need.
At the same time, people are spiritually hungry and longing for genuine community and belonging. All of these realities raise fundamental
questions about the nature and purpose of the church and the shape of
its ministry and mission in the world. The increase in the number of bi-
vocational ministers and congregations reflects the church's response
to what some experience as threat, and others as opportunity for a
more faithful witness in the world.

My experience in the seminary and the mainline denomination
where I minister, combined with my research, have convinced me that
bi-vocational ministry *is* the future of the church in North America.[2]
Even now, observes one Presbyterian tentmaker, "the demand for tent-
maker pastors far exceeds the supply at this time in the history of our
denomination."[3] The shift from the paradigm of a full-time minister
serving a congregation to a minister who is bi-vocational and (likely)
part-time is an invitation to churches, seminaries, and divinity schools
to discover how best to prepare the *whole* people of God—clergy and
laypeople—for ministries and other public vocations that bear witness
to and participate in the manifestation of God's reign in the world.

Of course, bi-vocational ministry is not new. Jesus was a carpenter, the first male disciples were fishermen, and the apostle Paul, a tent-maker. Many North American church traditions that ordain persons to the office of minister[4] have long relied on bi-vocational clergy to lead congregations, most notably in varieties of Baptist, Methodist, and free-church settings. Presently, there are growing numbers of bi-vocational ministers in these traditions and other mainline denominations in which full-time clergy have been normative, including Lutheran, Presbyterian, Episcopalian, and various Reformed churches.

As suggested above, the increase in bi-vocational clergy reflects the fact that shrinking congregations are unable to provide the salary and benefits required to support a full-time minister. In these situations, the move to call a part-time, bi-vocational minister is experienced as a significant, unavoidable loss. There is a sense of having settled for less and anxiety about how the work of the ministry will be fulfilled. Indeed, there is anxiety about the survival of the congregation altogether. Without intentional effort to frame a new paradigm for ministry, both the part-time pastor and the congregation are likely to be disappointed in each other as they continue to function with the norms and expectations of the good old days when there was a full-time pastor to "run the church."[5] Many a student in bi-vocational ministry has sat in my office, exhausted and frustrated, because the congregation expects them to do everything. When the toilets are clogged or the boiler shuts down, when a cancer diagnosis is received, and a marriage tilts toward divorce, the bi-vocational pastor is called in.

There are many resources that detail the struggles and joys of serving as a bi-vocational clergyperson, including firsthand accounts and research studies. Those interested in a comprehensive view of the experience and practical advice on how to thrive in bi-vocational ministry are encouraged to consult the bibliography included under Further Reading at the end of this chapter. For my purposes, I will highlight three theological themes that can support ministers and congregations who intentionally choose bi-vocationality in response to God's call. These theological foundations will also strengthen the lives and ministries of full-time clergy and the congregations with whom they serve. But I believe bi-vocational clergy and congregations, through their shared worldly and ecclesial vocations, are uniquely placed to participate in the Holy Spirit's ceaseless labor to make *all* things new. Following discussion of these theological themes, I will consider what all of this might mean for theological seminaries and divinity schools.

The Missional Church

The 1998 publication of *Missional Church: A Vision for the Sending of the Church in North America* is part of a movement that has begun to impact the church's self-understanding—its sense of identity, call, and purpose.[6] The central aim of the missional church movement is to remind the church that God *has* a universal mission and that the church *is taken* up into God's own mission and *sent* into the world as sign, instrument, and agent of that mission. The church does not initiate this mission, nor is the church the ultimate goal of God's mission. Rather, the goal of God's mission is to establish God's kingdom, that is, God's reign, on earth as it is in heaven. Jesus came to earth proclaiming and demonstrating that in and through him God's kingdom was present, with lifegiving power to reconcile, heal, restore, and liberate persons and communities from the powers of evil, sin, and death.

Here and now the church is an imperfect sign of God's reign and an imperfect instrument, and still God chooses the church and gives it the power to be the missionary agent who in word and deed proclaims the good news in Jesus. The mission is God's, and its scope extends to every square inch of creation. The Spirit draws the church to receive, respond to, and participate in God's mission, both in the church and in the larger world, where the Spirit also labors to bring God's kingdom on earth.[7]

Within this framework of God's comprehensive kingdom, we find a unifying reality that holds together body and soul, sacred and secular, public and private, individual and communal. If all of these realities are encompassed by God's mission, then in its gathering and in its being sent, the church is a sign, messenger, and servant of God's vast kingdom concern—clergy and laypeople together. Bi-vocational ministers, by virtue of their own "worldly" labors, enjoy a special solidarity with every person in the congregation who goes into the wider world on Monday morning carrying God's benediction and returns to the church on Sunday, carrying the people and concerns of the world.

The Priesthood of All Believers

With regard to the whole people of God participating in God's mission, a key doctrine, born from the Protestant Reformation, is the priesthood of all believers. With biblical foundations in Romans 12:1, where Paul invites Christians to present themselves as living sacrifices, and 1 Peter 2:4–9, which describes the church as a "holy" and "royal" priesthood called to offer spiritual sacrifices and to proclaim the mighty acts of God who called us out of darkness into marvelous light, the doctrine stresses the response-ability of Christians together and as individuals to offer themselves, their praise, their prayers, and their proclamation through Jesus, who has reconciled and made them acceptable to God.

One Reformation catechism expands on the notion of the priesthood of all believers, teaching that Christians, through baptism, are anointed to participate in the threefold office of Christ, who is prophet, priest, and king or ruler.[8] Christ's work through his threefold office is perfect and non-repeatable, but now, through the Holy Spirit, Christians respond to what Christ himself has done and is doing in them and in the world. The work of the whole church and the individual believer flows from and follows after Christ. It takes place in the church and in society where the reign of God is breaking in.

Building on the idea of the Christian's participation in the threefold office of Christ, Maria Harris, a scholar in religious education, describes the educational/formational ministry of the church as preparing all people to grow into their individual and communal pastoral vocation: to be priests who know for themselves and can "hand over" the core stories of God's liberating, redeeming love; to be prophets who listen for the cries of the marginalized and then speak and act from the very pathos of God; and to be rulers who order the life of the church and society—institutions, policies, and structures—to reflect God's own desires for the ordering of human life.[9]

To fulfill their threefold pastoral vocation as sign and servant of God's mission, Christians need to be deeply and creatively, seriously and playfully, engaged with God's stories so that they can get the story straight in the face of many alternative versions of reality! They need to welcome *and* speak the prophetic Word that shatters false peace and settles for injustice. On this point, bi-vocational pastors express joy in the freedom they find to preach prophetically, because their livelihood does not depend solely on the congregation. And, finally, Christians need to be wise and discerning every day as they seek to order the church and society, their homes and their workplaces, in ways that foster life, peace, liberation, and vocation for every person.[10]

The call to nurture congregations and Christians for their three-fold pastoral vocation goes beyond the normal process of using "gift inventories" to identify spiritual gifts listed in Romans and Corinthians that may be used in the ministries of the church. In this three-fold paradigm, "spiritual gifts" are most fully defined in terms of talents, dispositions, education, experience, passion, and desire that are offered and taken up by the Spirit of the living God for the fulfilling of God's mission in the church and the world. Bi-vocational ministers and congregations know better than anyone that the minister cannot fulfill the church's ministry alone and that even shared church ministry does not answer the breadth of God's call to love and serve God and neighbor. The bi-vocational pastor will be *especially* focused on building up the body of Christ for its pastoral vocation and participation in the expansive mission of God. Some will have gifts for preaching, teaching, and word evangelism, others for child care, farming, social work, and politics.

Calling and Vocation

At this point in our exploration, it should be fairly clear that what Christians do in their daily lives and labors has everything to do with their participation in the mission of God. During the Protestant Reformation, theologians like Martin Luther and John Calvin insisted that not only monks and priests but every Christian has a calling ordained for them by God. This includes the general calling by God to become members of the body of Christ, and a particular calling and vocation through which every person serves God and neighbor.[11] In the last several years numerous books have been published concerning a theology of work, calling, and vocation[12] in response to the reality that the social and cultural milieu of America no longer supports the Protestant tradition's sense of calling and vocation that "infuses the mundane secular life with religious meaning" and purpose.[13]

Corporate greed, exclusive focus on the bottom line as the measure of success, a globalized economy, rising unemployment especially among racial and ethnic minorities, and patterns of permanent overwork that rob people of a Sabbath all point to a crisis in the world of work. God's calling and a sense of vocation both include and are larger than our daily jobs. They also embrace being life partners, sons, daughters, parents, grandparents, friends, and neighbors, even to our enemies. For this reason, a central task of the church's ministry is "to evoke and sustain a sense for all of life as an integrated response to God's callings."[14] It has become urgent for the church to enable Christians to understand their total daily lives as a response to God's ongoing work in creation, providence, redemption, and new creation.

Bi-vocational pastors and congregations can lead the way in this as they participate together in the six plus one pattern of daily work and Sunday worship, which joins liturgy to life and recognizes every day as a self-offering to the Triune God. They are also in a position to more readily identify and nurture partnerships between the church and other public institutions and agencies with which they are engaged, for the sake of ordering all of human life in ways that honor the image of God and presence of Christ in every man, woman, and child.

By considering bi-vocational clergy and congregations in relation to a theology for the missional church within the reign of God, the formation of every Christian and congregation for participation in the threefold office of Christ, and a theology of calling and vocation in daily life, I have attempted to provide the bi-vocational paradigm of ministry and mission a theological framework that unifies all of reality under the rule of a sovereign Triune God. It is a perspective that holds together sacred and secular, body and soul, public and private, church and larger world, individual and communal. All of these things are encompassed by God's eternal mission, and the church is, in its gathering and sending, a sign, messenger, and servant of God's vast kingdom of concern—clergy and laypeople together in all of the places they live, labor, and love. As previously stated, this unified view of the world and the church as God's servant within it defines the nature and purpose of *every* congregation. But I believe that bi-vocational ministers and congregations are uniquely placed to shape their ministry and mission in ways that manifest this theological perspective. In my own short time as a bi-vocational minister, when I gathered with other members of the church for night meetings to plan for our shared worship and service, it was natural for us to reflect theologically on our days and offer our daily labors and prayers to the God who has given us life and being and guides the world by divine providence.

Theological Education

Given my daily work as the dean of New Brunswick Theological Seminary and professor of practical theology, I cannot conclude this essay without a word about what it might mean for seminaries to prepare women and men for bi-vocational ministries. At New Brunswick Theological Seminary we have been doing just this for many years. Over the years I have learned that just because folks are, or will be, engaged in bi-vocational ministries doesn't mean they don't need a thorough theological education. It does mean that the time for such deep, sustained study will be precious, and we have done our best to make seminary education accessible to students who work all day and can study only at night or on weekends. We have not moved toward online education, which though convenient, doesn't allow for the kind of face-to-face encounter with others that characterizes the heart of Jesus and the church's incarnational ministry and mission. We have been intentional about offering graduate degrees for those who will serve as ordained ministers and certificate programs for laypeople who want to deepen their faith and action. But my reflection on bi-vocational clergy and congregations has shown me that we have been, at least partially, missing the mark.

In the 1960s and early 1970s, when radical theologians were criticizing the church's failure to touch and transform the total life of society to reflect God's new creation,[15] and the Catholic Church was recommending that priests prepare for and engage in secular human services vocations alongside church work,[16] New Brunswick Theological Seminary instituted an experimental curriculum.[17] Although it is too complex to describe in great detail here, the chief innovation of the curriculum was to have students spend their first year of seminary reflecting biblically and theologically on the whole scope of human existence. Students were assigned to small "core" groups, with one faculty member leading, and together they served with the local police, in social service agencies, and in public schools, and they hung out in bars having conversations with the locals at night. While also teaching the core theological disciplines, the seminary collaborated with other institutions and agencies to "experience theological insights while ... engaged in assessing the needs of contemporary situations" in human existence.[18] Students were encouraged simultaneously to complete course work at Rutgers University, which surrounds the Seminary, in order to increase their grasp of the human situation.

The great irony is that these students in the 1970s were coming straight from college without "secular" vocations or broad experience of the world. Now we have students coming from their work as prison wardens, teachers, law enforcement officers, lawyers, social workers, doctors, and nurses, to name a few of the professions, not to mention their lives in families and neighborhoods. So, why not begin seminary education exactly where they live, not with reflection on the church, but on society and culture? Why not assist them in understanding their own and the church's vocation in light of the reign of God? Why not encourage them to create the kind of partnerships between church and society that can address the whole scope of human need and celebrate the super-abundant gifts and expressions of human cultures? Why not use pedagogies that prepare them to work with teams of people in the church and in the world through the development of community organizing skills and exposure to models of conversation as strategies for effecting change?[19] Why not prepare them to prepare congregations to embrace their call to share in the priestly, prophetic, and ruling offices of Jesus Christ, the risen Lord, through their service in church and other daily vocations? Why not be intentional in naming their call to bi-vocational ministry as a superb, integrating, holistic, and powerful response to the ceaseless labors of the Triune God who is making all things new? We are already on this road, so why not venture further, starting now?

Notes

1. See, e.g., Leonardo Boff, *Ecclesiogenesis: Base Communities Reinvent the Church* (Maryknoll, NY: Orbis Books, 1986); Hal Taussig, *A New Spiritual Home: Progressive Christianity at the Grass Roots* (Santa Rosa, CA: Polebridge Press, 2006); Jonathan Wilson-Hartgrove, *New Monasticism: What It Has to Say to Today's Church* (Grand Rapids, MI: Brazos Press, 2008).

2. This observation is based on my own experience as a minister in the Reformed Church in America, conversations with colleagues and students in other denominations and church traditions, and publications such as Linda Lawson, "Tentmaking Ministers Predicted to Become Southern Baptist Norm," *Baptist Press*, August 11, 1999; L. Ronald Brushwyler, "Bi-Vocational Pastors: A Research Report" (Westchester, IL: Midwest Ministry Development Service, 1992); and Evan Silverstein, "Short of Clergy and Money, Churches Take to the Tentmakers," *Episcopal News Service*, www.episcopalarchives.org/cgi-bin/ENS/ENSpress_release.pl?pr_number=2000-208.

3. Linda Kuhn, "Some Guidance to Churches from the Association of Presbyterian Tentmakers," www.pcusa.org/media/uploads/ministers/pdfs/tentmakerguidance.pdf.

4. The distinction here is between certain Anabaptist traditions in which no persons are ordained to a distinct office for ministry and other traditions in which persons are set apart for this office.

5. For an example of one denomination's efforts to frame and support the paradigm of bi-vocational ministers and congregations, see the Presbyterian Church (USA), Association of Presbyterian Tentmakers (www.pcusatentmakers.org), which produces resources and offers annual conferences and other forms of support.

6. Darrell L. Guder, *Missional Church: A Vision for the Sending of the Church in North America*, The Gospel and Our Culture Series (Grand Rapids, MI: Eerdmans, 1998).

7. David J. Bosch, *Transforming Mission: Paradigm Shifts in Theology of Mission* (Maryknoll, NY: Orbis Press, 1991), 391.

8. *Heidelberg Catechism*, Question & Answer 32: "But why are you called a Christian? Because by faith I am a member of Christ and so I share in his anointing. I am anointed to confess his name [prophet], to present myself to him as a living sacrifice of thanks [priest], to strive with a good conscience against sin and the devil in this life, and afterward to reign with Christ over all creation for all eternity [king]." In Christian Reformed Church, *Ecumenical Creeds and Reformed Confessions* (Grand Rapids, MI: CRC Publications, 1988).

9. Maria Harris, *Fashion Me a People: Curriculum in the Church* (Louisville, KY: Westminster/John Knox Press, 1989).

10. For an elaboration of an educational process that is suited for nurturing the church in its priestly, prophetic, and political (ruling) vocations, see Walter Brueggemann, *The Creative Word: Canon as a Model for Biblical Education*, 4th ed. (Minneapolis: Fortress Press, 1982); and for a model of education for liberation and vocation, see Anne Streaty Wimberly, *Soul Stories: African American Christian Education*, rev. ed. (Nashville: Abingdon Press, 2005).

11. William C. Placher, ed., *Callings: Twenty Centuries of Christian Wisdom on Vocation* (Grand Rapids, MI: Eerdmans, 2005), 205–7.

12. For example, Robert J. Banks, *Faith God to Work: Reflections from the Marketplace* (n.p.: Alban Institute, 1993); Darrell Cosden, *A Theology of Work: Work and the New Creation* (Eugene, OR: Wipf & Stock, 2006); David H. Jensen, *Responsive Labor: A Theology of Work* (Louisville, KY: Westminster John Knox Press, 2006); Douglas Schuurman, *Vocation: Discerning Our Callings in Life* (Grand Rapids, MI: Eerdmans, 2004).

13. Schuurman, *Vocation*, xii–xiii.

14. Ibid., xiii.

15. J. C. Hoekendijk, *The Church Inside Out*, trans. Isaac Rottenberg (Philadelphia: Westminster Press, 1964).

16. John C. Schwarz, "Modern Tentmaking: A New Leadership," *The Christian Century* 90, no. 6 (February 7, 1973): 170–76. The article describes the Catholic worker-priest movement.

17. The model for the curriculum was developed by the Association of Theological Schools (ATS). For details, see *Theological Education in the 1970s: A Report of the Resources Planning Commission* (Pittsburgh: ATS, 1968).

18. New Brunswick Theological Seminary, *Catalog* (1972–1973), 4.

19. See Jaunita Brown and David Isaacs, *The World Cafe: Shaping Our Futures through Conversations That Matter* (San Francisco: Berrett-Koehler Publishers, 2005).

Further Reading

Association of Presbyterian Tentmaker's Manual. Louisville, KY: Church Vocations Ministry Unit, Presbyterian Church, USA, 1991.

Bickers, Dennis W. *The Tentmaking Pastor: The Joy of Bivocational Ministry.* Grand Rapids, MI: Baker Books, 2000.

Bonn, Robert L., and Ruth T. Doyle. "Secularly Employed Clergymen: A Study in Occupational Role Recomposition." *Journal for the Scientific Study of Religion* 13, no. 3 (September 1974): 325–43.

Dorr, Luther M. *The Bivocational Pastor.* Nashville, TN: Broadman Press, 1988.

Elliott, John Y. *Our Pastor Has an Outside Job: New Strength for the Church through Dual-Role Ministry.* Valley Forge, PA: Judson Press, 1980.

Fuller, John, and Patrick Vaughan, eds. *Working for the Kingdom: The Story of Ministers in Secular Employment.* London: SPCK, 1986.

LaRochelle, Robert R. *Part-Time Pastor, Full-Time Church.* Cleveland, OH: Pilgrim Press, 2010.

Reko, Karl H. *Shared-Time Pastoral Ministry: A Workbook for Congregations and Pastors.* Minneapolis: American Lutheran Church, 1986.

Thompson, M. Greg. "Confessions of a Bi-vocational Baptist Preacher." *Baptist History and Heritage* 40, no. 2 (Spring 2005): 46–50.

About the Contributor

Rev. Renee S. House, MDiv, PhD, an ordained minister in the Reformed Church in America, has been serving on the faculty of New Brunswick Theological Seminary since 1987 in a variety of roles including six years as dean of the seminary. Presently, she serves as associate professor of practical theology. She also ministers at the Metuchen Reformed Church, working with educational ministries and small groups, and leads retreats and workshops through the Reformed Church in America. Her publications include a number of essays and articles related to the theology and practice of ministry and mission. She received her master of divinity degree from New Brunswick Theological Seminary and holds a PhD from Princeton Theological Seminary.

7

The New Business Model for the Non-Profit Organization

Ronald Thomas, MHCS, SWP

"Well, we can just worship in the dark. The Lord will make a way somehow." That is when I knew that I would be leaving soon. This statement was a rebuttal to my strategic plan that we could not continue financially to just depend on the tithe, when you had basically 1 percent of the membership adhering to the tithing principal. My plan was twofold: increase membership and produce more revenue-based programs. Step out of the past into a new and vibrant congregation that was geared for growth.

My view on congregational financing and marketing was based on the foundations of business. If a business is not growing and revenues are down, the leadership team develops a plan to increase revenue and grow market share, which in this case is new members.

Houses of worship going forward post-recession are going to have to realign their thinking around the basics of business. This model revolves around selling a service or product to produce enough revenue so that once all obligations are paid, the remainder is defined as profit.

Sounds simple enough; however, when it comes to religion/spirituality, a large part of a congregation does not want to come to terms with this truth.

Religion/spirituality is the brand that encompasses the product or service that your house of worship offers. This is what attracts people to this entity. The money they donate is the same as the purchase of goods and services. This "revenue" is what allows you to maintain salaries, services, and obligations. When this drops, it causes a domino effect to the other areas of the house of worship.

This is a dilemma that all houses of worship are facing—declining revenue, declining members, and so on. So how do leaders in the future operate in this environment?

Houses of Worship as a Business?

There seems to be a reluctance today to embrace houses of worship as a business. However, when you see houses of worship that are growing, such as the mega-congregations, this is the type of model that they are using.

Every house of worship cannot become a mega-house of worship, but every house of worship has the ability to grow and prosper. The basics of business require the new leader to embrace it and use tools that have been time-tested to produce results.

The use of the terms "business" and "house of worship" in the same sentence should not be seen as sacrilegious. The reason is that when you view the physical plant and the need for funds to keep the mission of the house of worship meeting its needs, it will require it.

You can't pay weekly and monthly bills if the revenue is not there. If you depend on tithes alone, you should do a means test to see whether you are on track. The leadership team may want to ask themselves the following questions:

- What percentage of your congregation is now tithing?
- What percentage is not? Can you get those who are not to transition to tithers?
- Does the weekly take create enough revenue to meet the monthly obligations (e.g., salary, utilities)?
- What is the amount left once all bills have been paid?
- Can you continue if the current state does not change?

If at the end of the month you break even or do not have enough to meet your monthly obligation, then that is a sign that you will need to develop another approach to raising funds.

The problem that I have always had with tithings is that you have no control over your main source of funding. Whatever the level of commitment will determine the amount of tithes. Committed members will contribute more than noncommitted members. If the majority of your tithers are elderly, what happens in time as these members get older? What steps are taken to motivate and convert other members to the status of tithers? As you are beginning to see, you can't just sit back waiting for it to happen on its own. There must be some type of plan in place.

Strategic Plan for Continued Success

One of the most important tools that the new leader must develop is a strategic plan. The strategic plan identifies where the organization wants to be at some point in the future and describes how it is going to get there.

This planning process is the continual attention to the status quo and current changes in the organization. Attention must also be paid to the external environment and how this affects the future of the organization. Strategic planning skills will be critical to the long-term success of your organization.

The strategic planning process includes the following:

- Taking a wide look around at what's going on outside the organization and how it might affect the organization (an environmental scan), and identifying opportunities and threats

- Taking a hard look at what's going on inside the organization, including its strengths and weaknesses

- Establishing statements of mission, vision, and values (some prefer to do this as the first step in planning)

- Establishing goals to accomplish over the next (usually) three years or so, as a result of what's going on inside and outside the organization

- Identifying how those goals will be reached (strategies, objectives, responsibilities, and timelines)

Strategic planning determines the overall direction and goals of the organization. Getting this process down will influence all aspects of the organization. This process will enable your organization to make strategic decisions as it relates to the following:

- The products and services that will be provided and how they will be designed to have maximum effect

- The way the roles and the organization will be designed for maximum operating efficiency
- The performance goals for positions throughout the organization
- The strategic roles within the organization and their importance (job segmentation)
- The resources that will be needed to achieve those goals

Membership Engagement

Numerous studies show that companies with engaged employees produce better overall results.

So what does engagement mean? It is an emotional connection that employees feel for their organization that will ultimately influence them to exert greater discretionary effort to their work within the organization.

The same holds true for members within your house of worship. It works on the principle of leaders engaging members, who then stay longer and are more involved in the organization and its mission, which leads to a more productive and beneficial organization.

You cannot be successful in the marketplace if you are not successful in the workplace. This workplace is defined as your membership within.

The following are questions to consider:

- What is the engagement level of your members?
- Break-even point: how long does it take for new members to get involved, such as joining a group within the organization?
- What is the average tenure of your members?
- What is the average age of the current membership?
- What is the average age of new members?
- What attracted this person or persons to become members of your congregation?
- Whom are we targeting?
- How can we better connect?

These types of questions will allow you to get a snapshot of your current membership, which will further allow you to understand how your membership plays a role in growing your organization.

Leadership Matters

Leadership does not mean just the clergy or head of the organization. Everyone who is in charge of a committee, whether it is a trustee, deacon, or head of a ministry, is part of the leadership.

This is extremely important because if these separate leaders are not knowledgeable about the strategy of the organization, you are missing out on a huge opportunity. If these leaders are not connecting in a positive way with the members of their group, they and the organization are missing out on a terrific opportunity. The dynamic relationship between leader and member will drive your engagement levels.

So how do we go about choosing leaders? In so many houses of worship, leadership is chosen not by rigor but by who is next up in the chain of command. This is a very flawed plan if you are seeking to grow your membership in the future. While leadership should not be limited to a certain group with prior management skills, care should be given to the development of the leadership pool.

A leadership development plan should be put in place to guide and shape the level of leaders for future opportunities. One unique way is to choose non-leaders within your organization and put them in a position to move seamlessly into roles as they arise.

Leaders will need to deliver results. These results will be the outcomes of leaders' actions. Leaders must buy into the vision of the organization as well as the vision of their ministry. They must inspire others and most importantly act with integrity and be authentic.

The clergy or head of the organization must clarify why leadership matters. They must explain their vision of the organization and show how leadership is responsible for attaining that vision.

In business, one of the most talked about corporate endeavors is the quality of the leadership pipeline. How deep is the bench of leaders?

Additionally, economic challenges are a reality of leadership. Leaders are evaluated on how they handle such challenges.

The New Leader Model

This new leader is an individual who is very humble on a personal level but who possesses a great deal of drive and desire to succeed, where "success" is not personal, but defined by creating something great that will outlast the person's time at the helm.

These are people with an unwavering will and commitment to do what it takes to drive their ministry or committee. They are the kind of people who do not point to themselves as the cause for their domains. There are many people within your organization that have this ability and the attitude necessary to attain that status.

It's about the Leaders

How can a house of worship transform itself into a great and growing house of worship? For any organization to be great, it must have the right people on the leadership team.

By having a strong team, these houses of worship avoid the pitfall of the "lone genius" leader. Great houses of worship are those that have a very solid foundation and don't depend on the brilliance of any one person.

Great teams are mostly composed of people who have a good sense of balance with the rest of their lives—family, career, and so on. Of course, they have a deep commitment to their houses of worship, but not one that blinds them to the other important things in their lives.

Are you making sound decisions? One of the key factors in the success of great houses of worship is a series of good decisions. The decisions flow from the fact that leaders all make a consistent and thorough effort to confront reality, internalizing the facts relevant to their situation. Having lofty goals can be good, but you can never lose sight of what the reality is on the ground, no matter how much you will it to be different.

It is necessary to create a climate where honesty is valued and honored. If people aren't telling it like it is, those at the top may not realize the truth until it is too late. Some tips to create this kind of climate are as follows:

- It's often better to ask questions rather than dispense "answers."
- Encourage healthy debate. It has to be real debate, not a show put on to make people feel included. It should also not just be argument for the sake of argument; reach a conclusion and move on.

- When things go wrong, investigate to avoid repeating the mistake, instead of assigning blame. If people are too worried about protecting themselves, it becomes difficult to honestly analyze and learn from failures.

- Create mechanisms, "red flags," that allow people to communicate problems instantly and without repercussions, and in a way that cannot be ignored.

Amid these "brutal facts" that must be faced, you must also have faith in your final goal. By maintaining this vision and keeping your ear to the ground, you won't need to motivate people; if you've got the right people, they'll be motivated of their own accord.

What makes your house of worship different? Can you see through the clutter and grab a few of the simple and unique things that give you the advantage? That is called your brand.

To succeed in branding you must understand the needs and wants of your members and prospective members. You do this by integrating your brand strategies throughout the organization at every point of contact.

If a person were to hear of your house of worship, what words would he or she use to describe it? Your brand resides within the hearts and minds of everyone that the house of worship or its members come in contact with. It is the sum total of their experiences and perceptions, some of which you can influence, and some that you cannot.

A strong brand is invaluable as the battle for members and growth intensifies day by day. It's important to spend time investing in, defining, and building your brand. After all, your brand is the source of a promise to your members and the ones that you are trying to attract. It's a foundational piece in your marketing communication and one you do not want to be without.

Passion, on the other hand, does not come from the rah-rah at worship services; it comes by doing things that make people passionate on their own. Passion isn't something that can be forced on people; it has to come from a mission that they truly believe in.

My suggestion would be to create a "strategic council" that would work with either of two approaches: a *SWOT analysis* or an *environmental scan*. Both of these methods are tools that corporations use.

A scan of the internal and external environment is an important part of the strategic planning process. Environmental factors internal to the firm usually can be classified as strengths (S) or weaknesses (W), and those external to the firm can be classified as opportunities (O) or threats (T).

The SWOT analysis provides information that is helpful in matching the firm's resources and capabilities to the competitive environment in which it operates. As such, it is instrumental in strategy formulation and selection. The following diagram shows how a SWOT analysis fits into an environmental scan:

SWOT ANALYSIS	
Strengths	**Weaknesses**
• What are your strong points? • What do you do well? Consider this from your organization's point of view and from the point of view of the people you deal with. Be realistic. What are you good at? What are you known for?	• What could be improved? • What is done badly? • What should be avoided? There are internal weaknesses as well as external. How do you compare with other individuals in your industry? Are you perceived as below or above average? Again, you must be honest with yourself in this exercise.
Opportunities	**Threats**
• What are the good opportunities facing you? • What are the interesting trends? Useful opportunities can come from such things as: • Changes in your donor base • Partnership opportunities • Changes in social patterns, population profiles, and lifestyles • Local events	• What obstacles do you face? • What is your competition doing? • Are the required specifications for your job, products, or services changing? • Is changing technology threatening your position? • Do you have bad debt or cash-flow problems? Performing this analysis can often be an eye-opening experience—in terms of both pointing out what needs to be done and putting problems into perspective.

Environmental scanning can be defined as a process that looks at the political, economic, social, and other events and trends that will influence your house of worship or organization. This is a more substantial tool in getting the overview of how you are positioned within your "market." The difference between the two strategic tools is that the environmental scan takes into account more of a global or outside view.

Houses of worship should have an entrepreneurial spirit and a sense of discipline. Both are necessary to drive new things. Without some sense of discipline, things begin to break down. The best companies have both latitude for individual action and a culture of disciplined behavior. This goes back to having the right people. You need to find people who have an innate sense of self-discipline.

Social Media

Social media will not create a fire about your organization unless you have something going on. However, where there is momentum, social media can accelerate it. The social media tools that should be addressed are Facebook, Twitter, and possibly YouTube. You must have a social media strategy that explains how you will use each medium.

Facebook allows you to connect with your members and allows people to connect with you or your organization.

Twitter, a 140-character platform, allows you to communicate and share. To me, Twitter is a more professional version of Facebook. If you read a great article, you can "tweet" it to your followers. In turn, they can retweet it to their followers. This is the multiplier effect of Twitter.

YouTube has a tremendous amount of promise. Imagine creating your own TV channel where you provide the content.

Changing Demographics

The United States is also expected to grow somewhat older. The portion of the population that is currently at least sixty-five years old— 13 percent—is expected to reach about 20 percent by 2050.

But even as the baby boomers age, the population of working and young people is also expected to keep rising. The number of children a woman is expected to have in her lifetime hit 2.1 in 2006, with 4.3 million total births, the highest level in forty-five years, thanks largely to recent immigrants, who tend to have more children than do residents whose families have been in the United States for several generations. Moreover, the nation is on the verge of a baby boomlet, when the children of the original boomers have children of their own.

This will have a tremendous effect on your congregation. How will you grow if the average age of your membership is skewed toward seniors? How will you attract and continue to attract this new demographic?

Final Words

Leaders of the houses of worship of tomorrow will face an avalanche of internal and external issues like nothing ever seen. They must be steeped in theology and be well versed and comfortable on the Monday-through-Friday business end. That will include growth, marketing, finances, and most of all, a solid leadership team.

This will require all cylinders to be operating at full throttle to manage houses of worship or organizations. It will also require managing the internal leadership pool that will be required to keep the fires burning so that the organization will look attractive to prospective members.

About the Contributor

Ronald Thomas, MHCS, SWP, is director of talent and human resources solutions at Buck Consultants in New York City. He is also a faculty member of the Human Capital Institute, facilitating two certification tracks (Human Capital Strategist [HCS] and Strategic Workforce Planning [SWP]). *HR Examiner* ranks him in the top twenty-five among both talent-management influencers and human resources influencers. He is the principal consultant at Strategy Focused HR in New York. He is a member of the *Harvard Business Review* Advisory Council, the Executive Online Panel at McKinsey Consulting, and the Human Capital Institute's Expert Advisory Panel on Talent Management Strategy. He is certified by the Human Capital Institute as a human capital strategist (HCS) and strategic workforce planner (SWP). His work has been featured in *Inc. Magazine*, *Wall Street Journal*, *Crain's New York Business*, *Canadian Business*, *Workforce Management*, and *Chief Learning Officer*. He is a graduate of Benedict College and New York University.

8

Teaching Worship

Rev. Gregg A. Mast, MDiv, PhD

Evaluating Your Sunday Morning Worship

This title feels almost sacrilegious! Worship is the sacred work of the church, and so to evaluate it feels like we are walking with heavy boots on holy ground. How can we measure how we sing and pray? How can we evaluate how present God is and how committed our congregation feels on any given Sunday? And yet, because worship is a unique act of religious communities and the central focus of many traditions, it is important to step back and reflect on our time with God and with each other every Sunday morning.

While many chapters in this book can be read and appropriated by many religious traditions with very little additional work, because of my own limitations, I have decided to create a model focused specifically on the worship of Protestant Christians. I hope this chapter will then allow you, the reader, to go back to your own faith tradition and repeat the exercise using the core of what is important in your worship. We will do so not by creating a laundry list of things we should do and say in every worship service, but rather by measuring ourselves with some core values that inform our worship. It is my hope that these values are embraced by many—if not most—Protestants and reflect the best of our common roots. I have imagined the exercise within this chapter as a strategy that the leaders of a congregation could use to reflect more deeply on their worship experiences together. I hope that the questions can be asked in religious school classes and on retreat, in women's and men's groups, in electronic surveys and with the pastoral staff of a large congregation. In a sense, the questions that follow are an audit of what happens in your worship experience, whether it is a gathering of a handful of believers or thousands who fill a single sanctuary.

A final word before we begin. The questions that follow do not in any way represent an exhaustive list. I hope that you will add your own concerns and core values that you believe ought to be dynamically present every time you worship. Far more important than the questions are the answers you hear together. God's voice and our discernment are often most clear when we listen and talk together. It is then that we hear the still, small voice of God in the irreverent words of a teenager or the whispered words of a very old saint, in the strong words of leaders and the reflective words of those who quietly go about the business of serving God.

How would you evaluate your Sunday mornings with God and each other? I invite you to think deeply, to speak honestly, to reflect carefully, and to smile again and again as we discover how God blesses us each time we gather and can bless us with new ways to worship in our favorite pews each and every Sunday morning.

Where Is God?

The woman sitting in the airplane seat next to me was a late-twenty-something and intrigued that I was a pastor. She talked about her childhood in the church with warmth but quickly confessed that she hadn't attended a church for some years except for weddings and funerals. She then spoke the words that have characterized her generation: "While I am not very religious, I am spiritual." When I suggested that the church was a community of people who were deeply committed to being spiritual together, she looked at me as if I had three heads. "That's not the church I remember," she observed. I invited her to tell me about the church of her memories. She shared that her childhood church seemed to be constantly interested in money, potlucks, and rummage sales. The sermons were long and boring, she observed, and had little or nothing to do with her life. Her observations were enumerated as if she were reading from a shopping list. Certainly she was not angry or even disappointed with the church; she just couldn't imagine that it had anything to do with her deep interest in leading a spiritually rich life.

After almost a decade, this airplane conversation still haunts me. What I assumed was self-evident—that the church had God at the very center of its life and worship—came as a great surprise to my traveling companion. I have come to the conclusion that my anonymous friend was far closer to the truth; her generation is voting with its feet in dramatic fashion and not finding a pew or a place in our congregations.

In thinking about the life and worship of the church, the story of Jacob comes to mind. Jacob was on the run from his brother Esau, whom he had betrayed. He lay down one of the first nights in the wilderness at a place called Bethel, where he used a stone for his pillow. It was there under the stars that he dreamed he stood at the base of a great ladder that stretched from earth to heaven and from heaven to earth, and the God of his grandfather Abraham and his father Isaac stood at his side. It is that wilderness ladder that represents the unique and essential architecture of worship. While it is vertical, representing our relationship to God, it undergirds the horizontal. This is a strange architectural principle, for in the "real" world, the horizontal always provides the foundation for the vertical. But in the worship life of the church, the up and down provides the structure for all the interpersonal edification and encouragement that is part of churchly culture.

If worship is to be timely and relevant, it needs to be tied to the timeless and eternally gracious presence of God. However, my airplane seatmate couldn't imagine that Sunday morning had anything to do with God and her spirituality. The thought that the church was a gathering of folk committed to walking up and down that staircase together, in prayer and service, was not even on her radar screen. Although she didn't, she could have easily asked, "Where is God in the church and in its worship?"

The first measuring stick for faithful and dynamic worship is to ask: Where is God in our worship? Where and how do we celebrate God's mysterious presence? How does our worship clearly communicate that this is not about us but about the God who was, is, and is to come?

Where Is the World?

The "none generation," those who increasingly fill out the word "none" in response to the question of church affiliation, often finds the church hypocritical, judgmental, insincere, or just hopelessly irrelevant. It is this generation that is also asking, where is the world in our worship? There are those who see Sunday morning as a cocoon, a place to insulate themselves from the problems of the world. I can't tell you how many folk have said to me that they are grateful for Sunday morning because it is an oasis in the wilderness of their week. They observe that it is the time when we don't have to worry about all that consumes the front pages of our newspapers or the incessant drumbeat of violence, pain, and trouble that fills the airwaves.

While I fully understand the need to escape the stress of the world, at its core, the worship of the church is not a time to live for a morning in heaven, but rather a time to understand how to live for a lifetime in our neighborhoods, nation, and world. The enormous need to escape the world, rather than love it and change it, is a second measuring stick of faithful and dynamic worship. The words of Jesus recorded in the third chapter of John make our call clear: "For God so loved the world that he sent his only Son ..." (verse 16). God's love, while celebrated in the worship of the church, is in no way limited to the church. Grace, God's unmerited love for the world, is radical. One theologian has observed that there is nothing we can do to cause God to love us more, and there is nothing we can do to cause God to love us less. We have no power over God's grace; we can only kneel in its presence and give God the glory.

And so, as you audit your Sunday worship, ask where the world is present as you gather. Is it found in your prayers for those who are sick and dying; for those caught in the deathly grip of war and hunger; for those who wander through life without hope and purpose? Is it found in preaching and in ministry, so the words of our mouths become the work of our hands? We cannot pray for peace without committing to the work of peacemaking; we cannot pray for justice without speaking truth to power that gives unearned privilege to some while it ignores others; we cannot pray for the hungry to be fed without finding our place on the Jericho road to reach out and heal a person, a neighborhood, a nation that has been stripped and left for dead. Where is the world in your worship?

Where Is Gracious Hospitality?

Everyone who worships with us wants to feel accepted and thus graciously welcome. The author of Hebrews, exercising a bit of wry humor and profound insight, wrote that we should not neglect to show hospitality to strangers, "for thereby some have entertained angels unawares" (13:2). The antecedent to this proverb is Abram and Sarai's welcome to the three strangers who came to their wilderness tent and shared the shocking news that in their geriatric years, they were about to welcome a child into their lives. The strangers shared news that Abram and Sarai could barely believe, and yet after nine months, Isaac (which means "laughter" in Hebrew) turned their sedate lives upside down.

Almost a decade ago, I left congregational ministry (which had been my life for nearly a quarter of a century) to work first in a denominational position and then in a seminary one. This grants me a number of Sundays when I lead worship for a congregation as a visiting pastor and almost an equal number of Sundays when I am free to visit other churches, where I am simply a stranger in the pew. While I have never "met" a congregation that would not describe itself as warm and friendly, the proof is often found in that time before and after worship when members are consumed with each other and oblivious to a stranger in their midst. I have decided that there is nothing lonelier than standing in a crowd of "warm, friendly" people who don't know you exist and have no expectation that you may be an angel with gifts and news that could change their world.

How are you intentionally welcoming strangers into your midst? How do you reach out to those who look different from you? Are you interested in visitors because you hope they will swell your membership rolls or because they may be anonymous angels with surprising news? How are the last and the least, the marginal and the newly arrived, embraced in your community and treated in your worship? Are there hints in the service or in its printed program that will make the singing and praying, the speaking and the listening, hospitable to those who have wandered in off the street or have never sat in a pew in their entire life?

Where Is the Community of Worship Leaders?

One of the great gifts of the Reformation was that the whole people of God were identified with the words of Saint Peter, "the priesthood of all believers." This has meant that each and every believer has direct access to God through the sole mediatorship of Jesus Christ. It has also meant that Reformation churches believe that all the baptized people of God are gifted and equipped to assist in the worship leadership of a congregation.

In the congregation I served in Albany, New York, the elders of the church traditionally entered the sanctuary together and sat as a community in the "elders' pews" which were constructed for exactly that purpose in 1798 when the church was built. I remember well teaching a new members' class in which I asked the group if anyone could identify who the folk were who entered and sat together. One woman truthfully admitted that she had no idea what role or title they had in the church, but it was obvious to her that the congregation highly valued the leadership of both lay members as well as clergy. Sharing the leadership of worship is a clear way for folk to utilize their God-given gifts and to clearly incarnate a community of leaders who are honored and respected by all.

Who leads your worship? Is there a diversity of people whom God has called and gifted to lead folk into the very presence of God?

Where Do All of the Senses
Get Used to Glorify God?

Another gift of the Reformation was the recovery of the preaching of the Word for a Sunday morning congregation. With the invention of the printing press, the scriptures became more available to those who sat in pews instead of literally being chained to the lectern so no one could steal the single copy owned by the parish. The unfortunate side of this gift is that there were some Reformers who believed that speaking and listening were the only God-ordained senses to be utilized in worship. While medieval worship had often turned worshippers into spectators, the speech-dominated worship of some Reformers (and many of their successors) meant that the senses of tasting, touching, and seeing became starved for attention.

How many senses do you use in your worship? Are all of the senses—tasting, hearing, speaking, seeing, touching, and smelling—part of the ways in which you offer a full and glorious worship to the God who created us, body, soul, and mind?

Where Is There Spontaneity and Intentionality in Your Worship?

Good and faithful worship is always a remarkable and creative harmony of freedom and form. Whether you worship with a printed bulletin or prayer book or follow the weekly rhythm of your "normal" worship, there is a mixture of spontaneity and intentionality. If a service becomes totally spontaneous, it begins to feel like anarchy, and the worshipping congregation looks to its leaders to provide structure and boundaries. If a service is so predictable that there is no opportunity for the Spirit to move, then the worshipping community either grows bored or corporate worship becomes the occasion for private devotion that happens quietly in the souls of those who attend.

How is your worship constructed? Is there a structure that allows the Holy Spirit to inspire leaders and people to respond creatively? Is there enough form that the congregation feels "safe" and knows that there are leaders who will guide them toward offering their best for the glory of God?

Where Is Our Worship Contextual/Indigenous to Our Community?

As I travel through parts of the global church, I expect that there will be some things that will be common no matter where I worship, and there will be parts that will be indigenous and thus contextual to the worshipping community. For instance, I expect that I will hear scripture read and prayers offered and songs sung in almost every service. At the same time, I would expect that the worship in Brooklyn would look and feel different from the worship in Borneo, worship in Chicago would feel different from worship in Cuba, and worship in Moscow would feel different from a service in Mumbai, India. The indigenous customs and gifts of each context should enrich the texture of the worship that is being offered to God. This truth is just as true within a nation as between nations. Worship in Appalachia should not look like worship in Anchorage, Alaska, worship in a city should not feel like the worship of a farming community, and worship of a Korean immigrant community should feel different from an African American service in Harlem.

What parts of your service are unique to your congregation? How have you utilized the indigenous gifts and perspectives God has shared with you to make "your" worship uniquely yours? At the same time, are you fully conscious of the need for the global church to embrace some common beliefs, customs, and sacraments that meld us into one?

Where Is the Word Central to Your Worship?

One of the most important gifts of the Reformation was the return of the Word of God—written, spoken, and incarnated—back to the center of the church's worship. In other words, the scripture (written) became central to the creation of the worship of the church. If a congregation or church had an opportunity to utilize the words or images of scripture, it would do so knowing it was honoring God through utilizing God's word. The sermon (spoken) became another opportunity for a congregation to hear, understand, and apply the scriptures to their common life. Finally, Jesus the Christ (incarnated) became for the church the Word of God in its midst. With the first words of Saint John echoing in its ears ("In the beginning was the Word ..."), the church again acknowledged that Jesus had never left them alone but that his Spirit was with them always, even to the end of the age.

How does your congregation use scripture in your worship service? Is the sermon and the scripture connected so the congregation participates in the Word coming to life in its midst?

Where Do We Turn an Audience into a Congregation?

This question, of course, is the key to this chapter. Those who come to worship can be treated as spectators as the preacher, liturgist, and choir perform on their behalf, or they can be turned into a worshipping congregation by making Sunday morning worship a gift offered to God from the whole people of God. It may be easier to leave them as an audience, but faithful and good worship brings each and every worshipper individually and corporately into the very presence of God. It is there that every tribe and tongue, every nation and language, will find a place at God's side as together we walk the staircase between heaven and earth, and between earth and heaven. The gifts that are carried in both directions will bring a smile to the very face of God.

Further Reading

Jones, C., G. Wainwright, E. Yarnold, and P. Bradshaw, eds. *The Study of Liturgy.* New York: Oxford University Press, 1992.

Long, Kimberly Bracken. *The Worshiping Body.* Louisville, KY: Westminster John Knox Press, 2009.

Schultze, Quentin J. *High-Tech Worship.* Grand Rapids, MI: Baker Books, 2004.

Van Dyk, Leanne, ed. *A More Profound Alleluia.* Grand Rapids, MI: Wm. B. Eerdmans Publishing, 2005.

Webber, Robert E. *Worship Old and New.* Grand Rapids, MI: Zondervan Corporation, 1982.

White, James F. *Introduction to Christian Worship.* Nashville: Abingdon Press, 1990.

About the Contributor

Rev. Gregg A. Mast, MDiv, PhD, is president of New Brunswick Theological Seminary. He has served as a pastor in Johannesburg, South Africa; Irvington, New Jersey; and Albany, New York. He has also served as minister of social witness and worship and as director of ministry services for the Reformed Church in America at different times in his career. He is the author of *The Eucharistic Service of the Catholic Apostolic Church and Its Influence on Reformed Liturgical Renewals of the Nineteenth Century, In Remembrance and Hope,* and *Raising the Dead,* among other books; was a monthly columnist for the *Church Herald* for thirteen years; and has published articles in popular and scholarly journals.

9

Teaching Ministry in an Urban World
Evaluating Your Curriculum

Rev. Warren L. Dennis, MDiv, DMin

In this chapter, I look at the defining characteristics for teaching faith leaders to engage in ministry in the ever-expanding urban world. The general purpose is to develop a common discourse of teaching and learning of the multiple dimensions of urban ministry. This chapter seeks not to be simply one more academic conversation about urban ministry. Rather, it reflects the post–World War II development of the urban ministry movement that has sought to be more collaborative and confessional while at the same time attempting to change pedagogical practices in seminaries, churches, and communities. Building on this brief pedagogical history of urban ministry, my aim is to discern the emerging curricula for community-based spiritual formation and public participation in theological education programs.

I am particularly interested in the theological reality of the empowerment of persons victimized by systemic oppression, violence, fear, and alienation to speak to the realized presence of God's affirming acts in their lives. These are the people Howard Thurman speaks of "having their backs against the wall."[1] They are willing to collaborate with the academy and the faith communities on common missional concerns and have put into practice the spiritual teachings of the community that makes them collaborative partners in the theological enterprise.

The central premise I wish to explore in this chapter is the need to bridge the gulf between learning, faith, and practice by implementing faith commitments through public engagement in the academy, house of worship, and community. Across the North American theological enterprise, a conversation is taking place about faith and public participation. The conversation is about teaching and learning, curricula development, credentialing, and the economic well-being of the community. In some cases, the conversation is within seminaries around the classical argument of theology and practices. In other instances, the conversation is an interdenominational and interfaith postmodern discussion focused on expanding urban theological education beyond the traditional boundaries to discern the best content and teaching practices for urban ministry. In urban neighborhoods, the conversation is about failed schools, police brutality, mass incarceration of black and brown young men, drive-by shootings, prostitution, child endangerment, drug abuse, domestic violence, gang recruitment, HIV/AIDS, and other issues of survival that differ profoundly in substance, subject matter, and style from those of the seminary. Urban ministry advocates in these conversations challenge seminaries to assume greater public responsibility for helping urban congregations and other private and not-for-profit institutions shape the character of effective urban ministry in this new century. The question is, how do we learn from the community where we are located?

A question is frequently asked of me: What is urban? Over the thirty years I have identified my calling to Christian ministry and to teaching urban ministry, the question has provided a pedagogical moment. But I have also come to recognize the political distraction of the question that keeps us from focusing on the real problems of the inner city over against an appreciative inquiry. It is a simple question complicated by location, ethnologies, demographics, and history. Who is asking the question and who is answering the question makes all the difference in how to respond. In these thirty years, I have seen a shift in the underlining implications of the question—from a dichotomy of black and white, and suburban and urban, to a revitalization of cities and a greater increase of immigration and other faith traditions. Ronald E. Peters, in his book *Urban Ministry*, flips the paradigm from a top-down theology of God-talk to a bottom-up theology of God-talk that values the voice of the poor, marginalized, and disenfranchised.[2]

This chapter introduces the reader to the question of theological education inherent in curricula to blend theory and practice in urban situations, and it examines the problem against the background of the urban landscape that gives rise to the inability of the academy and the urban church to address the crisis of spirituality and pedagogy in urban communities. Two critical questions are addressed throughout: Is the current paradigm of theological education the most effective for urban house of worship / faith revitalization and the transformation of urban communities? How do seminaries cultivate leaders to mobilize and empower urban communities to be self-defining and self-reliant? It is my opinion that institutions of theological education must establish an urban ministry body of knowledge that connects faculty, students, and pastors to the systemic realities and challenges faced in our inner-city neighborhoods. Faculty in particular are in positions to illustrate this connection by engaging in contextual critique of their course material. The point is, seminaries understand themselves to be about the cognitive and spiritual formation of men and women who will provide the necessary leadership for the church (and non-Judeo-Christian communities) to continue its mission and ministries in cities. By their very nature, seminaries are the repositories of new approaches, technologies, and methods of ministry that must be valuable to the entire religious community. At the core is the question, should urban ministry be a theological discipline in its own right, or should it be more intentionally woven throughout the whole curriculum? The emerging vision of a discrete field of urban ministry studies raises all sorts of possibilities in terms of curriculum development.

The theoretical and practical framework and content of this chapter validate the concerns and values from a lifelong learning journey couched in urban language and categories. It is written to engage both the academy and the faith community in a common dialogue about issues affecting the urban grassroots community. I realize, though, that an invitation to dialogue with *nontraditional* partners of theological education may be disconcerting for some of my colleagues and encouraging to others. This nontraditional approach to the context of learning is found in "the debate of North America Theological Education."[3] It calls into question the clerical paradigm of theological education that is oriented to monastic education, that is, education in matters of faith best happens in retreat from the distraction of the everyday world. This practical application of religious insight gained from such experience is not always possible in the actual practice of ministry. This is especially the case in ministry in the urban context, where it has been widely reported that many seminaries' curricula are simply insufficient when it comes to addressing the needs of today's metropolis. A close examination of all seminaries accredited by the Association of Theological Schools in the United States and Canada shows that nearly two-thirds offer no courses related to urban ministry. I contend that for theological education to engage beyond its traditional walls of education into practical arenas of the twenty-first century, it must be open to new dialogical partners.

With that said, I place a greater value on non-campus-based theological inquiry in urban situations. This non-campus-based theological focus incorporates the philosophy, methodology, and structure of traditional theological education. Efrain Agosto, former academic dean for the Hartford Seminary, pushes the boundaries of such a provocative approach when he argues to "bring the classes, the class schedules, the professors, the readings, the administrators, the advisors, the accreditation mechanism to the context where neighborhood women and men already exercise leadership."[4] Eldin Villafane, founding director of Gordon-Conwell's Center for Urban Ministerial Education (CUME), further notes:

> The urban theological education should be structured to train both clergy and lay persons. While distinct tracks can be provided for each, the best programs will provide for interaction by way of a flexible curriculum. In other words, the curriculum will provide courses and projects where both the potential clergy and lay person participate jointly.[5]

The curriculum in local class settings emerges from the community's understanding of God incarnated in the faith and the resistance of the people to deal with the sociopolitical and economic problems through contemplation and lived experiences in church and community. Its quest is to bring together the theoretical and the practical as a worthy discipline of urban theological education in the academy, church, and community. Such synthesis supplies the academy and the urban faith community with a new way of teaching and doing ministry that integrates issues contextually.

A Personal Reflection

My personal involvement in urban education goes back forty years as a trainee in the Action Training Movement.[6] During this time, I witnessed the importance of community empowerment through leadership development. I saw firsthand the significant contribution made by dedicated clergy who saw the city as their calling. These women and men stood on the margin of the institutional church and modeled for me a ministry of teaching and learning that is the foundation for much that is espoused in my teaching of urban ministry today. The Action Training Movement—or church-based urban ministry—encouraged direct engagement in and systematic reflection on the inner working of the social, political, and economic systems that shape the policies that work against a community's best interests. The paradigm shift of the Action Training Movement was its emphasis on contextual analysis and the inclusion of racial ethnic concerns as integral to theological reflection on issues of ministry and mission. It attempted to establish a knowledge base and language that furthered the exploration of systemic analysis and reflection as forms of instruction.

Cincinnati's Community Human and Action Resource Training (CHART), in conjunction with the Urban Planning Department of the University of Cincinnati, played a significant role in my formation and adherence to the philosophy of the Action Training Movement. CHART emphasized the importance of building community from the inside out. Being a part of this unique urban training program, whose purpose was to train teams of local citizens for planning community change, taught me the importance of cooperative theological education where the community is the pedagogical center. It is where we begin—with the community's own description and understanding of its condition and state of being. Whether these sources of knowledge are found in myths, rituals, metaphors, poetry, prose, or biographical narratives from the mouths of common folks, these folks happened to be the community's intellectuals.

When I began my curious obsession with the idea of integrating community organizing, social work, and urban planning and ministry while at the Interdenominational Theological Center (1977–79), I frequently had to defend my interest in these areas against skeptics who claimed that I was being "too social." Now, thirty years later, the climate has changed. The mainline Protestant churches and seminaries are eager to learn about the subtleties of urban ministry as mission and as a discipline. My research in the area is a profoundly different understanding of urban from when I committed my life to God's service with intelligence, passion, and imagination. Of all the career paths ventured, the Gospel ministry in an urban context has brought me the greatest fulfillment. I believe firmly that God has prepared me through a montage of lived experiences for a special teaching ministry. What this means personally and professionally is having an urban ministry identity grounded in an interdisciplinary body of knowledge of theory and praxis, thought and faithfulness. Knowing and doing are crucial to how one effectively ministers in urban settings. It also means that getting to this level of integrative consciousness requires one to be intentional and committed to learning about urban ministry.

Teaching urban ministry, for me, is a culmination of lived experiences and the reflection of God's self-disclosure and God's revelation in my life. Looking back over my life, several factors have played a significant role in my calling to teach urban ministry. They are family, teachers, and mentors on the one hand, and the church and community on the other. Together, they shaped and reshaped for me an urban curriculum and instruction that gave me a unique perspective and commentary on the church and the community. I shall never forget a mentor saying to me thirty years ago, "You cannot firebomb systemic violence." Ever since then, I have spent my adult life learning and working inside and outside various institutions and organizations addressing the systemic issues affecting urban communities. It is these experiences, along with my formal education, that I bring to the seminary classroom in its traditional structure and its nontraditional structure.

Defining Theological Education

By standard definition, the term "metro-urban" refers to a metropolitan area that has a core city population of fifty thousand or more according to the Standard Metropolitan Statistical Analysis (SMSA) with a surrounding suburban area that relates economically to it. Beyond simply signifying a population threshold, "urban" suggests the deeper connotation of an environment that is multicultural, multilinguistic, multiracial, and economically diverse. These cities are arenas for complicated interactions among economics, physical structures, information networks, systems of social organizations, and collective human communities. "Urbanization" refers to the ever-growing phenomenon worldwide in which people are migrating to urban centers, thereby increasing their geographic area (i.e., "sprawl"), political importance, cultural impact, and economic vulnerability.

Without question, the world is more populous and more urban every day. It is estimated that in 1800 the world's population stood at about 1 billion people, and by 1900 that figure had nearly doubled to about 1.7 billion. In 2000, however, the earth's human population had jumped to over 6 billion, and by 2025, it is projected that this figure will increase to more than 8 billion. Between 1800 and 2000, the proportion of US citizens who lived in urban areas went from a mere 6 percent to 79 percent.[7] There should be no doubt that we are living in an urban world.

Contextually, "urban ministry" refers to a theological understanding of the life work of the church in core city communities, but also including neighborhoods and suburbs, as they are economically related to cities and experiencing similar patterns of population density and cultural diversity. Urban ministry, therefore, has to be both intensely local in its focus as well as metropolitan in orientation for understanding and addressing larger issues. It is at once encompassing of the vitality of congregational life and the intentional engagement within its context. It is difficult to extricate the pastoral care of members who live in substandard housing, for example, from mission strategies that include community development. At the base is a theology of mission in which the Gospel is proclaimed in community and made manifest with it.

This then becomes the task of "urban theological education": to ground leaders in solid biblical theological study that will clarify their missional theology and commitment. Rather than moving them from the context for the purpose of theological education, only to reinsert them at the conclusion for their training and leave the responsibility on the students to integrate their theology with the urban reality, the very process of theological education needs to take place more intentionally in dialogue with the urban context. Thus, it is missional, contextual, structural, theological, and pedagogical.

It requires greater mastery, discipline, and leadership as its central modality. Additionally, given the complex nature of the city and the calling of the faith community to be effective in its witness and ministry, theological education includes exposure and competence in a number of areas of effective analysis and organization. This means that it is interdisciplinary in nature and could include such fields of endeavor coming together as urban sociology, urban planning, public health, public policy, social welfare, economics, and community organization—selected and integrated in a paradigm of reflection and engagement. It is a process of teaching and learning about the nuance of systemic change in both the church and the community.

The pedagogical commitment is a process of learning and doing, research, and reflection with the practice of ministry. It is a cultivation of passionate, prophetic leadership to advance the effectiveness of ministry in urban settings. Its methodology is dialectic and dialogical, interdependent and interdisciplinary. As an educational value, it affirms multicultural and religious diversity and the value of collaboration, transformation, and empowering approaches to theology.

The goal of urban theological education is the cultivation of passionate and effective leadership for ministry in cities—from the smaller and midsize cities to the mega-metropolises. Its approaches to theology within any faith tradition is necessarily one of empowerment and transformation. Those who come through it must be able to both provide pastoral care and do social analysis, while recognizing the relationship between the two. Urban theological education is not exclusive to pastors, however. This recognition of the potential priesthood of all believers should not dilute the process of theological training but, in fact, enrich it.

Urban ministry, then, is not a commentary or pronouncement on the urban predicament. Rather, urban ministry is the systematic study and knowledge of those interlocking systems that prevent persons from experiencing productive urban living. It is a comprehensive and systematic approach to the problems facing urban America, bringing together the collective energy, resources, and thinking of every entity affecting urban life. Hence, urban ministry is no single approach or method. This is of particular importance when we consider the magnitude of problems in the city.

Authentic Urban Ministry

The issues of ministry in urban centers of the United States mirror challenges facing the church in non-Western, large cities globally: employment, housing opportunities, access to quality health care and good education, and environmental and safety concerns. These issues are far more complex than simply assuming old philosophical postures of theory versus practice or academy contrasted by community polarities. The reality is that some of the devastating human and environmental challenges of the new global market reality and postmodern society are to be found in North American urban centers, where traditional approaches to theological education have not proved effective in preparing clergy to address these urban realities. Theological education needs to move beyond its traditional bifurcation of theory and practice—often at the expense of practice. Urban complexities will require a more comprehensive and creative approach to theological education.

The technological advances and global economic shift of the past sixty years have created a climate of uncertainty for inner-city communities across the country. Once thriving industrial communities are now vast ghettos and toxic wastelands. Work has disappeared, according to William Julius Wilson in his seminal work, *When Work Disappears*.[8] In contrast, we have moved from being a labor-intensive society to a market-driven service economy that relies more on information and knowledge as its economic product of the future. *New York Times* journalist Thomas Freedman once said, "The world has become flat and the United States no longer is the premier economic power."[9]

Thus, in this new century, authentic urban ministry in urban context(s) presents some of the most complex and challenging opportunities for seminaries, pastors, and congregation. This means that for urban theological education to be authentic in its engagement and reflection, it must be more theoretical, missional, liberational, spiritual, multicultural, antiracist, womanist, Afrocentric, prophetic, collaborative, empowering, and transformative.

In urban ministry, interdisciplinary analysis involves theological dialogue with non-faith-based disciplines or sciences: civil and criminal justice, sociology, business, medicine, education, anthropology, psychology, and so forth. The aspirations of the broad spectrum of constituencies, institutions, and individuals that compose the city become the classroom where ministry is learned. In essence, the seminaries must be able to discern God's self-disclosure and self-revelation in the lives of the people, whether or not they are members of the church.

The uniqueness of urban theological education in this case is its collaborative method of teaching and learning beyond the traditional classroom. Rooted in the political, multiracial, church-based community organizing philosophy is Saul Alinsky's "golden rule" (you never do for others what they can do for themselves).[10] Alinsky is founder of the Industrial Are Foundation (IAF), which was started in the backyards of Chicago in the 1940s and aimed to engage in direct action with what was not always a comfortable solution for all. The key distinction of Alinsky's organizing model was the use of confrontation and power as ingredients in every community transaction. For Alinsky, theology has the potential to become empowering and transforming when done in relationship to personal experiences of injustice. Community organizing represented a paradigm shift from service to empowerment. Up to this point, churches had been instrumental in the establishment of schools, hospitals, community centers, and other forms of social service.

Lastly, congregations and other faith communities in urban contexts are not necessarily urban. In many instances, the members have mentally disconnected from the community, and in most cases they travel *in* to worship and leave with no intimate relationship with the neighborhood. They may not be in touch with the social, cultural, and spiritual life of the community. Some congregations physically located in an urban area have little notions of the prayers of the people. True urban congregations, however, are teaching and learning congregations. While worship is central, these congregations also have an acute understanding of the theological, ecclesiastical, and historical, as well as an appreciation of religious plurality, an awareness of the evolution of urban land use and public policy, and urban approaches to pastoral ministry. Inner-city congregations benefit from knowing the historical intersection of faith and public life.

Final Words

In conclusion, my hope is to encourage and inspire others in urban seminaries, churches, and faith communities to collaborate, to make connections, and to pose new questions about the responsibilities and commitments that sometimes seem irreconcilable, all of which will assist them in undertaking the challenge of urban ministry in the twenty-first century. My objectives as an educator will be accomplished only when the conversation of urban ministry and urban theological education is continued well beyond the scope of this writer in this time and place.

Notes

1. Howard Thurman, *Jesus and the Disinherited* (Richman, IN: Friends United Press, 1981).
2. Ronald E. Peters, *Urban Ministry: An Introduction* (Nashville: Abingdon Press, 2010).
3. Edward Farley, *Theologia: The Fragmentation and Unity of Theological Education* (Philadelphia: Fortress Press, 1983).
4. Efrain Agosto, "The Gifts of Urban Theological Education: A Personal and Professional Reflection," *Theological Education* 33 (November, 1, 1996): 93–105.
5. Eldin Villafane, *Seek the Welfare of the City: Reflections on Urban Ministry* (Grand Rapids, MI: Wms. B. Eerdman Publishing Co., 1995), 78.
6. George D. Younger, *From New Creation to Urban Crisis: A History of Action Training Ministries 1962–1975* (Chicago: Center for the Scientific Study of Religion, 1987).
7. Peters, *Urban Ministry*, 7.
8. William Julius Wilson, *When Work Disappears: The World and the New Urban Poor* (New York: Alfred A. Knopf, 1996).
9. Thomas Freedman, *The World Is Flat* (New York: Farrar, Straus, and Giroux, 2005).
10. Saul Alinsky, *Reveille for Radicals* (New York: Random House, 1969).

Further Reading

Alexander, Michele. *The New Jim Crow: Mass Incarceration in the Age of Colorblindness*. New York: The New Press, 2010.

Conn, Havie M., and Manuel Ortiz. *Urban Ministry: The Kingdom, the City and the People of God*. Downers Grove, IL: InterVarsity Press, 2001.

Fluker, Walter E. *The Stone That the Builders Rejected: The Development of Ethical Leadership from the Black Church Tradition*. Harrisburg, PA: Trinity Press International, 1998.

Fullilove, Mindy Thompson. *Root Shock: How Tearing Up City Neighborhoods Hurts America, and What We Can Do About It.* New York: Ballantine Books, 2004.

Gornik, Mark R. *To Live in Peace: Biblical Faith and the Changing Inner City.* Grand Rapids, MI: Wm. B. Eerdmans Publishing, 2002.

Green, Clifford J., ed. *Churches, Cities and Human Community: Urban Ministry in the United States 1945–1985.* Grand Rapids, MI: Wm. B. Eerdmans Publishing, 1996.

Jacob, Jane. *The Death and Life of Great American Cities.* New York: Vintage Books, 1961.

Jacobson, Eric O. *Signs of the Kingdom.* Grand Rapids, MI: Brazos Press, 2003.

Jensen, Robert. *The Heart of Whiteness: Confronting Race, Racism, and White Privilege.* San Francisco: City Light Publishing, 2004.

Linthicum, Robert. *Building a People of Power: Equipping Churches to Transform Their Communities.* Federal Way, WA: World Vision Press, 2005.

Liverzey, Lowell W. *Public Religion and Urban Transformation: Faith in the City.* New York: New York University Press, 2000.

McRoberts, Omar A. *Streets of Glory: Church and Community in a Black Urban Neighborhood.* Chicago: University of Chicago Press, 2004.

Perkins, John. *Restoring At-Risk Communities: Doing It Together and Doing It Right.* Grand Rapids, MI: Baker Books, 1995.

Pierce, Gregory F. *Activism That Makes Sense: Congregation and Community Organization.* New York: Paulist Press, 1984.

Robinson, Eugene. *Disintegration: The Splintering of Black America.* New York: Doubleday, 2010.

Wuthnow, Robert, and John H. Evans. *The Quiet Hand of God: Faith-Based Activism and the Public Role of Mainline Protestantism.* Berkeley: University of California Press, 2002.

About the Contributor

Rev. Warren L. Dennis, MDiv, DMin, is ordained in the Presbyterian Church (USA) and is the Dirk Romeyn Professor of Metro-Urban Ministry at New Brunswick Theological Seminary, New Jersey. He earned the master of divinity degree from Johnson C. Smith Seminary in Atlanta and doctor of ministry degree from United Theological Seminary, Dayton, Ohio. His specific interest is examining issues of poverty, race, and culture in urban theological education.

10

Congregations and Communities
in Transition

Rev. Earl D. Trent Jr., MDiv, DMin

In the twenty-first century, it is inevitable that congregations and communities will periodically find themselves in major transition. Globalization—the tying of the world together as a giant global village—the mobility of persons, the transient nature of work, and the ever-quickening pace of life make change inevitable. However, it is the very nature of congregations and communities to seek a homogeneity and stasis point where change, if it takes place at all, is very slow or barely evident. As you can see, there is an inherent conflict between the cultural reality and the desires of both congregations and communities. How does one lead a congregation in a time of transition? What are the pitfalls and conflicts that develop? What denotes a successful transition? These are some of the questions to be addressed in this chapter.

To begin a discussion on congregations and communities in transition some definitions are necessary. I am defining "congregations" as those members who attend their house of worship at least twice a month. While all houses of worship count members from an official roll standpoint, the core of the congregation are those who attend regularly. The occasional member exhibits a different behavior and attitude from the core. These core persons are more involved in the life of the community. They are the officeholders, the ones who plan and get things done, and they have the most at stake when it comes to change and transition.

The "community" I define as a group of people who physically live in the same area. A "neighborhood" I refer to as a subset of this community where the area is more constricted in terms of real or perceived boundaries inside of a given area. A community may consist of several neighborhoods or be as simple as two neighborhoods.

"Globalization is the process of increasing the connectivity and interdependence of the world's markets and businesses. This process has speeded up dramatically in the last two decades as technological advances make it easier for people to travel, communicate, and do business internationally."[1] While this is a business definition, globalization has its mercurial social and cultural effects, and it is at the root of much of the change we see in our communities and therefore our congregations. I bring this up because it is important for faith leaders to know the root cause and that it is not a passing phenomenon, but an ongoing one. The acceptance of this reality is critical to understanding the dynamics of transition.

My observations and strategies are based on the pastoral experience of two congregations undergoing transitions as communities changed. One was in a setting of a semirural county transitioning into suburban development. Cornfields and cow pastures rapidly were becoming single-family developments. Farms were transformed into shopping malls. Businesses in the technology and service industry began to relocate to the area. The church was located in a town known as a college community. Political parties referred to this community as the county seat (the administrative center of a county). The courthouse was located there and it was the place where legal paperwork was filed.

The second experience was in an urban setting where the church resided in the "'hood." It was best characterized by the practice of vacating the neighborhood by 9:30 p.m., at which time the junkies, prostitutes, and dealers took over the turf. In a period of three years, with a united effort of Howard University, Fannie Mae, and Bell Atlantic (now Verizon DC), fifty dilapidated homes were renovated and sold to staff, faculty, and members of the community. After five years, the owners were then allowed to sell, and many did, taking advantage of a booming housing market and sparking another wave of transition.

Dynamics of Transition

In 1956 the science fiction classic *Invasion of the Body Snatchers* was released. The plot of the movie was that aliens had invaded the earth and were replacing people with physical look-alikes grown from giant pea pods. Although these pod people looked like their replacements, they had neither the warmth nor the individuality that the original people had. In a semirural setting transition to a suburban one, the principal dynamic can be described as an invasion of the body snatchers outlook. They look like us, but they are not like us.

A cursory look at this particular congregation in the late 1980s would have revealed a growing African American congregation that looked like a homogenous group. However, it was anything but homogenous.

The black population of this small town barely exceeded 8 percent of the population, and in the county the black population was barely 3 percent. The larger population of the town was due to the proximity of two universities. Historically, this congregation was nearing one hundred years and was the oldest African American Baptist church in the county.

The majority of the congregation was native to the area. Most of the members were domestics, farmworkers, and various degrees of skilled laborer and office workers. They worked in various positions at one of the universities, and some held teaching positions or administrative positions. It was a solid working-class congregation.

One distinction made clear was that those who traced their roots back three generations or more considered themselves native to the area. It was a significant badge of honor to them and a closed circle. Outsiders never really became insiders. One family had been in the area for twenty-five years but was still considered an outsider. A small professional class of mostly teachers did not emerge until the early 1970s. As the area began to change from rural to suburb, a professional group of mid-level managers began to move into the area. And the tension entered as well.

These new blacks were viewed as strange phenomena by the native blacks of the area. "They looked like us, but they were not really us." "They come from different places." "They did not talk like us." These expressions, while seemingly innocuous, were indicators of three major areas of tension.

Because the black population for many years was less than 3 percent of the county population and the income and wealth differential between the black and white populations was so great, a clearly subservient attitude had developed among blacks. In general, blacks were accommodating and passive in their interactions with the majority population, which led to a passive-aggressive style of behavior in resolving conflicts. There would be passive assent and seeming consensus, followed by aggressive undermining and other forms of surreptitious noncooperation.

New blacks had new attitudes and were less passive, less accommodationist, for they were the pioneers. A number of them were the first blacks in their companies or respective positions. It sparked a subtle clash of attitudes that was never outright but simmered behind the scenes in ongoing interactions. Both sides noted their differences.

Differences and tensions were reinforced by housing patterns. Those who were native or near native lived in town. Those who moved into the area seldom resided in town but moved into nearby townships and increasingly into new developments. Those who moved into the single-family developments acquired the nickname "the mink and Mercedes crowd" by the older members. It was an acknowledgment of the economic differences, with accompanying envy on one side and oblivious arrogance on the other.

In many cases, it was not just class or economic benefits. The new blacks were more educated, more articulate, better skilled, and used to leadership in a style and manner that emphasized completing tasks, with less emphasis on inclusive participation and sensitivity to others' feelings and thoughts. Men who became members of the congregation were generally younger and more athletic; however, there was less tension among the men than among the women.

As more women moved into the area, slow-building resentment began to take place between older and younger women. It centered on the older women having been denied the opportunity that these young black professional women had. The older women were as ambitious as these younger women, and though they were encouraging to the younger women on the one hand, resentment built up on the other. This was compounded by the obliviousness of these younger women to the impact that denial had had upon the older women. It was only at a retreat of women that a skillful facilitator helped the older women articulate their feelings. Once articulated and once the younger women became more aware of their own behavior, the tension died down substantially.

Urban Transition

Gentrification can loosely be defined as the arrival of wealthier people in an existing urban district, a related increase in rents and property values, and changes in the district's character and culture.[2] The dynamics of urban transition are best depicted in the staple of the science fiction film genre: aliens have invaded. The 1996 movie *Independence Day* personifies the dynamics. Aliens who have been watching us for years have finally invaded our planet. They are intent on destroying us and our way of life. They do not belong. They do not look like us. They do not know us.

The church I presently pastor, the Florida Avenue Baptist Church, is an urban church and has experienced a series of transitions within the past fifteen years. Historically, it has known stability. I am the fourth pastor in one hundred years. Historically, it has been a church going through various transitions. During the 1920s to 1950s, it was in a highly sought-after segregated neighborhood in the shadow of Howard University. At that time the church was one where all its members lived either within walking distance or in a nearby neighborhood. After segregation ended and redlining was somewhat curtailed, that way of life tapered off and the congregational makeup began to change. Fewer people lived in the area. After the 1968 riots following the assassination of Dr. Martin Luther King Jr., there was a significant drop in the population. The area was depressed. Howard University bought almost fifty properties in the neighborhood and let them languish in disrepair for more than twenty years. With the arrival of a new president, Dr. H. Patrick Swygert, which coincided with my own arrival as pastor, a partnership among the university, business entities, and the community was formed that resulted in the renovation of the fifty homes that were sold to faculty, staff, and members of the community. Those who moved in after the Howard renovations initially had a good relationship with the church, because the meetings for the renovation project took place in the church.

This was a significant transition for the community and congregation. Renovated homes meant less crime. The congregation became more active during the week, and the church was open later hours on the weekend. Members were less apt to leave by 9 p.m. The church saw outreach as part of its mission. The outreach of the church included voter registration, adopting a school, and the expansion of youth activities. Jazz concerts became a monthly activity on the fourth Sunday evening. However, now parking became a premium. With only a small lot owned by the church, there was vying for the on-street parking that had previously been readily available. Tension began between church members and the new neighbors. There grew an increasing intolerance for lingering church programs, resulting in excessive ticketing as neighbors complained. An invasion mentality began to take shape among church members: "They knew we were a church before they moved in."

After five years of ownership, the original homeowners were allowed to sell their renovated homes, and many of them did, as it was the height of the real estate boom and the equity had in many cases doubled. With this second wave, more white singles and young white families began to populate the neighborhood. The transformation of the neighborhood changed it from "'hood" to "hot spot."

The new young land gentry knew little of the history of the neighborhood and community and did not seem to want to know. They did not look like us and were preoccupied with their own way of life, which translated into a destruction of the original culture. Our safe haven as a historic African American neighborhood was no more.

Impact of Race

The major dynamic of this transition surrounds race. The post-racial society is a myth. It fits a convenient scenario, but the reality is a complex, covert, semiconscious tension. Although the neighborhood's racial makeup has changed, the congregation has not. We are still African American. The civic association is now almost evenly populated by whites and blacks, and two of the last four presidents have been white. The association continues to meet in our fellowship hall, but whites seldom attend our church on Sundays. Some will come by personal invitation to a special service or concert, but if there are white visitors, we usually find they have accidently walked in thinking that we are a Southern Baptist or evangelical church.

Although the congregation is about one-third senior citizens, age is a nonfactor. The neighborhood age demographic is mostly forty and under. Class has always made a difference, but in a more subtle way. The new neighbors would at one time be called "upwardly mobile," and with this there is a sense of privilege. This breeds an arrogance that has caused its own tension between community and congregation.

The new ethnic and religious mix of the city, which is highly diverse overall, has had an interesting effect. Where at one time the churches and synagogues were the sole religious institutions and highly respected, the diversity results now in a "one among many" attitude and a lessening of respect for churches, even to the point that many clergy believe there is a growing anti-church sentiment.

Leadership in Transition

Leadership is critical in an environment of transition. Without strong, purposeful leadership, chaos will ensue, possibly resulting in a congregation's demise. The following are emphases that have proved useful in both contexts of transitions in congregations and communities.

The question of purpose is the primary question that the leader must ask and clearly answer. What is your purpose as a congregation or religious institution as you see God moving in this transition? Is it to increase diversity? Is it to integrate or dominate the neighborhood? Is it simply to survive as an institution? Answering these questions determines strategy and the key measurement of success.

Jawanza Kunju identifies three types of churches: the entertainment church, the containment church, and the liberation church. The entertainment church is where there is a lot of whooping, hollering, and singing to the exclusion of teaching and working. It is a church that makes you feel good for the moment but does not address social issues. The containment churches are similar but only open on Sundays and are closed the remainder of the week. The liberation church is based on Luke 4:18–19 and understands the need to clothe the naked and feed the hungry, to be actively engaged in social justice and mission outreach.[3] Which one or combination of church types do you want to become? Will you be a family church, a tourist church, or something else? One thing is nonnegotiable—you cannot stay the same. Change is inevitable, and churches do die.

Pews do take their cues from the pulpit. Most congregational churches seek to build around consensus. Christians are nice people and endeavor to be liked. It is not a bad thing, but in critical moments the flock looks to the leaders. Transitions are critical moments, and it is important to remember that members take their cues from the leadership.

Clear goals must be set and articulated. Goals are not quotas, but the measurable objectives revolving around your purpose. Many organizations, but especially churches, operate in a casual, unintentional manner. Transition cannot be coped with casually but must be intentionally addressed.

Dos and Don'ts

1. Do not abdicate leadership. Times of transition are a time of crisis, and whatever your leadership style, your mark as a leader must be clear and decisive. Your opinions and actions matter.

2. Do not make obvious and blatant favorites of one group over another. Partiality is a reality, but blatant favoritism will cause endless conflict. You will be accused of favoritism anyway, but you should be able to articulate your objective statements and behavior as well as what you are partial to if you have to.

3. Do not ignore a house of worship's history and a community's history. We are the products of our ancestors. Historical roots are often overlooked in our present focus, but cross-generational and cross-cultural appreciation opens the doors to genuine fruitful relationships.

4. Try out your assumptions. A group of varied persons should be consulted or used as a focus group to ensure your assumptions are valid.

5. Be patient; think agricultural model, not technological. We are often fooled and expect a quick fix. There is none.

6. Expect conflict. There is no magic about handling transition and people. Their very nature causes conflict. Get comfortable with the existence of conflict, misunderstanding, and misinterpretation.

7. Pray unceasingly for guidance and wisdom.

Notes

1. www.investorwords.com/2182/globalization.html#ixzz1bkROhdzE.

2. Benjamin Grant, "What Is Gentrification?" *Documentaries with a Point of View*, Public Broadcasting Service, June 17, 2003, www.pbs.org/pov/flagwars/special_gentrification.php.

3. Jawanza Kunjufu, *Adam! Where Are You? Why Most Black Men Don't Go to Church* (Chicago: African American Images, 1994), 23.

About the Contributor

Rev. Earl D. Trent Jr., MDiv, DMin, is the fourth pastor in the one-hundred-year history of the Florida Avenue Baptist Church in Washington, DC. He also currently serves as chairman of the board of Church World Service (CWS), a US-based global relief, sustainable development, and refugee assistance agency, and is active in both the American Baptist USA and the Progressive National Baptist Conventions. In a model of cooperative neighborhood improvement, Dr. Trent led the church in revitalizing the LeDroit Park Civic Association, resulting in a multimillion-dollar fifty-home renovation and rebuild investment by Howard University, Verizon, and Fannie Mae in the LeDroit Park neighborhood. He has served on many boards with special commitments to economic reform, including justice for black farmers, workers' rights, women ex-offenders, and the battle against sickle cell disease. Author of *A Challenge to the Black Church* as well as many journal articles, he is married to Dr. Janice Ray Trent, the owner of Hearing Healthcare Services in Bowie, Maryland. They are the parents of three adult daughters.

PART III

How Do You Care for Others?

11

Pastoral Care as a Foundation for Leadership

Rabbi Stephen B. Roberts, MBA, MHL, BCJC

A Cautionary Tale

My parents were active and involved members of a synagogue for more than fifty years. Everywhere you walk within the building you see something they contributed or helped build. The art in the lobby was donated by them as well as the mezuzah (a key Jewish religious object found on all entrances to buildings) in the main sanctuary. Both my parents served on the board and numerous committees of the congregation. All six of their children were brought up in the congregation, and a number of them were married in the sanctuary. Family members' funerals were held at the synagogue. This religious community was the center of our family's life for decades.

This is past tense. Why? A key part of the separation was pastoral care and the lack of it by the senior clergy member over the past decade. For this clergy member, "leadership" is almost exclusively about preaching and teaching—which he is well known for, both locally and nationally. He is a "preacher" and "teacher," but not a "pastor." Further, he did not train members of the congregation to visit the sick or create a "caring community." Rather, he left pastoral care to another clergy member of the synagogue. He felt it was enough that he was good at teaching God's word and preaching God's teachings. Visiting the sick, the infirmed, the homebound was not "required" and thus not something he did.

The local hospital is five minutes from the synagogue. The senior clergy member must drive by it every day to get to the building. Over the past decade, on numerous occasions when my father was hospitalized for major and serious life-threatening illness, the senior clergy member almost never visited. On the one or two times he did, the visits were very brief and perfunctory, no real pastoral care. God's concern, compassion, love, and presence were not expressed to my father and our family during these visits. Ultimately, my parents left the congregation when the clergy member who did all the pastoral work of the synagogue left, as did many other longtime members.

Four generations of connection to a house of worship broken—a direct result of a senior clergy member not thinking that pastoral care needs to be a high priority to be an effective religious leader. And finally, this was also extremely poor financial congregational stewardship, because my parents also removed from their wills the significant gifts to the congregation they had planned to make.

An effective religious leader looks at and understands the big picture of congregational life. Pastoral care is at the heart of that life. It is most often the direct experience people have of God's presence during difficult times. No matter how good a preacher or teacher you are, without effective pastoral skills, ultimately people no longer turn to you, because they do not find God present in their hour of need, and thus your religious leadership is over.

What Do We Need to Know to Be Effective Leaders?

In a phrase, it's effective pastoral care. So what is "pastoral care" versus "spiritual care" and "chaplaincy care" (terms that are often used synonymously and without specific definitions)? In writing their Standards of Practice, the Association of Professional Chaplains (APC) created a glossary that proposed to separate these terms.[1] The definitions from the glossary are as follows:

> **Chaplaincy care:** Care provided by a board certified chaplain or by a student in an accredited clinical pastoral education program [e.g., Association for Clinical Pastoral Education (ACPE) in the United States; Canadian Association for Spiritual Care/Association Canadienne de Soins Spirituels (CASC/ACSS) in Canada].

Examples of such care include emotional, spiritual, religious, pastoral, ethical, and/or existential care.

Pastoral care: Coming out of the Christian tradition, "pastoral care developed within the socially contracted context of a religious or faith community wherein the 'pastor' or faith leader is the community's designated leader who oversees the faith and welfare of the community and wherein the community submits to or acknowledges the leader's overseeing. The 'faith' they share is a mutually received and agreed upon system of beliefs, actions, and values. The faith leader's care for his or her community is worked out within a dialectical relationship between the person's unique needs, on the one hand, and the established norms of the faith community, as represented by the pastor, on the other." Pastoral care may form part of the care provided by a chaplain.

Spiritual care: "Interventions, individual or communal, that facilitate the ability to express the integration of the body, mind, and spirit to achieve wholeness, health, and a sense of connection to self, others, and[/or] a higher power." Spiritual care forms part of the care provided by a chaplain.

It is clear from the definitions that congregational leadership includes pastoral care, *yet almost no one is born with this skill*. It is a skill with many aspects and parts. All of the various parts must be developed intentionally. Congregational leaders do not have to "like" this work, but they must learn to be able to do it compassionately, consistently, and with a strong zeal driven by a personal commitment to do God's work and to be the living embodiment of God's presence on earth to those who are ill and hurting. They must also learn how to teach members of the congregation to do this work as well and to make this a priority of the community. When members of a congregation get sick, they *expect* the congregation's religious and lay leadership to reach out to them.

What are the core minimum components of effective pastoral care that congregational clergy must learn? They include at a minimum the following:

- Foundational listening and responding skills
- Assessment

- Creating and implementing a spiritual care plan
- Life review
- End-of-life pastoral care—for both the person dying and that person's family

Foundational Listening and Responding Skills

Reverend Robert Kidd, a past president of the Association of Professional Chaplains, writes about this critical skill:

> Spiritually supportive listening is different and takes a great deal of intentionality, skill, and restraint. Allowing a spiritually supportive conversation to unfold naturally does not come easily to many and requires a foundational skill set.... Effective listening and responding entail absorbing what the speaker says and then offering it back in order to bring the dialogue to a deeper level. Such transformative listening involves attending to the entirety of the speaker's message, hearing the speaker's words, and discerning the emotions behind them. In such healing interactions, the speaker feels more valued and respected and experiences an emotional completeness unrealized in other forms of discourse. This kind of listening and responding takes practice, patience, and significant respect for the speaker. Such attending is by nature reflective and serves to hold up a mirror for the speaker to hear his or her words in a different, deeper way.[2]

Assessment

What is assessment and how does it work? Chaplain D. W. Donovan provides a concise answer: "The role of the clinically trained pastoral professional is to [1] assess the degree to which the client's emotional and spiritual equilibrium has been disturbed [2] by a particular event and to [3] determine what interventions would be appropriate to help the client restore that equilibrium and [4] when such interventions should be employed."[3]

Congregational clergy must look at themselves as *pastoral professionals*. Congregants do! The steps listed by Chaplain Donovan are essential in pastoral work. Each religious leader must be both familiar with this process and comfortable with it.

Creating and Implementing a Spiritual Care Plan

Listening to and assessing the needs of congregants is not enough. Clergy must then create and implement a plan to meet the needs. A plan does not need to be long or detailed. It does not need to be written down. A plan needs to help you do the following:

- Focus on the spiritual/pastoral issues assessed that need your focus during the visit.

- Understand how long the various issues have been going on (did it start as a result of this hospitalization/illness, or was it there previously?) so you can better work with them.

- Set goals for working with this specific congregant and his or her family. Goals should be related to specific spiritual issues that have arisen. Examples of spiritual issues include the following:[4]
  - Grief/loss
  - Guilt
  - Hope/hopelessness/despair
  - Serenity
  - Suffering

- Plan interventions to help you reach the goals you have set.

Life Review

This is a key and needed resource when working with both elderly congregants and congregants who have life-threatening illnesses. Reverend Nancy Osborne sums up the spiritual impact of life review very powerfully and beautifully. Her words demonstrate why this is an essential skill for pastoral leadership:

> And what is it that we learn about God as we do this life review, life synthesis, reminiscence work? We experience the holiness of life, torn and tattered, sewn together by listening and love. We can never return the cloth to its original form, but we experience the power of the One who can hold everything and the gift of being one of the number in the communion of saints, encircling all that we can only pick up with tenderness but cannot stitch together yet—to hold and see or hear, to smell or taste, to feel in the mysterious moments of life. We experience a God who can stitch forgiveness and eternity into every quilt, can find a balance

and sometimes a fierce beauty in the fullness of it all. As spiritual care companions, perhaps we hold a weary hand as the stitching happens, perhaps we help sift through the scraps for a matching or contrasting or fitting pattern to balance the life of the one with whom we commune. And hopefully we experience the warmth of shared life, heightened by the pause or brief stop in this portion of the journey even as the larger journey continues.[5]

End-of-Life Pastoral Care—for Both the Person Dying and That Person's Family

End-of-life pastoral care includes the following:[6]

- Guide the dying person through the stages of grief.
- Assist the congregant with spiritual distress.
- Provide reassurance of God's active presence and redemptive hope for the suffering or other spiritual comfort consistent with the person's spiritual frame of reference.
- Facilitate a life review and/or advance directives conversation.
- Encourage the involvement of a palliative care team when appropriate.
- Assist the person in articulating what a good death would look like for him or her.

Who Should Be Providing Pastoral Care in a Religious Community?

First and foremost, the senior religious leaders of faith communities must provide effective, caring, compassionate pastoral care. They must set the example for all within the community. They must, through their actions, indicate that this is an important religious value. No matter the size of the congregation, the senior leaders must make pastoral care an important part of their daily lives and of the life of the congregation.

Next, all those whom the congregation considers "clergy" should also be trained to provide effective pastoral care. In larger congregations with multiple clergy, each one should be trained to provide pastoral care. The youth "minister" ("minister" is used here to designate all clergy, whether priest, imam, rabbi, minister, and so on) needs to be trained so that when a youth, who feels that this particular person is his or her minister, indicates that someone is sick in the family, this minister will have the skills and training to work with these families. If the congregation has a health ministry / caring community team, the clergy who oversees this area must have training. The cantor or person in charge of the congregation's music, to whom people may turn on a regular basis for counseling, needs training.

Do not overlook, depending on the community and their own traditions, the "pastor's wife" or "rebbetzin." In certain communities, these are working titles with real pastoral expectations. This person may not have had formal theological education, but within her own community, particularly for many women, she is the one they turn to most often for pastoral help.

Finally, in the best of congregations, there is an active lay group who visit the sick, the infirmed, and the homebound. This group has many names depending on the faith tradition—health ministry, caring community, *bikur cholim*, and so forth. Those laypeople who have committed to this work also need training, and not just a single hour or two of training, but rather training that runs hundreds of hours.

How Do We Learn the Skills of Pastoral Care to Become Effective Leaders?

Very few clergy are "born" natural preaches and teachers. Rather, most religious leaders spend a minimum of three years learning to be effective preachers and teachers. In some religious traditions, such as my own, the training lasts at least five or six years past college.

Equally, very few people are born with both an effective and a large set of pastoral skills. This is no different than preaching and teaching. Yet, unlike with preaching and teaching, many people can be ordained and never have had training in this area. Others have had minimal education. Like preaching and teaching, these are skills that need to be learned, practiced, and developed.

The best developed system to learn these critical skills is clinical pastoral education (CPE). CPE is based on an "action, reflection, action" model. It is a very practical model, which states that people can learn and develop good pastoral skills. They do not have to "like" this work to be effective leaders in this area. They just need to accept that these skills are important and learnable and then set out to develop these skills.

CPE training is most normatively offered in a "unit" of four hundred hours. The largest and oldest organization offering CPE in North America is the Association of Clinical Pastoral Education (ACPE). The objectives for clinical pastoral education as stated in the ACPE Standards are as follows:

Pastoral Formation

- To develop awareness of oneself as ministers and of the ways their ministry affects persons.

- To develop awareness of how one's attitudes, values, assumptions, strengths, and weaknesses affect their pastoral care.

- To develop the ability to engage and apply the support, confrontation, and clarification of the peer group for the integration of personal attributes and pastoral functioning.

Pastoral Competence

- To develop one's awareness and understanding of how persons, social conditions, systems, and structures affect their lives and the lives of others and how to address effectively these issues through their ministry.

- To develop one's skills in providing intensive and extensive pastoral care and counseling to persons.

- To develop one's ability to make effective use of their religious/spiritual heritage, theological understanding, and knowledge of the behavioral sciences in their pastoral care of persons and groups.

- To have one learn the pastoral role in professional relationships and how to work effectively as a pastoral member of a multidisciplinary team.

- To develop one's capacity to use pastoral and prophetic perspectives in preaching, teaching, leadership, management, pastoral care, and pastoral counseling.[7]

A key part of CPE is that it is open to all within a community, not just those "ordained." Those taking the training do not have to have attended a seminary. Fees are low, and all programs have scholarships. Training is found in all areas of the country. It is a great way to prepare the various leaders within a congregation to provide effective pastoral care, whether ordained or functioning with the community or clergy's blessings.

Notes

1. Association of Professional Chaplains, *Standards of Practice for Professional Chaplains in Acute Care Settings*, www.professionalchaplains.org/uploadedFiles/pdf/Standards%20of%20Practice%20Draft%20Document%20021109.pdf.
2. Rev. Robert A. Kidd, "Foundational Listening and Responding Skills," in *Professional Spiritual & Pastoral Care: A Practical Clergy and Chaplain's Handbook*, ed. Stephen B. Roberts (Woodstock, VT: SkyLight Paths, 2012), 92–93.
3. Chaplain D. W. Donovan, "Assessments," in Roberts, *Professional Spiritual & Pastoral Care*, 44.
4. A more complete list can be found in Roberts, *Professional Spiritual & Pastoral Care*, 69.
5. Rev. Nancy Osborne, "Life Review," in Roberts, *Professional Spiritual & Pastoral Care*, 159–60.
6. Adapted from Rev. Brian Hughes, "End-of-Life Chaplaincy Care," in Roberts, *Professional Spiritual & Pastoral Care*, 163–64.
7. Association for Clinical Pastoral Education, *Standards and Manuals* (Decatur, GA: Association for Clinical Pastoral Education, 2010), 13.

About the Contributor

Rabbi Stephen B. Roberts, MBA, MHL, BCJC, is the editor of *Professional Spiritual & Pastoral Care: A Practical Clergy and Chaplain's Handbook* and coeditor of *Disaster Spiritual Care: Practical Clergy Response to Community, Regional and National Tragedy* (both SkyLight Paths Publishing). He is a past president of the National Association of Jewish Chaplains. Most recently he served as the associate executive vice president of the New York Board of Rabbis, directing their chaplaincy program, providing services in more than fifty locations throughout New York, and serving as the endorser for both New York State's and New York City's Jewish chaplains. Prior to this he served as the director of chaplaincy of the Beth Israel Medical System (New York), overseeing chaplains and clinical pastoral education (CPE) programs at three acute care hospitals, one behavioral health hospital, and various outpatient facilities served by chaplains.

12

Leadership at the Borders of Difference

Rev. Brita L. Gill-Austern, MDiv, PhD

Before us is a massive ugly wall with barbed wire all around, cutting this town in two like a knife slicing through the heart of a body. Nogales, sometimes called Nogales Ambos ("both Nogales"), because there is now a Nogales on each side of the wall, one in Mexico and one in the United States, is a city of sorrow. Before the wall, there really was one town, one rhythm of life, families living on both sides connected more than separated by the border. Now families come to the wall and try to peek through an opening to see their family living on the other side. Now there are no celebrations that bring both communities together. Now there is division, the militarization of the border, ugly bright lights protecting the divide of the border at night; now there is an "other" on the other side of the wall.

What difference does it make when you look at the issues of immigration, economic policy, and human rights when you are Mexican looking over at the other side, forbidden to cross into the land of plenty? How do you navigate the complex realities of immigration policy and understand the meaning of the biblical commandment of hospitality to the stranger after you have spent time with those who have traveled more than a thousand miles with virtually nothing but the hope to cross the border so they can simply make enough money to send home so their family can eat? How do you hold their truth while simultaneously remembering the meeting on the border with the US rancher who has compassion and sympathy for the condition of those who cross, but whose livelihood and life are radically altered by the continual crossing on his land?

There are no fast and easy solutions to these questions. Leaders who will move us from where we are to where we need to be will be those who are able to hold the truth of more than one reality while seeking common ground even in the midst of staggering complexity and difference.

For the past five years I have been taking seminary students to the Mexico-US border with the organization Borderlinks to learn about the border, to investigate issues of economic justice and human rights related to immigration, and to confront students with the moral complexity related to immigration. At the seminary where I teach, Andover Newton Theological School, I direct a program called Border-Crossing Immersions, a requirement for all our master of divinity students. This requirement grew out of the conviction of our faculty that leadership today requires not only learning about differences but also acquiring skills to build bridges across divides. Leaders of faith communities have to model how to make the world safe for differences.

This cannot happen without preparing students to step into unfamiliar terrain, without having to struggle with others' perceptions of them that are contrary to their own, without having to see the assumptions in which their own lives are drenched, without seeing the world through a cultural context radically different from their own. One way we begin to move toward making the world safe for differences is to begin to see yourself through the eyes of another, usually an inevitable consequence of really stepping across a border, be it social, economic, cultural, religious, and so on. You learn to see not only the "other" with new eyes, but also your own life and your own social world through the eyes of the other.

What does all this have to do with leading congregations? What does all this have to do with being an effective leader of a faith community today? This program was developed with the belief that you cannot lead responsibly in today's world without seeing clearly how partial our knowledge often is, particularly when dealing with radical difference. Leaders in a global, ever increasingly connected world cannot lead without having to take on the viewpoint from another standpoint and see the world or, even more challenging, their own world through another's lens.

Leadership in the twenty-first century requires the capacity to have the nimbleness that can only come from some experience in crossing borders of race, ethnicity, nationality, sexual orientation, culture, economic class, religious faiths, political orientation, and language. Difference is often the occasion of conflict, but conflict is not evil, only the desire to subjugate, assimilate, ignore, or expel the difference in our midst.[1] Ronald Heifetz, cofounder of the Center for Public Leadership at the Kennedy School of Government at Harvard University, reminds us that excellence in leadership belongs to those who see the creativity that comes from conflict, that is, differences honestly faced, rather than avoided or subjugated.[2] It takes courageous leaders to see reality as it is, to see the differences that divide us, and not simply view the world from an idealized perspective. Courage to face reality and help others face reality is what Heifetz calls the heroic aspect of leadership.[3] Leadership requires seeing and naming the reality of how we move toward the demonization of the "other" in order to protect the borders of our own worldview. We cannot move our world in the direction of more harmony and cooperation and less division and fighting unless we face honestly the differences that divide us.

One of the realities leaders need to face is the gap between espoused versus lived values.[4] My faith speaks eloquently about being One, the inclusive love of Jesus, and the Gospel as promoting the value and worth of each and every human being. Yet the reality of our churches is that we are far from embodying what we believe, especially when it comes to our attitudes and actions toward difference.

To become leaders who understand and celebrate difference, we need to learn some critical skills for understanding and relating across differences. I am deeply indebted to the work of Visions, Inc.,[5] and William Kondrath, in his book *God's Tapestry: Understanding and Celebrating Differences*, for their work and insight in developing some key practices that can assist leaders in understanding and celebrating difference, thereby creating bridges across rather than walls between difference. I would like to share five of ten practices they speak of that can help us in this critical work.

The first practice they call "try it on." This is a practice that invites us to new learning by practicing not forming judgments in the first five minutes. To learn to see something from a new perspective, we must take a moment to suspend judgment long enough to risk trying on a different viewpoint.[6] The students at the border have to "try on" multiple perspectives, getting inside the skin of the other for a moment, to try to stand outside their own references points in viewing reality. Like the story of the elephant and the blind men, each touching a part of the elephant, each believes that they know what it is. But each mistakes a part for the whole. But when you see what part of the elephant they have access to, it makes sense. The one touching the tail thinks he has a rope, the one touching the skin on the side thinks it is a wall, and the one touching the trunk believes it is a snake. If that was your experience of the "elephant," you too might say the same thing. To "try it on" is a practice of suspending judgment long enough to be able to experience reality from the perspective of the other. If we cannot do this, we cannot open ourselves to receiving knowledge outside our own experience.

The second practice is to model that it is okay to disagree, but it is not okay to shame, blame, or attack.[7] All too often when differences appear, the first thing we do is judge the difference negatively and react by shaming, blaming, or attacking the other. If differences are not allowed to be expressed, then we are shutting down development of the character trait of curiosity, which is essential in creating openness to learn about the other and developing the capacity to entertain the possibility of legitimate differences. Because people fear conflict, we don't talk about the things that threaten to divide us. But this very fear requires that differences be muted or nullified so that we seldom know the creativity and imagination that can be ignited by openness to difference. This requires learning ways not to put people on the defensive. We say, "Can you tell me more about that?" rather than a more hostile "Why do you believe or think that?"[8] Without creating environments where difference is invited and people do not fear being blamed, shamed, or attacked, imagination and creativity will be severely diminished.

The third practice for understanding and celebrating differences is to practice "self-focus," which means simply to speak in the first person, that is, with "I" instead of the collective "we" or "they."[9] This allows conversation to develop from our own personal beliefs, thoughts, feelings, and actions, rather than unsupported generalizations about the other. Self-focus requires us to pay attention to our feelings and what is arising cognitively. To practice self-focus is to practice self-knowledge. This allows us to take responsibility for our own thoughts, feelings, and actions and to listen more attentively to ourselves. It also allows us to respond rather than react to another. Self-focus is a way to increase self-transparency and offer some level of vulnerability in a conversation, which assists tremendously in the development of empathy and connection with another.

The fourth practice for understanding and celebrating difference is to practice "both/and" versus "either/or" thinking.[10] This helps moves us beyond binary, dualistic thinking that creates opposition and places us over and against another. It helps eliminate thinking that moves quickly to evaluation of superior/inferior and allows us to entertain complexity. This kind of thinking fosters openness to differences, allows for more than one truth about a given reality, and allows us to respond to another nondefensively or without canceling the other out.[11] This practice is essential in a world where it is all too easy to fall into dualistic, black/white thinking, which may give us a false sense of control, but more often than not simply reduces truth to our own myopic vision.

The fifth practice critical in understanding and celebrating difference is to become aware of the difference between intent and impact.[12] We can have a good intention toward another but not understand the unintended impact on another. Whereas the intent is my motive for saying or doing something, the impact concerns how the other receives my act or speech or its consequences. Even though our intent and impact are often not in alignment with one another, we need to acknowledge to the other the impact our words and actions have on them, even when it is contrary to our intent. This is often the case when someone experiences a remark as racist or sexist when the speaker had no intention of making a negative evaluation of the other, but the unintended consequence may still be hurt, anger, or shame on the receiver's end. To facilitate dialogue that can go deeper, speakers needs to acknowledge the impact of their words on another, without defending their intent.[13]

These practices are not all that is needed in learning to communicate and interact across differences and divides, but they are excellent places to start practicing how to welcome difference and create fertile soil for in-depth dialogue that opens new horizons for all involved. Only as we learn ways to open ourselves to receive and hear difference can we find ways to deal with the conflict of differences creatively and empathically in our congregations and in our communities.

The ability to welcome difference is an essential component of learning how to move to see and respond to some problems as "adaptive challenges." Ronald Heifetz speaks about one of the key tasks of leaders today being the capacity to distinguish between technical problems, problems we confront for which we already have the solutions, and adaptive challenges, which require us to think beyond our current frame, to think outside of the box, to go beyond our current narratives and metaphors for meeting a new challenge. So, for instance, we have the technological capacity to repair a blocked artery through surgery, but the adaptive challenge of learning to live a new lifestyle that puts a priority on exercise, healthy eating, and the avoidance of smoking and excessive alcohol will be much more difficult than having the surgery. One is a problem that has a sophisticated medical solution; the other requires the adaptive challenge to find a whole new rhythm and way of life. Adaptive challenges require a response that is beyond our current repertoire, where our current know-how is simply insufficient to respond. In adaptive challenges, you cannot take the problem off the shoulders of another, but rather you have to be able to see how you yourself may in fact be part of the problem.[14] How, then, do we begin to develop such skills to prepare us for the kind of leadership that is being called for in our complex and global world? Heifetz speaks of adaptive challenges requiring us to learn new ways that make us move beyond our normal borders of thinking. In a global world, to learn new ways leaders will have to acquire skills to cross borders at many levels. This is going to require that we learn some new skills in how we relate to others different from ourselves.

After listening to pastors and alumni in focus groups and interviews concerning the question of what skills future leaders of congregations will need, the faculty at Andover Newton, in designing the Border-Crossing Immersion program, identified some key factors for learning.

The following were seen to be central in enhancing the capacity of leaders to understand difference and work across borders of all kinds:

- Find approaches to create hospitable ways to relate to difference that eliminate making an "other" out of those who are different from us.

- Develop greater understanding and sensitivity to the dynamics of privilege, power, and disadvantage as they are seen in patterns and structures in one's own and others' contexts.

- Learn tools for social analysis, theological reflection, and deeper self-knowledge.

- Create experiences that allow students to view the world and themselves through a larger lens than their current one.

- Cultivate multicultural sensitivity and skills that help leaders become more agile, knowledgeable, and respectful in border crossings.

- Understand in depth how our assumptive worlds influence what we see and make it difficult to be open to perspectives that really challenge those assumptions.

The Border-Crossing Immersion program was developed on the premise that the leadership we need in today's world must be one that works for the common good. In their powerful and insightful book *Common Fire: Leading Lives of Commitment in a Complex World*, Laurent Parks Daloz, Sharon Daloz Parks, Cheryl Keen, and James Keen conducted interviews with more than a hundred people who had sustained a commitment to the common good in their professional and personal lives for more than twenty-five years. Their research focused on understanding the critical factors that influenced this kind of commitment. One of the most important discoveries among the people interviewed was that all of them had at some formative period in their life had what the authors called "a constructive engagement with otherness." The authors state, "Whenever and however it occurs a constructive engagement with otherness defuses tribal fear of the outsider, and for many anchors an enduring sense of a wider belonging."[15] They write that such a constructive engagement with otherness is not a single event after which everything else appears different, but rather a crystallized moment of memory in a larger pattern of engagements with otherness. Usually it is such experiences over a period of time that create a way of being in the world that is continually open to discovering and rediscovering that "we" and "they" share common bonds.[16]

Given that many seminary students come from rather provincial backgrounds and have often had few experiences of encounter with radical difference, the faculty at Andover Newton created a program where Border-Crossing Immersions would be a requirement for an integrative catalyst in our curriculum. We hoped this "constructive encounter with otherness" would provide students with their first encounter among others to follow or a different engagement with "otherness" to build upon ones previously experienced. As seminary students are exposed to contexts vastly different from the ones they know, their curiosity about the other grows by leaps and bounds. Without curiosity about what we don't know and who we don't know, we cannot learn new things. Without this kind of learning, we cannot develop the skills to meet "adaptive challenges." Learning curiosity and openness are among the most important qualities to cultivate in today's leaders of faith communities. Leaders of congregations will need to embody the very attitudes and ways of being they hope to call forth in their congregants.

To cross over into terrain where we have never been is always a risk. We do not know what we may confront or face. We may, with the best intentions, cross over in the hope of establishing relationships of mutuality and trust but find ourselves failing in the very areas that propelled our journey. Heifetz reminds us that leaders have to have a stomach for failure, that in baseball no one gets on base more than 40 percent of the time,[17] and therefore we have to be prepared that failure and disappointment will also accompany our border crossings. But without failure we do not learn how to let go of our assumptions, we do not learn how to see what is inadequate about the frame we brought to analyze a situation, we are not forced to think anew and with greater flexibility than before.

After crossing a border, we need to go home, but home is never quite the same, for now we see it from a whole new perspective. Leaders of our faith communities need to be among those who model and show others the way to understand and celebrate differences so that we can create a world safe for differences and learn the joy, imagination, and creativity that come as we open ourselves to people, perspectives, and truths that take us beyond the borders of our own lives. A part of the job of seminaries in the formation of leaders of faith communities is to provide experiences that prepare leaders of faith communities for this role in our society.

Notes

1. For more on ways of reacting to difference, see Miroslav Volf, *Exclusion and Embrace* (Nashville: Abingdon Press, 1996).
2. Ronald Heifetz, "Leadership, Adaptability and Thriving" (address to Convocation and Pastor's School, Duke Divinity School, October 8, 2008).
3. Ronald Heifetz, *Leadership without Easy Answers* (Cambridge, MA: Harvard University Press, 1994).
4. Ibid.
5. Visions, Inc., provides multicultural training and consultation to corporations, ecclesial institutions, educational institutions, and nonprofits. William Kondrath is a program consultant for Visions, Inc.
6. William Kondrath, *God's Tapestry: Understanding and Celebrating Difference* (Herndon, VA: Alban Institute, 2008).
7. Ibid.
8. Ibid.
9. Ibid.
10. Ibid.
11. Ibid.
12. Ibid.
13. Ibid.
14. Ronald Heifetz, www.youtube.com/watch?v=CSZId1VlYxc.
15. Laurent Parks Daloz, Sharon Daloz Parks, Cheryl H. Keen, and James P. Keen, *Common Fire: Leading Lives of Commitment in a Complex World* (Boston: Beacon Press, 1996), 71.
16. Ibid.
17. Heifitz, "Leadership, Adaptability and Thriving."

Further Reading

Gunderson, Gary. *Boundary Leaders: Leadership Skills for People of Faith.* Minneapolis: Fortress Press, 2004.

Heifetz, Ronald. "Leadership, Adapability and Thriving." Address to Convocation and Pastor's School at Duke Divinity School, October 8, 2008.

———. www.youtube.com/watch?v=CSZId1VlYxc.

Jones, L. Gregory, and Kevin Armstrong. *Resurrecting Excellence: Shaping Faithful Christian Ministry.* Grand Rapids, MI: Wm. B. Eerdmans Publishing, 2006.

Kondrath, William. *God's Tapestry: Understanding and Celebrating Difference.* Herndon, VA: Alban Institute, 2008.

Volf, Miroslav. *Exclusion and Embrace: A Theological Exploration of Identity, Otherness, and Reconciliation.* Nashville: Abingdon Press, 1996.

About the Contributor

Rev. Brita L. Gill-Austern, MDiv, PhD, is the Austin Philip Guiles professor of psychology and pastoral theology at Andover Newton Theological School (ANTS). She is faculty director of Border-Crossing Immersions and has led border-crossing trips to Nicaragua, El Salvador, and the Mexico-US border. She is committed to interfaith dialogue and work between Jews, Christians, and Muslims. She is a founding member of the Interreligious Center for public policy. As a board member of Communities Without Borders, she is active in work to stop the spread of global AIDS and to educate AIDS orphans and other vulnerable children in Zambia and India, to ensure a more hopeful future for them and our world. She has also led a dual narrative immersion to Israel/Palestine and is designing one in the US criminal justice system. She is an ordained United Church of Christ pastor and served in three parishes in Pennsylvania and California for eight years before joining the faculty at ANTS in 1988. In a coedited volume, *Feminist and Womanist Pastoral Theology*, she and Bonnie Miller McLemore lift up the contributions of feminism and womanism to the discipline of pastoral theology. She has contributed many articles and chapters to the field of pastoral theology.

13

Healing Those Who Hurt

Mary Pender Greene, LCSW-R, CGP, and
Terrie M. Williams, LCSW

Pastoral Counseling

Pastoral counseling is the ministry of care and counseling provided by pastors, chaplains, and other religious leaders to members of their congregation and the community. It is the intersection between spirituality and psychology. Religious communities have traditionally sought to provide spiritually based solutions for individuals in crisis. Clergy have listened intently to personal problems for centuries and have cultivated a spiritual counseling response to those who suffer from mental and emotional illness.[1] Traditional spiritual counseling continues to help many; however, it was recognized more than a half century ago that in many cases, professional psychological care was necessary for effective treatment.

The integration of religion and psychology for psychotherapeutic purposes began in the 1930s when Norman Vincent Peale, a minister, and Smiley Blanton, MD, a psychiatrist, formed the American Foundation of Religion and Psychiatry (the Blanton-Peale Institute). The role of pastoral counseling, once only religious or spiritual counseling, has evolved to pastoral psychotherapy, which integrates theology and the behavioral sciences. Carl Jung, Abraham Maslow, and William James all brought spiritual aspects to therapy. Psychiatrist Karl Menninger, a pioneer in the integration of the psychological and theology, believed in the "inseparable nature of psychological and spiritual health."[2]

According to the American Association of Pastoral Counselors (AAPC), pastoral counseling accounts for three million hours of treatment annually in institutional and private settings, and the number of certified counselors has tripled in the past twenty years.[3] The onset of managed mental health care has brought a reduction in available counseling services. As a result, many people seek clergy for advice with personal issues. For the working poor and those without insurance benefits, pastoral counseling offers free or low-cost help from a trusted source. Pastoral counseling addresses such issues as marital discord, divorce, parenting, dating and premarital counseling, illness, job loss, and grief. Some counselors provide individual counseling for victims of crime or abuse. It is a service that is both effective and in demand.

A 1996 *USA Today* survey found that 79 percent of Americans agree that faith can help recovery from illness. According to another survey, 77 percent of patients feel their physician should consider spiritual needs. In a 1994 *Newsweek* poll, 58 percent of respondents said they feel the need to experience spiritual growth. The Gallup Organization and the Lilly Endowment reported that 96 percent of the population said they believe in God.

Compassion Fatigue

Adversity is the major reason people seek help, and it is the mission of the pastoral counselor to provide guidance to the wounded and suffering. The hazard of the job is stress and compassion fatigue, the long-term consequence of working with and caring about individuals in crisis. Pastoral counselors are constant witnesses to anxiety, sadness, grief, fear, and anger. One hazard of the role is that giving too much can take its toll. There is a great need for pastoral counselors to practice self-care. It is crucial that they listen to their body's clues, which often warn when downtime is needed. Learning to recognize the complex symptoms of compassion fatigue in themselves and in others can prove priceless in their role.

There must be a clearer distinction between psychotherapy and pastoral counseling. Pastoral counselors are trained in both psychology and theology. They provide psychological as well as spiritual guidance, counseling, and companionship. They may also work with hospital staff to provide ethical and spiritual direction and instruction on religious practices and beliefs.[4] According to the Mississippi Hospital Association, pastoral counselors differ from other mental health professionals in three distinct ways: (1) they are trained in two disciplines, psychology and theology; (2) the educational requirements are different, usually requiring a master of divinity degree plus other academic work; (3) they are not doctors and cannot prescribe medication.[5] They work closely with other medical professionals as part of a team and must maintain counselor-client confidentiality.

Mental health professionals are health care practitioners who are trained to improve an individual's mental health or treat mental illness. This includes psychiatrists, psychologists, psychiatric social workers, psychotherapists, psychiatric nurses, pastoral psychotherapists, mental health counselors, and other health professionals. Specialized training enables them to address complex and multidimensional psychological problems. They perform a clinical assessment to evaluate a client's mental condition and then develop, implement, and monitor a treatment plan based on their data and findings. They also assess the need for medication and suicide risk.

Resources and Referrals

Further, triaging is an important part of the role of mental health professionals, who often act as the client's advocate when coordinating required outreach services or resolving crisis situations. Therefore, the collaboration of pastoral counselors with them and other treatment programs is essential to the optimum care for congregants. Clients are prone to be dishonest by omitting certain truths about their situations, because while they need help, they are extremely concerned about losing esteem or favor with their pastoral counselors. This further complicates pastoral counselors' ability to be of genuine service to them. Just imagine how difficult it would be for board members to admit to their clergy that they are abusing their spouse or having an affair. Privacy and anonymity play a vital role in treatment, especially during the engagement phase; having a person who is both unknown and neutral to the client is most valuable.

When clergy alone continue to see a congregant who is in need of a higher level of care, this can lead to a sense of hopelessness and prevent the person from obtaining the help needed. The pastoral coun-selor's role is the key to the referral process. In sermons and in private sessions, congregants need to hear that their clergy believe in mental health. People often repeat the things that were said during a service when it impacts their self-esteem or sense of hope. Messages that sug-gest that pain is punishment for the prior evil deeds of their ancestors will make them feel (1) faulty in the eyes of God, (2) that this is their destiny and nothing can be done, or (3) that prayer is the only answer.

Many clients may need prayer, clergy support, and mental health services all at once; therefore, collaboration is essential to best meet the needs of the client. Clients often seek services only when their situation has reached crisis level. Pastoral counselors must accurately assess both their professional and their personal limitations, because most people are drawn to ministry out of an innate desire to help, which causes a vulnerability to practicing beyond the scope of their role. Being clear about their role restraint and the professional skill set of a psychother-apist can be helpful in determining at what point a referral is indicated. The greatest gift a pastoral counselor can give is "permission" so that the congregant knows that in addition to prayer, all forms of help that enhance wholeness and wellness are encouraged.

There are many resources within the community to partner with and refer to, such as 12-step addiction programs. Addictions often grow out of a person's attempt to self-soothe when faced with life stress and pressure. It is important that pastoral counselors expand their defi-nition of addiction, because it can come in many forms and cut across all levels of society. It can impact the clergy, their supervisees, or their congregants. In addition to traditional substances (e.g., marijuana, alcohol, pills, cigarettes), people can develop addictions to everyday behaviors, such as eating, working, sex, shopping, gambling, or play-ing the lottery. These behaviors are persistent and maladaptive; they are clearly unproductive for the individuals and damaging to their families. They undermine people's ability to function normally, yet they con-tinue to engage despite the problems caused. The pastoral role can be greatly enhanced by hosting 12-step meetings within the house of wor-ship and openly demonstrating the value of addiction resources (e.g., during supervision, mentioned in sermons, and practiced in self-care).

Clergy Supervision

New clergy interns need both supervision and mentorship. Renown supervision researchers and authors, Bernard and Goodyear, defined supervision as "an evaluative relationship between a senior and a junior member of the mental health profession whose purpose is to enhance the professional functioning of the supervisee."[6] Supervisors are the culture carriers for the profession and are responsible for directing and nurturing the development of the supervisee's skills and professional identity. Supervisees who have unrealistic expectations for themselves are more apt to experience burnout and despair. This is why clergy supervisors being open and presenting their true selves as whole human beings with shortcomings and doubts is so crucial to the development of pastoral interns if they are to be well prepared for the realities of the profession. Supervisors should share both their wisdom and their shortcomings and emphasize that they are both a spiritual leader and a human being. This relationship will set the stage for the intern's future.

Points to Consider

- Seek to understand supervisees as whole, complex people. Don't limit your focus to work issues.
- Encourage their emotions; they need to know that you see them as a whole person and not just an extension of their role.
- Keep an eye out for signs of distress or compassion fatigue.
- They want your approval, so share both your approval and your concerns.
- They will doubt their faith at times; let them know about times when you've had doubts.
- They may omit or downplay things that shine an unfavorable light. Be open to hearing mistakes; share your own and let them know that lessons are learned from mistakes.
- Be honest. Respectfully share your concerns. Be clear and direct about expectations.
- Make "office politics" a regular part of your discussions. New leaders often struggle with newfound status, boundaries, and authority.

- Encourage and model self-care. Help them develop a plan to avoid burnout and compassion fatigue. Make this a regular part of the supervision.

- Reiterate that experienced leaders need continuing education and supplemental training to meet new challenges and that collaboration with peers is a career-long process. Model this by continuing your own education and supervision.

- Let them know that becoming a successful clergy leader is not a destination but a journey and that supervision is required throughout the trip.

- Remember that the quality of their future leadership skills is closely related to the quality of the supervision they received.

Support and Evaluation for Clergy and Lay Leaders

Clergy are often faced with complex and difficult issues, such as domestic violence, substance abuse and addictions, troubled teens, infidelity, under/unemployment, foreclosures, depression, and chronic illness. This creates a unique set of challenges for spiritual leaders. Ask for referrals and partner with supportive organizations such as Divorce Cares, Marriage Encounter, Engaged Encounter, and other specialized programs for deeply troubled relationships. Invite mental health professionals into your facility to discuss these issues.

A house of worship can be a truly comforting and supportive environment. It can also be an unforgiving and critical environment. While spiritual leaders themselves may feel they answer to an even higher authority, it is important to remember that clergypersons are human beings just like everyone else. Not grasping this concept can lead to the "imposter syndrome," where the isolation, overwork, and feelings of guilt compel negative behaviors such as the hiding of pain. Be aware that congregations often expect clergy to have "godlike" qualities, which is unrealistic and stressful. Spiritual leaders must ask themselves whether their role as a constant source of compassion is taking a toll. Compassion fatigue causes physical, emotional, and spiritual fatigue and exhaustion that can cause clergy, management, lay leaders, and congregants to become overwhelmed. Compassion fatigue can put stress on the entire congregation.

Questions to Ask

- How do we address the personal and professional needs of clergy leaders?
- Where do the clergy go for professional support and assistance?
- Do we have appropriate referral resources to help our congregants get their needs met?
- Why are ministers, clergy, and lay leaders especially at risk for burnout?
- How can we learn to identify the impact that compassion fatigue has on our congregation?

Over time, the constant output of emotional energy can lead to a decline in both morale and productivity. The organization is at risk for suffering the far-reaching symptoms of stress: friction among committee members, congregant-management tension, increased absenteeism, and loss of membership. Addressing compassion fatigue within an organization requires time, patience, and vision. Clergy must assess themselves and their organization for signs of compassion fatigue and create a plan for positive change and healing.

Symptoms of Compassion Fatigue within the Organization

- Inability for committees to work well together
- Desire among members to break rules
- Outbreaks of aggressive behaviors among committee members
- High degree of loss of members
- Inability of committees to complete projects
- Lack of flexibility among members
- Negativism toward clergy, administrators, and leadership
- Strong reluctance toward change
- Inability of congregants to believe improvement is possible
- Lack of a vision for the future

Accept that despite the special nature of the role of clergy, it is still a job that must begin and end each day and have breaks in between to avoid burnout and compassion fatigue. Also, because it is a job, the time may come to move on. Clergy must perform regular self- and career assessments to determine their level of effectiveness, satisfaction, and compassion fatigue and whether the work continues to be a match to their goals. Seeking their own therapy is crucial, as people cannot give what they do not have. Often, spiritual leaders fear that seeking help is an admission of their lack of faith, inadequacy, a weak character, or dependency. In reality, therapy can help people learn more about themselves, gain a new perspective, and identify their strengths, as well as recognize and change destructive behavior patterns.

Red Flags for Clergy

- Feeling that there is no room for mistakes and that you must always be "on"
- Soothing pain with substances that lead to addictions
- Prescription drugs, food issues, relationship issues
- Feeling that you must be "loved" by everyone
- Noticing a lack of time for self-care or nurturing personal relationships
- Trying to be everything to everybody (husband substitute for widows and divorcees; father to fatherless children, a hero to all)
- Your mate and children are suffering from jealousy, resentment, and lack of attention
- Engaging in harsh self-judgment and negative self-talk ("if people only knew")

Working with a licensed psychotherapist is the most effective method of overcoming chronic depression, fears, trauma, and anxiety and breaking unhealthy patterns. It can provide clergy with a safe space to explore their spiritual doubts and dilemmas. Unlike colleagues, who may not really know their personal issues, or loved ones, who are too personally involved to challenge their ideas, a therapist can complement their work by lending objective support, helping discover new resolutions, and assisting in exploring solutions in a different way.

Questions for Clergy to Ask Themselves

- Am I suffering from compassion fatigue?
- Are my feelings of fatigue, stress, and worry starting to affect the quality of my work?
- Is my relationship to my work uplifting and positive?
- Do I need to examine how I am relating to this difficult and important work that I do?
- What is self-care, and how can I use it to be a more effective leader?
- Could I be more effective in my work and personal life if I practiced self-care?
- What can I do to restore and sustain the zeal, enthusiasm, and joy for service?
- How can I learn to clarify my role in the healing process?

The therapeutic journey can help clergy become their best personal and professional selves. Unresolved personal issues can create obstacles and prevent them from fulfilling goals, dreams, and potential. A combination of prayer, self-care, supervision, and therapy is the best recipe for success.

A Note from the Editor

One aspect of healing those who hurt is black pain. In many black neighborhoods, mental illness is a topic that you do not discuss. Best-selling author and mental health advocate Terrie M. Williams writes about black pain as an illustration of healing those who hurt.

Black Pain: Talking about the Taboo of Mental Illness

Many health care professionals refer to hypertension as "the silent killer," and that is an accurate assessment, for if the illness goes undetected, it can result in paralyzing strokes and death. However, there is another silent killer that is not spoken of because it's considered taboo to do so. It suffocates an individual's will to live, paralyzes its victims by killing their joy of life, and causes suicidal thoughts and tendencies in its victims. This silent pain—or what I refer to as black pain—is clinical depression. My own harrowing experience with depression and my numerous talks around the country have convinced me has that there needs to be transparent, real conversation about this illness, because the deafening silence around the issue is killing us.

The Silent Scream

The critically acclaimed book *Black Pain: It Just Looks Like We Are Not Hurting* came out of my experience with depression. Another reason for sharing my experience with depression was due to the overwhelming response by the public to an article in *Essence* magazine in 2005 when I first openly shared my experience. I received more than ten thousand letters from men and women suffering with depression who confessed to me that they "thought they were alone." That response caused me to hear the silent scream of individuals affected by this illness who previously had no name for how they felt.

Depression is that dark place in all of us. The danger for us, especially those in the black community, is that we were taught to hide our pain. We mask our pain because we feel that this is what we need to do to survive daily. It's a mask that reassures the world that we are fine, accomplished, and confident. The Harlem Renaissance poet Paul Laurence Dunbar once said, "We wear the mask that grins and hides / it hides our face / it shades our eyes." Dunbar was illustrating the assumed subservience of blacks as a radical strategy for survival during slavery and Jim Crow. Even Ralph Ellison points to the subterfuge in his short story "Battle Royale" when the grandfather, on his deathbed, encourages the protagonist to wear the mask and play the game in order to dupe the dominant culture. Masking is deception and duplicity; when we mask, we are hiding because we can't give anyone in the highly competitive world an edge over us. So you dare not say or even hint that you are less than perfect, because there goes your edge.

Moreover, mental health issues are not the topic of conversation at the family's barbecue reunion. It's not talked about in the black community because it's considered a sign of weakness—a character flaw. If you hint at the issue, people will think you are weak. To talk about it may ruin your career and hurt your family. Because we are a faith-based people, to do anything other than pray to God is considered a "betrayal."

This mask we wear, in some ways, prohibits anyone from truly checking out our emotional and mental state and, ironically, keeps us from obtaining the help we need. It's an effective camouflage against detection; we tend to perceive it as a mask of self-preservation and survival in a competitive world.

Recognizing There Is a Problem

However, recognizing there is a problem is the first step toward recovery. I have suffered from low-grade depression for more than half my life. In retrospect, I now recognize that the signs were there when I was in graduate school. I slept a lot in my room, during the day, with the blinds drawn. I went to a therapist but was not diagnosed with depression. Many of us are either undiagnosed or underdiagnosed. We have all inherited the unresolved pain and scars of our parents, no matter how loving and well intentioned they were. They did the best they could, and we inherit their gifts and talents, but it's the pain and oppression that many of us have experienced that have left an indelible mark. So if you don't talk about the things that have happened to you, it sits inside you and it festers.

For example, I am still traumatized by my experience with my first-grade teacher, who didn't give me an opportunity to correctly pronounce a word I had mispronounced. She stopped me from reading and called on someone else. And that experience has had repercussions in life. I developed a "Pollyanna syndrome"—a Miss Goody-Two-Shoes persona. It was always work, work, and more work; I had to be the best student, and the class officer for three years.

I put other people's needs before my own; I was last on my own "to-do" list. All of this, unresolved past experiences, coupled with an inherent obsession with overachieving, resulted in my major breakdown. For nine months, I literally could not function. It was a difficult time. I woke up feeling anxiety and dread with no desire to face the world. I slept excessively, and then I often lay in bed crying, in a fetal position, with the sheets pulled over my head. I did not even answer the phone. It took a lot of energy for me to get up, shower, get dressed, and put the mask back on. *So it wasn't just how I was feeling, it was the stress of pretending I was fine when I was just literally "the walking dead."* I was highly irritable. I would snap at people. I ate excessively but not the right foods. I wasn't exercising. However, I have always marveled that I was able to wear the mask—the game face—and no one saw my true emotional/mental state.

The game face—the act—was in full effect whether I was attending a business meeting or an award show; I would be smiling, laughing, and I would say to myself, "Two hours ago, you were on the floor in tears and had no idea how you were going to get here." I know that it was God who ordered my steps because I was clearly not operating under my own strength. The best illustration I can think of to describe that experience is that it was like trying to walk with concrete taped around your ankles. It was a very tormenting experience. It felt like a death sentence. Even now, talking about it often makes me emotional, but what I have discovered is that speaking about it, unveiling the issue and making it visible, is an essential step in the process of recovery.

The Importance of a Support System

For those suffering from depression, community plays an important role. Seven years ago, it was some friends who rescued me. They recognized something was wrong when I wasn't returning phone calls. They came to my house and banged on the door and seeing the condition I was in told me that I had to make an appointment to see a psychiatrist. In my effort to mask my depression, I lied to my parents. I called and left messages when I knew no one was home because I didn't want to talk. We lie because we don't want to seem weak, or we don't think that people would be willing to stop and listen to what we have to say about how we truly feel.

Get the Help You Need

I started seeing a therapist regularly, and she prescribed medication that I chose to take because I wanted to stabilize, but I started to sabotage myself by not keeping regular appointments. I canceled several sessions with her because my work was more important. I decided to change therapists and found an extraordinary psychiatrist in the person of Dr. Denise Shervington, but I started to skip appointments with her as well. It was she who helped me see how I was sabotaging myself. She said, "Let me see if I understand this. It's more important for you to go to these events, be a fraction of who you want to be than to commit to coming here each week to heal." She called me out and I totally got it.

Resources: Making the Issue Visible

The national campaign Sharing Ourselves ... Healing Starts with Us and Used2BeMe.net are the initiatives we, at the Stay Strong Foundation, use to make the issue visible and generate public dialogue about depression. It's a health initiative to break the stigma and shame related to mental health issues in the black community. We need to talk about the taboo because mental illness is not just our problem—it's a universal concern. I went through the fire, came out on the other side, and found out what I was called to do.

Our work has positively impacted thousands of lives through programs such as Sharing Ourselves ... Healing Starts with Us (a collaboration with the Ad Council and the US Government's Substance Abuse and Mental Health Services Administration). The campaign garnered $2.5 million in donated national advertising space and $11 million in media results to significantly heighten the awareness and importance of mental and emotional health.

Notes

1. American Association of Pastoral Counselors (AAPC), "Brief History on Pastoral Counseling," www.aapc.org/about-us/brief-history-on-pastoral-coun-seling.aspx?.
2. Ibid.
3. American Association of Pastoral Counselors (AAPC), "Pastoral Counseling Today," www.aapc.org/about-us/pastoral-counseling-today.aspx?.
4. Mississippi Hospital Association (MHA), Health Careers Center, "Pastoral Counselor," www.mshealthcareers.com/careers/pastoralcounselor.htm.
5. Ibid.
6. Janine M. Bernard and Rodney K. Goodyear, *Fundamentals of Clinical Supervision*, 2nd ed. (Boston: Allyn and Bacon, 1998).

Further Reading

American Association of Pastoral Counselors (AAPC). www.aapc.org/content/brief-history-pastoral-counseling.
Association for Clinical Pastoral Education (ACPE). www.acpe.edu.

Bernard, J. M., and R. K. Goodyear. *Fundamentals of Clinical Supervision*. 4th ed. Upper Saddle River, NJ: Merrill/Pearson, 2009.

Boorstein, Sylvia. *Don't Just Do Something, Sit There: A Mindfulness Retreat with Sylvia Boorstein*. San Francisco: HarperOne, 1996.

Buxbaum, Yitzhak. *Jewish Spiritual Practices*. Northvale, NJ: Jason Aronson, 1990.

Davis, Avram, ed. *Meditation from the Heart of Judaism: Today's Teachers Share Their Practices, Techniques, and Faith*. Woodstock, VT: Jewish Lights Publishing, 1997.

Mississippi Hospital Association (MHA), Health Careers Center. "Pastoral Counselor." www.mshealthcareers.com/careers/pastoralcounselor.htm.

Shapira, Rabbi Kalonymus Kalman. *Conscious Community: A Guide to Inner Work*. Translated by Andrea Cohen-Kiener. Northvale, NJ: Jason Aronson, 1996.

Smith, Patricia. *To Weep for a Stranger: Compassion Fatigue in Caregiving*. Charleston, SC: Createspace Publishing, 2009.

BOOKS FOR CLERGY AND LAY RELIGIOUS LEADERS

Gilligan, Stephen, and Robert Dilts. *The Hero's Journey: A Voyage of Self-Discovery*. Carmarthen, UK: Crown House Publishing, 2009.

Kabat-Zinn, Jon. *Wherever You Go, There You Are: Mindfulness Meditation in Everyday Life*. New York: Hyperion, 1994.

Morrissette, Patrick J. *The Pain of Helping: Psychological Injury of Helping Professions*. New York: Brunner-Routledge, 2004.

Myss, Caroline, and C. Norman Shealy. *The Creation of Health: The Emotional, Psychological, and Spiritual Responses That Promote Health and Healing*. New York: Three Rivers Press, 1993.

Saakvitne, Karen W., and Laurie Anne Pearlman. *Transforming the Pain: A Workbook on Vicarious Traumatization*. New York: W. W. Norton & Company, 1996.

OTHER RESOURCES

American Association of Pastoral Counselors, 9504A Lee Highway, Fairfax, VA. info@aapc.org, 703-385-6967, www.aapc.org.

The Compassion Fatigue Awareness Project. www.compassionfatigue.org/pages/symptoms.html.

Elat Chayyim: A Jewish Spiritual Retreat Center, 99 Mill Hook Road, Accord, NY. 800-398-2630, www.elatchayyim.org.

The Spirituality Institute at Metivta, 2001 S. Barrington Ave., Suite 106, Los Angeles, CA.

About the Contributors

Mary Pender Greene, LCSW-R, CGP, is an accomplished individual and group psychotherapist with more than twenty-five years of experience and a thriving private practice. She is a dynamic professional speaker, coach, and clergy consultant. She has been instrumental in advising clergy and religious organizations on compassion fatigue, supervision, referrals, and other mental health issues. The goal is for clients to have healthier, more satisfying relationships with themselves, loved ones, and colleagues. Her inspirational keynotes and leadership development programs include workshops, seminars, and training on a variety of topics. Her background includes executive and management responsibility for a large nonprofit organization.

Terrie M. Williams, LCSW, one of *Ebony* magazine's "Power 150" for Activism and *Woman's Day* magazine's "50 Women on a Mission to Change the World," is an advocate for change and empowerment. For more than thirty years, she has used her influence and communications expertise to educate and engage audiences in causes. She launched the Terrie Williams Agency in 1988, with superstar Eddie Murphy and the late jazz legend Miles Davis as her first clients, and has continued to represent some of the biggest personalities and businesses in entertainment, sports, business, and politics including Prince and Mo'Nique. Her book *Stay Strong: Simple Life Lessons for Teens* addressed challenges our youth combat everyday. Her critically acclaimed book *Black Pain: It Just Looks Like We're Not Hurting* recounts her personal struggle with depression and the impact the stigma of mental illness has particularly on the African American community. Her creation of a mental health advocacy campaign led to a collaboration with the Ad Council and the Substance Abuse and Mental Health Administration (SAMHSA) on a national initiative of mental health recovery.

14

Safety in Sacred Spaces

Rabbi Diana S. Gerson, MAHL

The story of *The Hunchback of Notre Dame* and the concept of sanctuary is familiar, thanks to movies, children's books, and Disney. The idea of running into a house of worship to find respite when fleeing from harm brings comfort and consolation to many. However, every spiritual leader should ask the questions, "Is there safety in our sacred spaces? How can we make our sacred spaces safe spaces?" Regardless of whether or not we have ever counseled a congregant or community member who is enduring or has survived abuse, we know that people within our congregations are suffering at the hands of loved ones and trusted individuals. To say that this is an overstatement is to live in a state of denial that the nationally recognized statistics are real. To be truly effective spiritual leaders and to build a ministry of presence, we must begin with the understanding that abuse does not only occur in someone else's community, but rather the epidemic of family violence occurs in every community. To be clear, family violence is a pattern of coercive behaviors, including physical, sexual, and psychological attacks as well as economic coercion, that adults or adolescents use against their intimate partners, children, or elderly relatives. While the numbers are overwhelming, they are imperative to gaining a full understanding:

- One in four women report being physically or sexually abused by an intimate partner at some point in their lives.[1]
- Every nine seconds a woman is assaulted by a loved one in the United States.[2]

- One in four girls and one in six boys are sexually abused in the United States. The average age of the victims is nine years old.
- Nearly four children die every day in this country as a result of child abuse and neglect.[3]
- Up to ten million children witness domestic violence each year.[4]
- It is estimated that for every one case of elder abuse, neglect, exploitation, or self-neglect reported to authorities, about five more go unreported.[5]

Spiritual leaders are an important key to the solution of this problem because, statistically, abuse victims will turn to their faith leaders first for help. They are also uniquely positioned to change community attitudes, such as denial, refusing responsibility, blaming the victim, or "maintaining the status quo." Leaders in faith communities can dispel the myth that family violence is a woman's problem and name it as a societal problem.

Recognizing Victims and Abusers

The statistics are overwhelming and necessary, but real understanding and transformation begin when clergy spend time with victims, survivors, and thrivers. The conversations are not about "How do I escape my situation?" They ask for help in "fixing the problem" because they are convinced that they are doing something to cause the abuse. In these cases, congregants and members of the larger community are usually disclosing their stories for the first time. It is important to recognize that people will not disclose until their spiritual leaders open the door to discuss this topic. Often, victims and survivors guard their wounds as classified secrets that should be divulged to "safe" individuals who will not pass judgment and will offer genuine support. When there is reason to believe that a person in the community is being abused, the spiritual leader should try to talk with the individual alone, without other family members present.

- Listen without being judgmental; believe the victim.
- Support and encourage the victim, but don't push or make decisions for the person.
- Make suggestions about where the victim can find help.
- Tell the victim that there is help and awareness in the community.

- Be ready to offer information about where to seek help. Social service and law enforcement providers are best equipped to assist a victim.

- Support the victim's decision about what to do. Respect the person's choice whether to leave the relationship or to stay. Make sure the individual knows that your door is always open to her or him.

- If the victim is a child or a disabled or elderly person, consult a family violence specialist about your legal obligations and mandated reporting requirements.

Just like the victims, there are no "typical" abusers. Anyone can be an abuser. On the surface, abusers may appear to be good providers, loving partners, law-abiding citizens, and trusted members of the community, but their abusive behavior toward their victims can lead to serious injury and even to murder.

To create a sense of safety where abuse can be discussed within a faith institution, leaders must seek out opportunities to introduce the topic. Offering sermons, articles, and community programs is a wonderful beginning but must be done routinely. Not everyone will be present to hear a sermon on abuse. Discussing these subjects should be done often to remove the stigma that surrounds abuse and build confidence that this is a community that addresses these issues. Posting local resources, distributing brochures, developing policies, implementing protocols, and providing regular staff and volunteer trainings send a clear message that this community is serious about safety.

Guiding Principles for Safety in Sacred Spaces

Every child dreams about happily ever after, and no one thinks that when they grow up they will be the victim of a crime. Victims and survivors of abuse are walking, working, and living alongside each and every one of us. They are our loved ones and sometimes we see them when we look directly into the mirror. Faith communities must seek to build safer sacred communities, because we know that everyone should be given the means and the tools to protect themselves.

Congregations are believed to be sacred spaces, and we affirm that they must be safe spaces for everyone. Developing a congregational safety initiative with comprehensive policies and protocols to create, maintain, and protect congregational safety on behalf of the membership, leadership, and staff is critical to making that belief a reality. Some denominations have begun to develop similar policies in response to the changing requirements of insurance companies around the country, but there is no standardized comprehensive plan that has been made available across denominations. These policies should address the federal and state policy guidelines and legal requirements.

Goals for Institutional or Congregational Safety

- Set standards for how staff and the congregation's members treat and behave toward one another.

- Develop and implement a mechanism to oversee proper conduct of all employees, members, and guests; investigate complaints; and take appropriate action when necessary.

- Protect alleged victims, survivors, witnesses, and reporters from recrimination, retaliation, and intimidation during the reporting and investigatory process; provide support for victims and survivors.

- Maintain confidentiality.

- Commit to communal training and educating the staff and the greater community about bullying, harassment, and abusive behavior.

Protecting Children Is an Adult Responsibility

The purpose of developing a child protection policy is to address the safety of our children and youth at all local congregations and faith centers and the organization's sponsored events. All organizations who serve children need to have a written policy with procedures in place (1) to help prevent the opportunity for the occurrence and/or appearance of abuse of children and youth and (2) to help protect workers from false accusations and/or suspicion. The following policy and procedures are not based on a lack of trust in workers, but are intended to protect our preschoolers, children, youth, workers, employees, volunteers, and the entire organizational body. Careful and confidential documentation is essential to show compliance with policies, to verify information as needed, and to have an accurate record in the case of an incident.

Purpose

The purpose of this policy is to ensure the fulfillment of the moral and legal obligation to protect minor children as vulnerable members of society and the obligation that is mandated by law. Specifically, this policy addresses the abuse of minor children.

Definition of Abuse

Abuse of a minor child includes serious endangerment of a child's physical or mental health due to injury by act or omission, including acts of sexual abuse. Abuse occurs between an adult and a minor or between two minors when one exerts power and control over the other. This can be a onetime occurrence or can happen repeatedly over a short or an extended period of time.

Sexual abuse includes contacts or interactions between a child and an adult when the child is being used as an object of sexual gratification for the adult. A child is abused whether or not this activity involves explicit force, whether or not it involves genital or physical contact, whether or not it is initiated by the child, and whether or not there is discernible harmful outcome. Non-contact acts of sexual abuse include exhibitionism, exposure to pornography, voyeurism, and communicating in a sexual manner by phone or Internet.

Child Maltreatment Statistics

- In 2008, US state and local child protective services (CPS) received 3.3 million reports of children being abused or neglected.[6]
- CPS estimated that 772,000 of those children were victims of maltreatment and approximately three-quarters had no history of prior victimization.[7]
- Seventy-one percent of the children were classified as victims of child neglect, 16 percent as victims of physical abuse, 9 percent as victims of sexual abuse, and 7 percent as victims of emotional abuse.[8]
- A non-CPS study estimated that one in five children in the United States experience some form of child maltreatment: approximately 1 percent are victims of sexual assault, 4 percent are victims of child neglect, 9 percent are victims of physical abuse, and 12 percent are victims of emotional abuse.[9]

- In 2008, an estimated 1,740 children ages 0 to 17 died from abuse and neglect (rate of 2.3 per 100,000 children).[10]

- Eighty percent of deaths occurred among children younger than age four; 10 percent among four- to seven-year-olds; 4 percent among eight- to eleven-year-olds; 4 percent among twelve- to fifteen-year-olds; and 2 percent among sixteen- to seventeen-year-olds.[11]

Child Sexual Abuse and Molestation

- Adult retrospective studies show that one in four women and one in six men were sexually abused before the age of eighteen.[12] Experts estimate that there are more than 42 million adult survivors of child sexual abuse in the United States.

- The primary reason that the public is not sufficiently aware of child sexual abuse as a problem is that 73 percent of child victims do not tell anyone about the abuse for at least a year; 45 percent of victims do not tell anyone for at least five years. Some never disclose.[13]

- Nearly 70 percent of all reported sexual assaults (including assaults on adults) occur to children ages seventeen and under.[14]

- Youths have higher rates of sexual assault victimization than adults do. In 2000, the sexual assault victimization rate for youths twelve to seventeen was 2.3 times higher than that for adults.[15]

- Most children are abused by someone they know and trust, although boys are more likely than girls to be abused outside of the family. A study in three states found 96 percent of reported rape survivors under age twelve knew the attacker. Four percent of the offenders were strangers, 20 percent were fathers, 16 percent were relatives, and 50 percent were acquaintances or friends.[16]

Definitions of Terms

The following terms and definitions were first identified by the General Conference of the United Methodist Church in their Safe Sanctuaries Policy adopted in April 1996, including the "two-adult rule" and the "five-year rule." Today, these definitions and rules are widely used by faith and non-faith-based institutions that serve children.

Adult: A person eighteen years of age or older.

Child: A person under the age of eighteen.

Staff person: Any person employed by the organization or programs using its facilities who is responsible for children's activities. This person has regular and direct contact with children, must be twenty-one years old or older, and is counted in the two-adult rule.

Leader: Any person who supervises a children's activity. This person has regular and direct contact with children, must be twenty-one years old or older, and is counted in the two-adult rule.

Volunteer: Any adult who assists in conducting children's activities under the supervision of a staff person and/or team leader, has regular and direct contact with children, and is counted in the two-adult rule.

Helper: Anyone who aids in programs and activities and is not counted in the two-adult rule, including a youth ages fourteen to eighteen.

Mandated reporter: A person who in the course of his or her employment, occupation, or practice of his or her profession comes into contact with children. Such persons include but are not limited to medical professionals, school administrators, teachers, school nurses, social workers, day care workers, mental health professionals, and law enforcement officers. Clergy are mandated in 50 percent of US states. Please check your state's laws.

Staff person in charge of children's activity: The organization's employee responsible for conducting this activity.

Supervision

To achieve compliance with this policy, it may be necessary to combine groups; recruit, train, and reference additional volunteers; or cancel an event. There is safety in numbers; children and youth should be instructed to use the "buddy system." There should be at least one staff member or volunteer present who is trained and certified in first aid and CPR at all daylong or multiday events.

Training is a requirement for all staff persons, leaders, and volunteers working with children in the organization's children's activities. An educational component should be part of the application packet and interview. Thereafter, the minimum training would be an annual orientation that includes information regarding this policy and procedures for supervision, as well as information on how to identify and report child abuse.

Minimum supervisory standards include the **two-adult rule**. The two-adult rule requires that no matter the size of the group, there will always be two unrelated adults present. This may include the presence of an adult "roamer" who moves in and out of rooms.

- *No child should be left unsupervised* while attending an organization-sponsored children's activity.
- Each room or space where children are being cared for should have a window in the door or the door should be left open (e.g., a restroom). All activities should occur in open view, be observable, and be interruptible.
- There are no organization-sanctioned events that permit one adult to be alone with one child.
- Staff and volunteers who accompany a child to the bathroom are to remain outside the bathroom while the child is inside. If a child needs assistance with zipping, buttoning, buckling, cleanup, wiping, and so forth, two adults must be present, one of whom can be a helper.
- No adult, staff, or volunteer should initiate or encourage physical or intimate contact with children. Setting boundaries is the responsibility of the adult. Should the children's activity be an outdoor program or occur in a setting that makes it difficult to comply with this policy, the staff person in charge of the activity should take appropriate measures to make sure that the *children are properly supervised*.
- Registration materials for activities in which children are outside of the direct supervision of their parents/guardians should require signed written permission forms.
- All participants who can understand a behavior contract should sign a code of conduct. This code of conduct can be in

the form of clear, posted, or printed rules that are explained to the participants at the outset of every program.

- No person should supervise an age group unless he/she is at least eighteen years of age or older and is at least five years older than the children being supervised.

- Accurate participation records must be maintained for all children's activities and include the date and hour of the activity, location, participants, adults involved, and early dismissal details.

- Staff and volunteers are not allowed to pick up children from home or bring them home from the organization, or be alone in a car with one child.

- There should be a minimum of two adults per room.

- Whenever possible, state child-care minimum standards should be followed, particularly in relation to the number of child-care providers to child ratio.

- If the group is sleeping in one large open space, two leaders should be present in the room.

- When staying at a hotel, leaders should sleep in separate rooms from children/youth.

Screening for Leaders Working with Children and Youth

Prior to employment or acceptance as a leader (paid or unpaid), each prospective applicant must complete the application/consent form. By signing the form, the applicant gives the organization permission to contact references and perform the necessary investigation to complete the review of the application.

The local organization is responsible for conducting reference checks and screening. All screening should be done in accordance with guidelines to be established and adopted by the organization.

The director should receive the completed forms and reports from the department director and review them. If any of the reports raise questions about the fitness of the applicant, the director should disapprove the application and notify the department director. The director reserves the right to turn away any persons for service.

If the applicant (paid or unpaid) is found to have been involved in any activity in which the applicant abused or exploited children or youth, the applicant should not be approved. Any conviction of a crime against children or youth disqualifies any applicant. Results of screenings should be kept confidential.

Negative Recommendation Guidelines

Persons having a criminal history of any of the following types of offenses should not be allowed to serve in any program with children and youth:

- Child abuse, whether physical, emotional, sexual, or neglectful.
- Violence offenses, including murder, rape, assault, domestic violence, and so on.
- Persons having a criminal history of DUI or DWI conviction within the last five years immediately prior to application should not be allowed to act as a driver.
- Persons having a criminal history of a drug-related conviction within the last five years immediately prior to application should not be allowed to participate in the program.

Training

The organization should implement orientation and training for all persons in leadership who work with children and youth at local or off-site activities and events. Training should include but is not limited to appropriate discipline, boundaries, leader misconduct, and this policy. No adult or helper should have any direct or indirect contact with children and/or youth until they have completed this training program. A review of this policy should be conducted at the beginning of an event or activity.

Discipline

Children and youth should be made aware of what kind of behavior is expected of them at all activities and events. While reminders are always necessary when working with children and youth, discipline might be required when these reminders don't work. When negative behavior has to be addressed, a designated adult should be notified. It is never appropriate to employ physical discipline as a measure to deal with disruptive or destructive behavior. Rather, a period of "time out" for the child or youth should be implemented, along with the necessary supervision as detailed by this policy.

It is important to keep parents involved. They must be informed of their child's behavior, good and bad. For serious offenses, the required response is to send the child or youth home immediately. Parents and the director are expected to work together on proper arrangements.

Developing Boundaries

Physical and emotional boundaries are critical when working with children and youth. Boundaries should be explained and respected by all staff, volunteers, helpers, and children at all times. Boundaries are specific to the age group of the children and youth participants, because their needs change as they grow older. As children grow older, it is important for all leaders to maintain appropriate emotional boundaries in relationships. It is important for those working with children and youth to not cross boundaries and allow the younger person to become too attached or overly familiar. Adults must be mindful of subject matter and avoid inappropriate discussions of private matters. When an issue regarding boundaries arises, the adult should be removed. If the problem persists, the leader should contact the child's parent/guardian to discuss and address the issue.

Leader Misconduct

It is a privilege to work with youth. Great responsibility is required. Those who violate the organization's policy should immediately be removed from contact with children and youth, and appropriate authorities should be notified immediately.

Reporting Procedures

Every state has legal mandates and requirements pertaining to how and when to report reasonable suspicions of child abuse or neglect. In order to meet the reporting obligation, as well as to provide appropriate protection for children, an organization's policy applies to abuse that allegedly occurs on-site, on property owned or leased by the organization, or while employees, members, or guests are participating in an organization-connected activity off-site.

1. A minor and/or his or her parents or guardians or anyone external to the organization who has knowledge about the

abuse of a minor that occurred on organizational property or that involved an organization employee, member, or guest during the course of an organization-connected activity off-site is urged to report the alleged abuse to the director in charge of the program in which the minor is involved or to anyone else at the organization with whom the reporting person feels comfortable speaking after following state reporting procedures.

2. An organization employee, member, or guest who has reason to believe that a minor has been abused on-site, on property owned or leased by the organization, or while employees, members, or guests are participating in an organization-connected activity off-site or who has received a report of such alleged abuse must report this information to the director. The alleged offender should be restricted from further access to minors, and a report with the appropriate law enforcement agency must be placed in accordance with the state's reporting laws.

3. An organization member who has reason to believe that a minor has been abused on-site or while members of the staff or membership are participating in an organization-connected activity off-site or who has received a report of such alleged abuse must report this information to the director in accordance with the state's reporting laws.

4. The executive committee and general counsel in conjunction with the director should develop written procedures for handling the investigation of allegations of abuse, for reporting it to the authorities if appropriate, and for resolving the situation, including imposition of sanctions, if appropriate. Such written procedures should be published in the organization's staff, employee, member, and parent handbooks.

5. If there is a finding that the alleged abuse occurred, the organization should assist in obtaining appropriate counseling for the victim and members of the victim's family, if appropriate. The greatest delay in supporting a victim of abuse is the time it takes to report the incident.

Notes

1. Tjaden, P., and N. Thoennes, *Full Report of the Prevalence, Incidence, and Consequences of Violence against Women: Findings from the National Violence against Women Survey*. Research Report (Washington, DC, and Atlanta, GA: US Department of Justice, National Institute of Justice, and US Department of Health and Human Services, Centers for Disease Control and Prevention, 2000), NCJ 183781.

2. American Medical Association, 1998, Georgia Department of Human Resources, 1999.

3. National Child Abuse and Neglect Data System. Child Maltreatment 2007. www.acf.hhs.gov/programs/cb/pubs/cm07/index.htm.

4. Bonnie E. Carlson, 1984. *Children's Observations of Interpersonal Violence.* 147–167 in A.R. Roberts, ed. *Battered Women and Their Families* (NY: Springer, Straus, MA, 1992), 147-167.

5. National Elder Abuse Incidence Study, 1998. Washington, DC: National Center on Elder Abuse at American Public Human Services Association.

6. US Department of Health and Human Services, Administration on Children, Youth and Families, *Child Maltreatment 2008* (Washington, DC: US Government Printing Office, 2010), www.acf.hhs.gov.

7. Ibid.

8. Ibid.

9. D. Finkelhor, H. Turner, R. Ormond, and S. L. Hamby, "Violence, Abuse, and Crime Exposure in a National Sample of Children and Youth," *Pediatrics* 124 (2009): 1411–23.

10. US Department of Health and Human Services, *Child Maltreatment 2008*.

11. D. Finkelhor, R. Ormrod, H. Turner, and S. L. Hamby, "The Victimization of Children and Youth: A Comprehensive National Survey," *Child Maltreatment* 10 (2005): 5–25.

12. Centers for Disease Control and Prevention, 2006. Adverse Childhood Experiences Study: Major Findings (Atlanta, GA: US Department of Health and Human Services, Centers for Disease Control and Prevention). Available from www.cdc.gov/nccdphp/ace/findings.htm.

13. D. W. Smith, E. J. Letourneau, B. E. Saunders, D. G. Kilpatrick, H. S. Resnick, and C. L. Best (2000). Delay in disclosure of childhood rape: Results from a national survey. Child Abuse & Neglect, 24, 273–287 and J.J. Broman-Fulks, K.J. Ruggiero, R.F. Hanson, D.W. Smith, H.S. Resnick, D.G. Kilpatrick, & B.E. Saunders (2007). Sexual assault disclosure in relation to adolescent mental health: Results from the National Survey of Adolescents. Journal of Clinical Child and Adolescent Psychology, 36, 260–266.

14. H. N. Snyder (2000). Sexual assault of young children as reported to law enforcement: Victim, incident, and offender characteristics. Washington, DC: US Department of Justice, Office of Justice Programs, Bureau of Justice Statistics. www.ojp.usdoj.gov/bjs/pub/pdf/saycrle.pdf.

15. US Department of Justice, Bureau of Justice Statistics. National Crime Victimization Survey, 1992–2000. Conducted by the US Department of Commerce, Bureau of the Census. ICPSR03140–v4. Ann Arbor, MI: Inter-university Consortium for Political and Social Research.

16. D. Finkelhor, "The Prevention of Childhood Sexual Abuse" in *The Future of Children.* 2009;19:169–194. B. Barrett, "The Impact of Childhood Sexual Abuse and Other Forms of Childhood Adversity on Adulthood Parenting" in *Journal of Child Sexual Abuse.* 2009; 18: 489–512. V.E. Kress, N.A. Adamson, and J. Yensel. "The Use of Therapeutic Stories in Counseling Child and Adolescent Sexual Abuse Survivors" in *Journal of Creativity in Mental Health.* 2010; 5:243–259.

About the Contributor

Rabbi Diana S. Gerson, MAHL, has been successfully advancing the New York Board of Rabbis' leadership role in confronting family violence in the faith community since 2005. As a recognized authority in the field, Rabbi Gerson has provided education and training to more than three thousand members of the clergy and faith leaders around the nation. She has also provided family violence prevention education to more than a thousand teenagers and adults through her extensive outreach in faith communities. In October 2009, Rabbi Gerson founded a new organization, Love Squared, which focuses on building leadership in faith communities to support and engage their members in fostering healthy relationships and healthy marriages. Love Squared will continue to work in partnership with the New York Board of Rabbis as its lead sponsor. She also has developed training programs for the New York City Mayor's Office to Combat Domestic Violence and has educated faith leaders for the New York City Family Justice Centers. Rabbi Gerson serves as a member of the board of directors of the National Coalition Against Domestic Violence (NCADV) and continues to chair its Jewish Women's Caucus. Rabbi Gerson is a recipient of the Faith Leaders Award from Affinity Health Plan and was named one of the "21 Leaders for the 21st Century" by *Women's eNews.* Her work in the faith community has been the focus of articles in the *New York Daily News, Hadassah Magazine, Moment* magazine, *Women's eNews,* and the *Mann Report.* Rabbi Gerson received her rabbinic ordination from the Hebrew Union College–Jewish Institute of Religion in New York City. She previously served congregations in Short Hills, New Jersey, and Atlanta, Georgia.

15

"Each Person Is Sacred"

Leading toward Full Inclusion in Faith Communities

Lisa V. Blitz, PhD, LCSW-R, and
Mary Pender Greene, LCSW-R, CGP

Assumptions about race, gender, and sexual orientation are deeply entrenched in American culture. Many of these assumptions reflect bias and stereotyping that can lead to painful discrimination and the perpetuation of oppression. The organizations and communities we create are both a process and a product of social constructions,[1] where bias can become embedded and go unrecognized. Faith communities, built on the foundation of centuries-old traditions, may reflect social bias and hinder the full inclusion of all people they seek to serve. In this chapter, we explore the experience of leaders of faith communities to identify ways to help others increase diversity and inclusion in their congregations. First, however, it is important to understand something of the complexities of the problem.

Racial and Ethnic Differences

Most congregations are monoracial and monocultural, and most existing literature on inclusiveness focuses on race and culture in Christian churches. One study of Christian church congregations in the United States showed that nearly half do not have a single member of another racial group, and only 12 percent had a moderate amount of diversity.[2]

Congregations that are multiracial or multiethnic, however, are often very diverse and include Hispanics and Asians and either blacks or whites.[3] Churches struggle with whether they should encourage new members to assimilate into the existing church culture or support the expression of a unique ethnic culture and language to enhance diversity.[4] Increased diversity, however, may impact the congregation in unexpected ways. One study found that in previously monocultural churches, as diversity increased, members who represented the dominant group were more likely to leave, causing instability within the congregation.[5]

Women in the Congregation: Are Women in Power?

While women are the majority among congregation members, they are not represented proportionally among the clergy.[6] Even congregations that have worked toward multiculturalism and may promote other types of diversity do not achieve gender equity. Theology may play a role in suppressing gender equity in conservative churches, particularly when the congregation is multiracial.[7] The value of women's participation is generally unquestioned, but interpretations of scripture may limit the degree of leadership and power women hold.

Lesbian, Gay, Bisexual, Transgender— and Not Included

It is probably of little surprise that a study found prejudice among conservative Protestants against lesbian, gay, bisexual, and transgendered (LGBT) people who were asking for spiritual care.[8] Homophobia and heterosexism are endemic in American culture. Religious ideas that oppose homosexuality can contribute to emotional distress and identity conflict, and the mental health field has not found a way to be fully inclusive of both religious ideals and non-heterosexual orientations.[9] This potentially leaves individuals with no community that responds to both their spiritual and their psychological needs. The issue of full inclusion of LGBT people of color into predominantly black churches may be even more complex. While homophobia is seen in many black churches, it ironically and painfully replicates the ways in which racism has demonized black sexuality,[10] but attempts to protect against racism may contribute to rigid ideas of masculinity that reinforce homophobia.

It's Not Just Diversity: Ministering to the Marginalized

To more fully appreciate the meaning of inclusion, it is helpful to understand the experience of marginalization. An individual's identity and social standing are defined by society in many ways. One way to understand this is to recognize that we live in social contexts created by the intersections of systems of power and oppression: race/racism, gender/patriarchy, class/classism, and sexual orientation/heterosexism.[11]

Racism, patriarchy, and heterosexism can be understood as a systemic power arrangement that provides people with unearned privilege based on being white, male, and heterosexual.[12] Members of these groups become the dominant culture and influence the norms, expectations, and attitudes of the larger society. Others are placed at a disadvantage, and their views, traditions, and experiences are marginalized by the larger society. Members of nondominant groups may pull back from multicultural relationships to seek comfort and camaraderie from members of their own group.[13] Beyond individual acts of meanness or prejudicial attitudes, the dominance of one culture can become woven into an institution. Thus, the prejudicial attitudes are perpetuated as a matter of course, regardless of the values of the individuals involved in the organization.

Inclusion in a faith community does not happen spontaneously. Racial inclusion needs to be intentional, with race relations programs that address social oppression.[14] Without attention to racial experience, the person of color is not understood "in a society where color has historically mattered in terms of physical, social, economic, and spiritual well-being."[15] The same can be said of processes of inclusion directed at women and people who identify as LGBT. A robust diversity paradigm considers a wide range of difference, includes cultural and social context and oppression, and identifies individual and collective strengths.[16] Leaders need to take responsibility for initiating, guiding, and supporting work toward organizational change that values and responds to individual diversity in the full context of social and environmental experience.[17]

Lessons from Leaders in Faith Communities

Very little existing literature provides guidance on how to enhance inclusion within a congregation. To learn more, we conducted interviews with eleven leaders in faith communities who have long-standing commitments to inclusion. Some also have roles outside of the congregation that inform their work: conflict mediator, social worker, and community organizer to name a few. All have held leadership positions for many years, with congregations ranging from 125 to 3,000. Most identified their congregation as multiracial, but all indicated that one racial group was dominant. Three identified with historically black churches, and one was from a church that had been exclusively white but is now predominantly black. Two were with congregations that intentionally reach out to the LGBT community. While some diversity exists in the group interviewed, it is not representative of the wide range of religious and social diversity found in the United States. Giving voice to the experiences of this group, however, is an important contribution to the dialogue on inclusiveness.

All of the leaders described a variety of issues related to inclusion in their congregation. Older respondents reflected on how issues of inclusion have changed over time, noting that the focus was on race in the 1950s and 1960s, then shifted to women in the 1970s and 1980s, and is currently on lesbians and gay men. Most admitted to not being quite

RESPONDENT DEMOGRAPHICS			
Gender	**Race and Sexual Orientation**	**Faith**	**Position**
Male: 8	White: 5 (1 gay) Black: 3	Christian: 6 Jewish: 2	Pastor (senior or associate, current or retired): 5 Rabbi: 2 Deacon: 1
Female: 3	Black: 2 (1 lesbian) Latina/black: 1 (lesbian)	Christian: 1 Interfaith/ nondenominational: 2	Reverend: 1 Youth minister: 1 Committee member: 1

ready to take on the issues of transgendered people yet and acknowledged that inclusion work has been difficult:

> Issues of inclusion have been controversial—it drew fire and continues to draw fire. (retired senior pastor, male)

A faith community leader who also spent many years as a community organizer discussed the difficulty with bringing antiracist work and anti-homophobic work together, stating:

> There is a social conservatism in the black community, which made acceptance of my work with gays and lesbians difficult. The white community had a problem with both aspects of my work. (retired pastor, community organizer, male)

But they agreed that their spiritual calling motivated their desire to pursue the challenge:

> If you are saying you are called by God, you need to be ready to serve everybody. You can't just pick and choose. You don't know who will show up at your doorstep. (reverend, female)
>
> We need to look at how we're modeling, what we're saying through our actions. People look at how we're going to respond to issues of inclusion, and we need to be in integrity while demonstrating to the community what we preach and teach. (youth minister, female)

The faith community leaders also noted a need to balance their obligation to provide spiritual care with their role as educators on issues that can enhance inclusion:

> When somebody comes to be taught, they are asking to be challenged to grow, but when somebody comes to a leader they come with [spiritual] needs. (rabbi/chaplain, male)
>
> You need to be there with the people in the congregation, through life, challenges, death.... There is still a job that you were hired to do [to provide spiritual care]. (retired pastor, community organizer, male)

Race

All of the leaders valued racial and cultural diversity but noted the complexities involved. In discussing his "typically white suburban" congregation, one pastor noted that although the members of the congregation were accepting, they did not make necessary changes to ensure the new members would feel genuinely welcome:

> They welcomed black people, but the black people didn't stay because they didn't get the communication, caring, and celebration that would have helped them feel genuinely connected and embraced.... There was no willingness to change in response to diversity. (retired pastor, male)

Leaders also noted that while racism still persists, the need for black churches is changing. They noted that greater inclusiveness, including racial diversity, is desirable to maintain the viability of the church and grow congregations:

> [The black church] is a past paradigm. The black church had to exist because of the culture that existed.... As we move into the new century, I would fully expect that the churches will have to embrace a diverse community. If we have a genuine purpose to serve, if we are interested in growing the church, we have to be open. (deacon, male)

Gender

All of the people interviewed supported full inclusion of women, stressing the vital role they play in the congregation:

> We have four women who sit on the pulpit on any given Sunday. They teach, preach, and when they get ordained they will [perform marriage ceremonies]. We get in trouble if only men are on the pulpit.... Women need to see other women in leadership. (senior associate pastor, male)
>
> Women have a big voice in our church. They work as treasurers, chairperson, working with the minister. (committee member, female)

One rabbi noted that as women take on more leadership roles, it may result in feminization of the role of spiritual leaders in a way that makes it less attractive to men or boys:

> All the women are reading the Torah and women are leading the service.... There is a concern that since women have been becoming the majority, sometimes extreme majority in rabbinical

classes, boys only see women as ritual leaders. This has implications for the boys' participation; it could be seen as a girly thing to do. (rabbi, male)

Others noted a tension that they attributed to gender and sexism, where women's leadership styles were not always validated or accepted. A female youth minister stated:

There is a drive from some of the men in leadership, a different energy—harder, faster, "do this now" type of energy—that the leadership in place just wasn't able to do; it wasn't how they moved. There was some frustration; women had the last word, and at some point it blew up. (youth minister, female)

Similarly, a male pastor noted:

Problems can manifest as gender difference, where men are expected to function more in the left brain [logic] and women more in the right brain [relational]. This is not always true, but because of the social expectations, men may discount women's left brain functioning because they are hearing, or expecting to hear, her right brain message. (retired pastor, male)

In discussing the decision-making process in her church, a female reverend noted the challenges to female authority:

Our pastor is female, and ... we have three other females and four ministers who are males and there's still issues around who's in charge. (reverend, female)

LGBT

Many respondents indicated that those who identify as LGBT are not discouraged from attending services, but are also not given a space to talk openly about their identity and lifestyle:

As long as they play the role in church they can be accepted, but if they show who they are in the church they are ostracized. (deacon, male)

One rabbi noted:

Our synagogue doesn't know who is gay and who is bisexual; it has a rainbow inclusive posture. (rabbi, male)

Some recognized the difficulty with a culture of secrecy or lack of support in coming out openly within the faith community and expressed the need to move toward genuine inclusiveness to ensure the faith community is providing safe haven and spiritual support for all:

> If they feel like they have to keep it a secret, it could be very painful. How do we help them take that risk to talk about themselves … in a way that people can hear and be supportive? (committee member, female)
>
> There's so many of our children struggling with their sexuality, and if they don't get support, they may consider suicide or disappear from church. If you can't work that out with church, where do you go? If your parents don't understand, where do you go? (senior associate pastor, male)

Many of the leaders reflected on the relationship between theology and homosexuality and expressed that their congregations are currently struggling with how to respond:

> There are items in the Bible that deal with homosexuality, and every church is trying to find out how to reconcile the Bible with what is going on today. (deacon, male)
>
> I don't know how they [the church] are going to deal with the law about same-sex marriage. I don't know how far they can go. (committee member, female)
>
> Abomination is used in connection with a man lying with a man as with womankind. In conservative tradition, what they sorted out is that the verse is talking about sex outside of a long-term committed relationship. (rabbi, male)

Spiritual Practice and Belief

In relating to issues of inclusion in general, the leaders often referred to stories from scripture or text to explore issues of diversity, acceptance, and inclusion. For example, the book of Ruth and the Christian Scriptures story of the Samaritan woman at the well were offered as illustrations of biblical messages supporting inclusion and acceptance. Other messages from sacred text were referred to as well:

> Jesus in his life was trying to say that in addition to the law there has to be a provision for love and compassion. Jesus portrayed a life of love and acceptance. (deacon, male)

Every year we read about the passionate relationship between David and Jonathan, and some see this as a gay relationship; there is a homoerotic connection. (rabbi, male)

John's Gospel tradition says he was the only disciple who did not marry, that he was responsible for Mary after Jesus's death. [In a sermon] I said something to the effect, raising the possibility that the beloved disciple might be gay. (senior pastor, male)

I love the stories in Genesis that give different pictures of families: Jacob, who had four wives; Abraham, whose wife brings another woman into the relationship so he can have his needs met; Rebecca as the person in charge, who makes all the decisions. Are these the traditional family? (rabbi/chaplain, male)

Ultimately, themes of love, acceptance, and nonjudgment were repeated:

My belief about salvation is that it is right now. I have to demonstrate love, compassion, and caring, and I have to demonstrate that right now. (retired pastor, male)

Each person is sacred, created in the image of God. Keep that foremost. That makes this person who disagrees with you important. (retired senior pastor, male)

We're asking the wrong question: does homosexuality make you a sinner? ... We need to ask, does being heterosexual make you righteous? (senior pastor, male)

As a leader, I always want to be in a place of love and loving honesty. (rabbi/chaplain, male)

Skills and Advice

When asked to offer suggestions for other leaders in faith communities to help them respond positively to inclusion issues, many focused on the need to talk about diversity and the related issues of oppression with members of the congregation:

The more we are inclusive in our conversations, the more we are educating one another and not hurting. (reverend, female)

Several of the faith community leaders stressed the importance of listening to understand as a foundation for increasing inclusion:

Use communication skills to understand differences and different positions.... Agree to disagree, understand where the other person is coming from … [do not] put down the other person's perceptions of the world. (retired pastor, male)

Leadership in my perspective is the command to listen…. Listening is about comprehending what is being said to me. (rabbi/chaplain, male)

One person suggested using the natural flow of the religious calendar as an opportunity to explore issues:

[Fall] is the season of change and renewal, the month before Rosh Hashanah through the High Holy Days, and this could be a great time to talk about structural racism, because we talk about misdeeds that are not conscious or intentional. (rabbi, male)

The need to build diversity within teams or work groups in the congregation was also discussed repeatedly:

You need a real voice, an intentional forming of leadership teams that are representative, and kind of instilling the people who are marginalized or underrepresented and doing leadership training in those segments of the organization…. I need to provide training and preparation so they are ready for leadership. (senior pastor, male)

The minister of music had a musical group … and they were mostly white. It was not that she had anything against black people, but she was reaching out to her own, and people of color were not being included. We need to look at how we're modeling, what we're saying through our own actions. (youth minister, female)

The need for education, continued learning, and peer support was also echoed:

[We] are not trained adequately to confront these issues. We might say we are supporting inclusion or equity, but we don't know how to work it, especially in settings that are more conservative. We need training that helps people understand issues of oppression and how to be organizers to work toward change. (retired pastor/community organizer, male)

I was helped in my understanding of issues by exposing myself to new things, things unfamiliar to me. (senior pastor, male)

You can't do ministry on your own; you need a support group. It doesn't have to be formal. Have lunch together. Talk each other through things and support each other. (senior associate pastor, male)

Final Words

Leaders in faith communities are called to balance many priorities, the most important of which is spiritual care. Providing this care to all members of a community, however, requires intentional action to create safe and welcoming congregations, particularly for those who do not experience safety and acceptance in other aspects of their lives. The path toward inclusion may create disruptions in the existing congregation, a risk some may hesitate to take if membership and donations are already shrinking. In the words of one leader, however:

> I have the responsibility to bring words of inclusion and hope into a world that is so easily divided. Inclusion may be the only true way to peace. (senior pastor, male)

Notes

1. D. Newberg, "Postmodernism: Implications for Organization Theory?" in *Handbook of Organizational Behavior*, 2nd rev. ed., R. T. Golembiewski (New York: Marcel Dekker, 2001), 525–45.
2. K. D. Dougherty and K. R. Huyser, "Racially Diverse Congregations: Organizational Identity and the Accommodation of Differences," *Journal for the Scientific Study of Religion* 47 (2008): 23–43.
3. M. O. Emerson, *People of the Dream: Multiracial Congregations in the United States* (Princeton, NJ: Princeton University Press, 2006).
4. K. Garces-Foley, "New Opportunities and New Values: The Emergence of the Multicultural Church," *Annals of the American Academy of Political and Social Science* 612 (2007): 209–24.
5. C. P. Scheitle and K. D. Dougherty, "Race, Diversity, and Membership Duration in Religious Congregations," *Sociological Inquiry* 80 (2010): 405–23.
6. R. A. Cnaan and A. L. Helzer, "Women in Congregations and Social Service Provisions: Findings from the Philadelphia Census," *Journal of Religion and Spirituality in Social Work* 23 (2004): 25–43.
7. G. Yancey and Y. J. Kim, "Racial Diversity, Gender Equality, and SES Diversity in Christian Congregations: Exploring the Connections of Racism, Sexism, and Classism in Multiracial and Nonmultiracial Churches," *Journal for the Scientific Study of Religion* 47 (2008): 103–11.
8. K. C. McLeland and G. W. Sutton, "Sexual Orientation, Mental Health, Gender, and Spirituality: Prejudicial Attitudes and Social Influence in Faith Communities," *Journal of Psychology and Theology* 36 (2008): 104–13.

9. E. Bartoli and A. R. Gillem, "Continuing to Depolarize the Debate on Sexual Orientation and Religion: Identity and the Therapeutic Process," *Professional Psychology: Research and Practice* 39 (2008): 202–9.

10. E. G. Ward, "Homophobia, Hypermasculinity and the US Black Church," *Culture, Health & Sexuality* 7 (2005): 493–504.

11. M. Bograd, "Strengthening Domestic Violence Theories: Intersections of Race, Class, Sexual Orientation and Gender," in *Domestic Violence at the Margins: Readings on Race, Class, Gender, and Culture*, ed. N. J. Sokoloff and C. Pratt (New Brunswick, NJ: Rutgers University Press, 2005), 25–38.

12. P. McIntosh, *White Privilege and Male Privilege: A Personal Account of Coming to See the Correspondences through Work in Women's Studies* (Wellesley, MA: Center for Research on Women, 1988).

13. B. D. Tatum, *Why Are All the Black Kids Sitting Together in the Cafeteria? And Other Conversations about Race* (New York: Basic Books, 1997).

14. Dougherty and Huyser, "Racially Diverse Congregations."

15. M. Hearn, "Color-Blind Racism, Color-Blind Theology, and Church Practices," *Religious Education* 104 (2009): 272–88.

16. T. Faist, "Diversity: A New Mode of Incorporation?" *Ethnic and Racial Studies* 32 (2009): 171–90.

17. M. Pender Greene and A. Siskind, "From a Multi-cultural Institution to an Anti-racist Institution: A Traditional Jewish Organization Meets the Challenge," *Racism and Racial Identity: Reflections on Urban Practice in Mental Health and Social Services*, ed. L. Blitz and M. Pender Greene (New York: Haworth Press, 2006), xxi–xxx.

About the Contributors

Lisa V. Blitz, PhD, LCSW-R, is an assistant professor of social work at Binghamton University. She brings years of experience as a licensed clinical social worker and advocate for social justice to her teaching and research. Her research focuses on effectiveness of school-based interdisciplinary intervention with elementary and middle school aged children; assessment of an antiracist/anti-oppression model to inform management and supervisory practices in social work and social services; and privilege as it impacts social worker performance in cross-racial interactions with clients, staff team members, and supervisors. Dr. Blitz earned her master of social work and PhD in social work from Columbia University.

Mary Pender Greene, LCSW-R, CGP, is an accomplished individual and group psychotherapist with more than twenty-five years of experience and a thriving private practice. She is a dynamic professional speaker, coach, and clergy consultant. She has been instrumental in advising clergy and religious organizations on compassion fatigue, supervision, referrals, and other mental health issues. The goal is for clients to have healthier, more satisfying relationships with themselves, loved ones, and colleagues. Her inspirational keynotes and leadership development programs include workshops, seminars, and training on a variety of topics. Her background includes executive and management responsibility for a large nonprofit organization.

16

People with Disabilities and Their Families

"Apart from" to "A Part of"

Rev. Bill Gaventa, MDiv

Hearing the Call: Stories, Facts, and the Hidden Presence

People with disabilities, their families, and those who work with and support them present pastoral leaders with both the challenge and the opportunity to embody the best of individual and congregational leadership. It's a challenge not because one needs to learn skills in "specialized ministry," but because it calls for a breadth of pastoral skills in an area of ministry that also plumbs the depths of theological questions and issues. The opportunity is that effective ministry with people with disabilities and their families can literally transform lives (including those of others within the congregation), lead to sensitivities and skills that are applicable to everyone else, and enable a community of faith to experience and live out the fundamental tenets of their own tradition.

The place to begin is where most pastoral leadership begins: listening. All that a pastor, priest, rabbi, imam, or faith community leader needs to start is to ask people with disabilities and their families to share their own stories with the disability, including their faith stories. With a group of individuals and families, the response is never lukewarm. People will talk about how important their faith and faith community has been to them on the one hand, or, on the other, about how they have been ignored, isolated, wounded, and/or rejected.

I asked that question once at a Down syndrome conference after my presentation. Several of the stories will be in this chapter, but the one that hit me the hardest was from a mother who approached me during the break, saying she could not stand up and tell the story because it was still too raw. They had recently moved from another state, where their daughter, labeled "moderately retarded" and "micro-cephalic" in the professional lingo of twenty-five years ago, had been doing extremely well. Through a supported employment program, she worked at a McDonald's, proud of her uniform and contribution. There was no such program in their new home. She ended up back at a large sheltered workshop, where she was much more segregated.

Like many moving to a new community, they had gone "church shopping," trying any number of congregations. Finally, one Sunday evening, they came home and it was clear something had happened when their daughter had participated in a young adult activity. The daughter said, "No more church, Mom. No church!"

Whereupon the mom confessed to me that she started playing the mother role, saying to her, "We need to have a church. It's God's house. We need to belong." To which this young woman, with all the labels above, simply and profoundly said, "It may be God's house, but God's not home!"

Fast-forward a few years later and a half-day workshop in another state that simply had a panel of people with disabilities or parents telling their stories. You will hear some of these as well, but two parents, one with a daughter with autism, and the other with a son with intense behavioral and psychiatric issues, told stories about how they had each been asked to leave congregations by its leadership. For the first mother, it happened thirteen times; for the second, seventeen. That pain reminded me of a Catholic mother in Rochester who summed it up by saying what any parent of any child would say: "When the church rejects my child, they reject me." These two mothers were back in congregations, one because of the pastoral leadership, the second because of her son's invitation when he found a small, new congregation that welcomed him.[1]

The good news is that there are now more and more stories on the other end, families who have told me that they went to a new church, expecting to find barriers or to contend with negative attitudes, but instead found congregations who had thought this through, prepared, and had supports built in so that their child was whisked away in fifteen minutes to a class, often with a support "buddy," and they were left standing there with what felt like pure grace. People with disabilities and their friends talk about the power of that welcome and participation, which is not hard to imagine given the ways that they have to deal with stigma, stereotypes, and marginalization in so many areas of their lives.

When either full inclusion or rejection happens, with the name of the Sacred associated with it through the leader or the community, it simply magnifies the impact.

Take those few examples and multiply them by the numbers. The World Health Organization, in a 2011 report, estimates that 17 percent of the people in the world are impacted by some form of disability.[2] The number often cited in the United States is fifty-four million. That includes the major categories of people with intellectual and developmental disabilities; physical disabilities; sensory impairments such as deafness, hearing loss, and blindness; psychiatric and emotional disabilities; traumatic brain injuries; and learning disabilities. Multiply that by family members and relatives. Recognize the growing numbers of people who acquire disabilities as they age. Disability is sometimes referred to as the world's most inclusive minority group: anyone can join, any time.

The numbers are changing. The definition is changing. Disability, once seen as a medical condition, is now defined in a social context. The World Health Organization defines it on three levels: (1) a physical condition, anomaly, or impairment, with multiple kinds of causes, which leads to (2) difficulty or inability/disability to perform some typical tasks or functions, leading to (3) inability to participate in many areas of community life because of attitudinal or architectural barriers.[3]

That definition points the way to pastoral and congregational leadership. The key issue is not what causes a disability, even though disability raises the profound theistic question "Why?" along with multiple issues of ethics as human technologies have more and more power to prevent and to cause disability (e.g., the largest single cause of disability in the world is violence and war). Confronting disability is an experience of confronting limitation and vulnerability. Human services and congregational ministries can certainly help with accommodations and technologies that aid those with a second level of disability (e.g., large-print bulletins, hearing loops, and a wide variety of assistive devices and learning strategies). But pastors and faith communities have a power almost unequaled by any other human organization to help change attitudes, value judgments, stigma, and stereotypes that keep people with disabilities apart from congregational and community life. Societies can pass laws that give people rights to have a space in community life. Faith communities can build relationships, transform hearts and minds, and build community where there too often is none.

The Core Leadership Skills and Roles

Four key pastoral roles have emerged for me in my work in ministries with people with disabilities, their families, and the communities and congregations in which they live:

1. **Be present:** Be there. Go there. Listen. Nothing takes the place of a face-to-face encounter. Pastoral presence represents to many the presence of the Sacred or Divine as well as the community behind that leader.

2. **Provide guidance and counsel:** Be with people as they struggle to understand the questions and meaning that a developmental or acquired disability has for their lives. The shift in expectations and plans, the loss of ability in one area or another, and spiritual/theological questions of identity, purpose, connections, and suffering are all areas for a wise presence that helps connect people with the universal human questions that are also embodied in sacred scriptures and stories.

3. **Be an advocate**, or, as one might say, shepherd, with the rod and the staff: Help individuals and families navigate what may be a desert of services and supports or a jungle of confusing educational, medical, and social services. Go help the one while others tend the ninety and nine. Advocate by addressing issues related to disability in scriptures and preaching. A pastor once told me that after the first time he included concerns related to mental illness in his pastoral prayer, his phone did not stop ringing the next day. It was finally safe for people to talk to him.

4. **Build communities of support:** Provide leadership that models and enables a faith community to welcome, support, and include people with disabilities and their families in all aspects of their life together.[4]

When to Use Them: A Life-Span Perspective

The questions and issues that arise over the life span of people with disabilities and their families lead to opportunities to walk alongside them with one or more of the skills above.

Birth and/or Diagnosis

Prospective parents are increasingly dealing with issues related to disability before birth compared to in the past, when people often did not know until after the delivery. Amniocentesis and ever more sophisticated prenatal screening tools may present prospective parents with huge ethical and spiritual dilemmas in a health care system that increasingly assumes there is only one response and answer. The issues are never clear-cut and simple. A person can be strongly "right to life" but struggle when the question hits home personally. I once heard a mother say, "I learned my child would have multiple disabilities. I went to my clergyman. He reminded me of our tradition's belief in the right to life and sanctity of all life. I decided to carry my baby to term. She was born, and the church disappeared. She had a right to life, but also a right to living."

An unexpected disability, either at birth or acquired through accident or illness, can shatter expectations about parenting, children, or one's life plan for the future. There are many parallels with other experiences of grief and loss, calling for sensitive pastoral skills that do not deny or presume a particular process or set of feelings. It is important that spiritual leaders be present, listen and guide through the valleys, help individuals and/or families find information and answers, know the importance of early interventions for children and effective rehabilitation services, and connect individuals and families with others who have been through the same territory through organizations like Parent to Parent or, perhaps, individuals and families in their own congregation or faith tradition. Most of all, pastoral leaders must proclaim by word and/or deed that each child or adult is beloved by the Divine and that the faith community will do what it takes to embody that love as well. It is a promise often embodied in rituals after birth, such as baptism, where each child is welcomed and blessed by the faith community, who also make a pledge to help them grow up surrounded by that community.

Childhood into Adolescence

Presence reverses itself here. Clergy must lead in ways that enable children with disabilities and their families to be present. That can mean guidance and learning for religious educators and others on the best ways to include and support these children so they, too, can learn and grow within the community.[5] We too often worry about what children with autism or other forms of intellectual and developmental disabilities can understand. Before understanding, any child has to experience the spirit and embrace of a faith community. This is another area where leaders can act as a guide and advocate, perhaps asking professionals who work with a child in other settings, such as school, to come and help teach members of the congregation what might work best with any given child.

Pastoral leaders' guiding roles may include helping the congregation better understand disability and deal emotionally, spiritually, and theologically with the questions that may arise on the journey to full inclusion. They model the attitude and behavior they hope others will follow. As they listen to families and parents, they may find ways to support them as they identify the right services or the right educational program. Another parent at the Down syndrome conference mentioned earlier stood up and said, "We took our minister with us to our child's IEP [Individual Education Plan meeting, where parents usually meet with an array of school professionals and often are in an adversarial relationship]. It was wonderful. We got everything we wanted … they thought he was our lawyer." For parents, that always gets a laugh, but think of the power of presence with parents, perhaps helping them find their own voice, and representing a community that is essentially saying, "We care about what you are doing here in this school and want to be able to do the best we can for their child in our community." The same thing can happen with annual planning processes in most systems that serve adults with disabilities.

Teenager to Young Adult

Spiritual leaders have a key role in promoting inclusion for the rites of passage of the teenage years: confirmation, bar or bat mitzvah, believer's baptism, and so on. There are wonderful examples in many faith traditions of the ways that children and youth with severe disabilities (e.g., kids with severe autism) are being taught with the best of educational and behavioral strategies to learn what they need to be included, leading to even more marvelous stories of the impact of that inclusion on the individual, family, and congregation.[6]

Beyond those rites of transition, clergy can help adolescents with disabilities find leadership roles within the congregation just as other teenagers are invited to do. The "best practices" of both faith traditions and current disability perspectives is that everyone has gifts and strengths in addition to limits. We must find ways to nurture and use them.

Because they work with youngsters who are at a life stage when huge peer pressures are the norm, pastoral leaders can guide and challenge other youth in the congregation to explore with eyes of faith the multiple ways by which adolescents with disabilities may be the target of attitudes that they all face: "Who's in, who's out?" "What's cool, what's not?" "Who to hang out with?" Helping the natural youth leaders in your faith community recognize these issues will provide models for other youth who already look up to them.

For individuals and families, in the wider world of education and early adulthood, this is the time known by the word "transition." Colleges are indeed open to most teenagers with disabilities, including a growing number of post-secondary programs for young adults with intellectual and developmental disabilities. For others, transition services work on helping individuals and families identify skills and passions that can lead to work opportunities. The faith community is a built-in network of employers and employees who may be contacts and bridges to multiple opportunities. Finally, transition can also mean helping look for places to live outside a family's home and guiding everyone through the emotional and physical parts of more independent living.

Adulthood

For many adults with disabilities, the hospitality that leads to inclusion as a full member in activities of congregational life, as receivers *and* givers, simply makes all the difference in the world. For people who acquire disabilities as an adult, a steadfast faith community can provide the support and affirmation of their continued value that can undergird a rehabilitation and adjustment process. For adults with intellectual and developmental disabilities who may begin to attend a faith community because of a new group home in the area or the congregation's own outreach, providing opportunities for them to learn and grow *into* the culture and traditions of the community can be a huge blessing.[7] Intellectual or psychiatric disability is often blamed as the reason some people don't follow unspoken rules of behavior in a congregation when the real issue may have been the lack of opportunity and practice that are typically there for anyone growing up within a given tradition. Faith communities believe in lifelong learning. They can help everyone participate and/or tailor opportunities in ways that address individual needs and gifts.

One of the strategies that has emerged from disability services and supports is the development of a "circle of support" around a person with special needs. It can be formal or informal, but the secret is an intentional group of people with different gifts who work together on building opportunities and supports for an adult with a disability. Faith communities are full of various circles and networks who often respond especially well in a crisis such as an accident or a death, but these are more long-term ways of sharing care together. A revised booklet from the Anabaptist tradition, *Supportive Care in the Congregation*, outlines circles of support beautifully.[8]

Aging and End of Life

Pastoral and congregational leaders know the importance and value of their presence and support when people age, lose family members, and/or begin to face the end of their own lives. One of the key roles for leadership here begins at any point someone with a disability is in the hospital for conditions that may or may not be related to the disability. Ask people with disabilities and their families to tell you their "hospital stories." Far too often, hospital staff do not have the experience or skills to communicate with people who do not use typical means. Individuals and families also encounter attitudes about a disabled person's "quality of life" that can impact recommendations and decisions. Pastoral presence and leadership can help medical staff both see and understand the people behind the labels and the ways in which their gifts and needs are recognized, plus the number of people who care about them.

That being said, people with disabilities get sick, age, and grieve over losses just like anyone else. Pastoral leaders should encourage families to include children and adults with disabilities in family situations of loss and death. Other caregivers can help provide support. Excellent new resources are available to guide caregivers working with people whom others are not sure will "understand" death or loss.[9] When a child or an adult with an intellectual or a developmental disability dies, it is important to remember their friends, who may or may not have disabilities, and the educational or human services staff who may have poured their care and love into their lives. Sensitive rituals of grief and loss that include everyone can reaffirm the impact and value of someone's life, just as they do for anyone else.

Finally, the often unspoken question that many families have is "Who will care for our child after we are gone?" The skill needed here is helping them find good future planning legal services for such things as special-needs trusts as well as determining the ways that the spiritual leader and faith community will continue to care and look out for someone no matter where he or she might live.

Things to Remember

- Never underestimate the power of pastoral and congregational leadership in all of its forms—presence, guiding, advocacy, and community building—over the long haul. There may be crisis points in the life span of people with disabilities and their families, but sustaining care over time is a model of the Divine.

- Profound spiritual and theological questions will be encountered and dealt with, such as issues of identity, cause and purpose, healing, and what it means to be a community. Learn to see the questions raised by or around a person with a disability as questions that everyone faces in one way or another, and help the whole community face them.

- Be very careful with some ancient interpretations that still manifest themselves, such as "What did you do that caused this disability or this disabled child?" and "If your faith was strong enough, you could be healed." Those are forms of avoiding the struggles to understand and can lead to what people with disabilities see as spiritual abuse. The questions are just as easily reversed: "What did we do as a society or world that caused a disability?" and as one man said to a stranger who diagnosed his problem as lack of faith, "If your faith was strong enough, you could cure me."

- The power of congregational inclusion and advocacy can be a more effective witness to the wider community than any words.

- Ministry and hospitality to the "stranger with a disability," in all of its forms, end up being about all of us.

Some Final Dos and Don'ts[10]

- Don't call people "special" just because they have a disability. Do look for everyone's unique gifts and figure out ways to affirm and use them. "Capacity vision" goes for the whole faith community.[11]

- Don't identify people with disabilities by their diagnosis only. Do use what is called "people-first language," e.g., "John, who has a physical disability or uses a wheelchair."[12] People who use wheelchairs usually do not see themselves as "wheelchair victims" or "wheelchair bound." They are, in fact, technologies of liberation. When in doubt about what to say about someone's disability, ask him or her.

- Don't generalize from one disability to another or within a diagnostic category. As people, families, and professionals who deal with autism say, "When you have met one person with autism, you have met one person with autism." As above, do see the individual and hear his or her own unique story.

- Don't plan for individuals and families; plan with them. "Nothing about me without me!" is a slogan of the disability movement.

- Do avoid simplistic euphemisms like "God does not give you more than you can bear." Your presence means more than words. Your questions to others that will help you understand count much more than your answers along with your offer to help with the things they have to bear. At times, the worst burdens are other people's attitudes.

- Don't assume disability equals suffering. It may, at times, but most want to get on with their lives and would like support in doing so. Many, in my experience, are much happier than so-called normal people.

- Don't interpret disability too quickly as evidence of a "broken world." Disability, illness, death, violence, and injustice may be all be seen as part of a broken creation, but don't make people with disabilities the scapegoats for that. Most people with disabilities are sick and tired of feeling like they are seen as broken people who need to be fixed. Do help them find ways to help and support others so they are not the "designated receivers" of care all the time.

- Don't say too quickly that "we are all disabled." That may be true, in terms of human limitation and vulnerability, but said too quickly implies you know what someone experiences and feels. If you have not dealt with the same issues they have, over time, you probably don't. Do recognize that the experience you may have had in common with people with disabilities is some form of social isolation or rejection.

- Do be intentional in addressing this area of ministry. People who have been hidden and apart from community may gradually emerge because they feel welcomed. Whole families may come with them.

- Do recognize and celebrate the ways that intentional and inclusive ministries may transform individuals and congregations. More and more congregations are attributing their spiritual and numerical growth to this form of hospitality that lives out the signs in the front lawn, "Everyone is Welcome."

Notes

1. William Gaventa, "The Power of One," 2010, http://rwjms.umdnj.edu/departments_institutes/boggscenter/projects/documents/ThePowerofOne.pdf.

2. World Health Organization and the World Bank, *World Report on Disability*, 2011, www.who.int/disabilities/world_report/2011/en/index.html.

3. World Health Organization, definition of disability, www.who.int/topics/disabilities/en.

4. William Gaventa, "Pastoral Care with Persons with Developmental Disabilities." *Thematic Conversations Regarding Disability within the Framework of Courses of Worship, Scripture and Pastoral Care.* (New York: National Council of Churches Committee on Disabilities. Monograph published by the University of Dayton, 1997). A sample module for seminary courses in pastoral care. http://rwjms.umdnj.edu/boggscenter/projects/documents/Introductiontopastoralcaremodule.pdf.

5. There are many good inclusive religious education resources. Check within your faith tradition. See a new one by the Rev. Susan Richardson, *Child by Child: Supporting Children with Learning Disabilities and Their Families* (Harrisburg, PA: Morehouse Publishing, 2011).

6. For example, see books by Kathleen Bolduc at www.kathleenboluc.com; or Mary Beth Walsh, Alice F. Walsh, and William C. Gaventa, *Autism and Faith: A Journey into Community* (New Brunswick, NJ: Boggs Center, 2008), http://rwjms.umdnj.edu/boggscenter/products/documents/AutismandFaith.pdf.

7. For one book to start with, see Erik Carter, *Including People with Disabilities in Faith Communities: A Guide for Families, Congregations and Service Providers* (Baltimore: Paul Brookes Publishing, 2007).

8. D. Preheim-Bartel and A. Neufeldt, *Supportive Care in the Congregation: Providing a Congregational Network of Care for Persons with Significant Disabilities* (Harrisburg, PA: Herald Press, 2011).

9. William Gaventa, "Resources in Developmental Disabilities and Coping with Grief, Loss, and End of Life," 2001, http://rwjms.umdnj.edu/boggscenter/projects/documents/EndofLifeResources11.11.11.pdf; and/or go to www.QualityMall.org and its section on grief, loss, and end-of-life resources.

10. Look for "disability etiquette" on the Internet; use a wonderful video called *The Ten Commandments for Communicating with People with Disabilities* (Challenge Publications, 2005), which you may be able to borrow from a local agency; and/or look up other lists of terminologies and words such as those at www.disabilityisnatural.com.

11. J. Kretzmann and J. McKnight, *Building Communities from the Inside Out: A Path toward Finding and Mobilizing a Community's Assets* (Evanston, IL: Northwestern University, 1993). Many other resources are available from www.abcdinstitute.org.

12. See www.aucd.org/template/page.cfm?id=605.

Resources

The Elizabeth M. Boggs Center, for brief one-page resource listings, such as
"Beginning and Strengthening Inclusive Ministries in Your Congregation" and
"New Resources from the Past Three Years," and much longer ones, such as
Dimensions of Faith (2009). Online products include interfaith booklets on
autism and brain injury and audio presentations by many leaders in disability
and theology from Summer Institutes on Theology and Disability, funded by
the Pennsylvania Developmental Disabilities Council: http://rwjms.umdnj.edu/
boggscenter/projects/faith_based.html.

The Congregational Accessibility Network, for a listing of faith group ministry
resource offices and resources: www.accessibilitynetwork.net.

The Journal of Religion, Disability, and Health (www.tandf.co.uk/journals/WRDH)
is moving into its sixteenth volume, with back issues offering a wide, interfaith
variety of perspectives and viewpoints.

Multimedia resources, such as the award-winning documentary *Praying with Lior*,
about Lior Liebling's bar mitzvah (www.prayingwithlior.com) and *A Place for
All*, an interfaith documentary exploring inclusive faith supports.

The Quality Mall, an online resource directory in many areas of life pertaining to
disability, including spiritual and faith supports: www.qualitymall.org.

About the Contributor

Rev. Bill Gaventa, MDiv, serves as director of Community and Congregational Supports at the Elizabeth M. Boggs Center on Developmental Disabilities and as associate professor at Robert Wood Johnson Medical School, University of Medicine and Dentistry of New Jersey (UMDNJ). In his role at the Boggs Center, Rev. Gaventa works on community supports, training for community services staff, spiritual supports, training of seminarians and clergy, aging and end-of-life/grief issues, and cultural competence. He has edited four books, written a number of book chapters and articles, and served as the editor of the *Journal of Religion, Disability, and Health* for fourteen years.

17

Working with Undocumented Immigrants

Rev. Seth Kaper-Dale, MDiv

A congregation is a crucible in which people of faith practice the actions and behaviors that God has said belong to a world made in God's image. A congregation is the place where a community of followers insist that the last are first, that the beaten down are inheritors of attention, love, and assets. A congregation is where the naked are clothed and the imprisoned are set free. A congregation can engage in ministries that support "the last" *outside* the congregation, but it engages most fully on behalf of the poor when the poor are invited to become full participants in the life of the community of faith. Leaders are those who proclaim this new order and who create ministries and mechanisms that bring the new order into being, in response to God.

When a congregation becomes increasingly populated by those who are last, the identity of the congregation itself changes, but it doesn't change entirely, for those who are last when they enter the community of God do not remain last. When the poor are given the love and compassion that is available in and through the congregation, they rise up, and one thing they "lose" is their status of being last. Instead, they are in a place where they can seek out others who are last—others who belong, for a time, at those highest seats of honor within the life of the congregation—on the right and left of God—seats reserved for the most lowly. In time, they too will move to another seat, freeing up the "best seats" for the "new last."

The process of the "last becoming first" is a faith community essential, but there are others, in the so-called secular world, who practice the same essentials. There are times when our government and institutions behave in ways that should make congregations proud, for the actions and behaviors are of God. When we see such practices, we should celebrate and partner with the government, for it is doing God's work. Leaders continually discern a congregation's relationship to the state around issues of justice. An important element of congregational leadership is to teach disciples how to discern the congregation-state relationship, so that they may also look for the movement of God's Spirit in and through the systems of this world.

There are times, however, when the practices of the nation run so painfully counter to the will of God and God's intentional community (congregations) that congregations need to truly take the lead in a counter-approach. *The treatment of undocumented immigrants in many parts of America is one such example.*

There are national movements of all sorts that address the issues associated with immigration. Denominations of many different religions have immigration offices, and there are wonderful nonprofits like Detention Watch Network and Human Rights First. These agencies and offices make essential contributions, but congregations, too, have an important role and their own unique angle. Strong pastoral leadership can lead a local congregation to become an essential community for undocumented immigrants, both for their personal care and support and for radical efforts that impact governmental practice and policy.

Since 2006, the Reformed Church of Highland Park has actively engaged in immigration issues, with significant successes. The groundwork for the activity of the past five years was five years in the making.

The best way for me to share suggestions for congregational leadership around the topic of immigration is to share our story of involvement with immigrants, while highlighting eight essential elements of our process. While these elements grew up organically, they can be understood as a structure around which pastors, church leaders, and the entire congregation formulated its immigration attitudes, understandings, and actions.

Each reader lives in a congregational context that is unique, but the essential elements for church leadership highlighted here in regard to immigration will apply in most contexts.

Getting to Know Undocumented Immigrants

In the year 2000, an Indonesian congregation began using the sanctuary of the Reformed Church of Highland Park for Sunday afternoon worship services in the Indonesian language. My wife and I became co-pastors in 2001, and we slowly began getting to know some of the families in the church. It was clear that most congregants were recent arrivals from Indonesia, as most spoke very little English. Within a couple of years we had become friendly with some members. We had no idea that of the one hundred or so participants in the church virtually all were undocumented.

In 2003, Attorney General John Ashcroft unveiled National Security Entry-Exit Registration System (NSEERS), an immigration program that required any male age sixteen to sixty-five, from twenty-five primarily Muslim countries, to report immediately to immigration offices or be considered fugitives. The policy was overtly biased and only acceptable in the post-9/11 climate. Indonesia is the largest Muslim country in the world and was, therefore, most definitely on the list.

Because of the relationships that had formed between leaders at the Reformed Church and the Indonesian Christian congregation, we were approached for support and guidance. Could we write letters vouching for the character of those who needed to report? Over the next year I submitted nearly one hundred letters, which were included in asylum applications. I also held a meeting with the congregation where I apologized to them for the behavior of our government in creating inconsistent immigration policies that were now resulting in such turmoil for families.

The letter writing was a *minor* job, as was the congregational meeting, but to those recent arrivals in this country, who needed to show their connection to America, this was absolutely essential for their applications and, most important, for their spirits. This small act of leadership told the entire congregation of Indonesians, "There is someone on this soil who is not Indonesian, and who is my brother in Christ, and who thinks I belong here." For many, it was the first positive welcoming voice they had heard from an American church.

A couple of years later, one of the Indonesian families—Harry and Yana Pangemanan—joined our American church. The church community soon came to love this young couple and their little girl (now two little girls!).

Since 2005, Indonesian music from Harry and Yana has graced our services, other Indonesian friends have joined our church, and we have had increased moments of contact with the Indonesian community—concerts, shared services, food fairs, and so on.

Ours is not a congregation that had (or maybe has) 100 percent agreement about immigration, but there is 100 percent approval of Harry and Yana Pangemanan and their children. And because they approved of Harry and Yana, and supported them, prayed for them, and fought for their rights, they had a much easier time supporting and praying for other undocumented immigrants.

Ideas for Leaders

1. Have you gotten to know undocumented people, recent immigrants? If it doesn't happen organically, speak a bold word about your open position on the full inclusion of immigrants, and that word will reach those in need!

2. Ask your congregants to introduce you, and to introduce the church, to undocumented coworkers, neighbors, family members, and friends. Ask congregants to share with their acquaintances your open views.

3. After you get to know people going through immigration turmoil, find ways to celebrate them for who they are—for their skills, their families, their faith.

4. Ask immigrants how you can help them with their case. Can you introduce them to a congressional member? Can you accompany them to an initial meeting with an attorney?

Unveiling Abuses So That Immigrants Don't Suffer in Silence

By the time 2006 arrived, many Indonesians who had reported for NSEERS had seen their immigration cases considered and denied. Virtually all cases from Indonesia were denied. This had to do with the fact that all were applying for asylum, but they were filing more than twelve months after arriving in this country. This late filing resulted in a "time bar" from filing. After approximately $15,000 in attorney fees, virtually all Indonesians (and those from other primarily Muslim nations) were at risk of detention and deportation.

One night, in 2006, thirty-five Indonesian men were arrested from the same apartment complex, with more than sixty children (most of whom were American citizens, having been born here) losing their fathers to detention and deportation. I received a call from Harry and Yana, who were hiding in their bedroom with their three-year-old. Yana was six months pregnant with their second child. Immigration Customs and Enforcement (ICE) was pounding on their door.

I called other church leaders, and immediately we started calling media outlets. I drove to the complex, arriving just after ICE had left. I shared the story with TV reporters and helped determine which immigrants were safe enough to be speaking to the media without ramifications. I then offered that if anyone felt fearful they could come and stay at the church. Over the next month some forty Indonesians "camped out" at the church and in the homes of congregants, afraid to return to their apartments.

In addition, I wrote a scathing article against American policy that was published in the newspaper, called Congress members, led an effort to distribute flyers about ICE's actions to our neighbors, and preached about these events.

These actions gave undocumented immigrants the clear message that the leaders of the Reformed Church were friends of the undocumented.

I called an emergency meeting of the elders and deacons to announce what I'd done (in terms of inviting undocumented immigrants to stay in the church)—not to ask permission. I asked for their blessing in regard to this decision.

Ideas for Leaders

1. Has God presented you with opportunities to respond to injustice against immigrants? If so, have you responded? Do you "tolerate injustice" toward immigrants?

2. Do undocumented people know and does the government know that you are fearless when it comes to speaking up for justice sake?

Celebrate When Your Congregation
Grows in Undocumented Status!

After I, as pastor, and the leadership board of the church started taking these actions, other members of our congregation, including some who had been involved for many years, started coming and privately sharing their own immigration stories. It turns out that we had many undocumented members from all over the world!

As the congregation became aware of this reality within our church, lay leaders formed an immigration committee, primarily to support those congregants who were experiencing great stress due to their immigration status. The first event held by this committee was a healing service—an anointing—and many people came forward and for the first time shared with other church members their immigration pains.

Throughout these years I somewhat regularly preached about immigration or referenced immigration in the liturgy. The sermons were unabashedly supportive of immigrants being here among us—regardless of status. Sermons celebrated that we are all included in God's family, that we are all "undocumented" here, for our home is ultimately with God. Most weeks prayers for the undocumented were included in our congregational prayer—often praying for congregants and their friends by name.

The more we celebrated the undocumented shape of our congregation, the more "undocumented" we became! We now have undocumented congregants from many countries throughout the world.

Ideas for Leaders

1. What tangible way can you celebrate undocumented members of your community? How can you show that the church is richer because of their undocumented presence? What theological themes can you invoke to celebrate these brothers and sisters?

2. What gifts can undocumented members share—talents and skills that are uniquely theirs?

Expect to Be Criticized

There is a strong voice against immigrants who arrive here without proper status. Some of the critique is legitimate, and some is completely unwarranted.

In our church community, one of the critical voices came from a union worker who has, over time, become very critical of undocumented workers. From his perspective, undocumented workers, because of their willingness to accept low wages and unsafe conditions and improper equipment, have driven down the value of his work.

Leadership on a controversial issue means sitting and listening to the critique of congregants. It also means reading the union policy on immigration and trying to facilitate conversation between undocumented congregants and the critic(s). Finally, it means maybe accepting the fact that you will disagree with some in your congregation.

Ideas for Leaders

1. Try to anticipate who will be troubled by your decision to publicly support undocumented immigrants, and don't be afraid to call up likely critics, so that they know they are on your mind and that you realize the potential ramifications of taking a particular stance on this issue.
2. Don't be defensive.
3. Don't force reconciliation … and don't promise a compromise.

Be Tireless in Support

On January 12, 2009, Harry Pangemanan was arrested and put into a detention center, awaiting deportation. His wife was also arrested, but they released her, temporarily, because of the children. The church, already knowing and loving Harry and Yana, snapped into action. Through our work over the past few years we had come to know immigration attorneys, and now we engaged them. We took special offerings on Sunday mornings, raising more than $5,000 to assist in the Pangemanan's legal battle. We got hundreds of signatures on a petition asking ICE to please allow Yana to move about freely, without a tracking device attached to her ankle. We visited congressional offices. Each night a congregant would go and stay with Harry and Yana's children, so Yana could continue a third-shift job. Each day a congregant would go and visit Harry in the detention center. Each week Harry would get upwards of fifty letters of support.

Many of these initiatives were pastor driven; all were pastor supported, but the work was only accomplished because of the multitude of emerging leaders who understood how to put *the last* first. When it came to supporting Harry and Yana, I felt like I was overseeing a whole system of small task-based committees, together working for the good of the family!

One day in late March Harry was moved, in the early hours of the morning, to Tacoma, Washington. He didn't know he was going to Tacoma. He thought he was being deported to Indonesia. He called me at 5 a.m. Emboldened by my church community and their tireless efforts, I drove to the airport and talked my way onto the airplane at Newark Liberty International. I got on the plane for one purpose—to pray with Harry and to tell him that we would keep the baptismal vows we made to his children and to him and his wife. I also promised to keep working for his freedom.

That evening the congregation held a vigil in front of the Elizabeth Detention Center, in Elizabeth, New Jersey, where Harry had been held for sixty-eight days before being sent to Tacoma. We celebrated Communion, asking God to be with us and with Harry in this broken place. We got the *New York Times* to come and cover the story (they took pictures but didn't use them for some months).

Two weeks later, after dozens of calls to the Obama administration, Harry Pangemanan was sent back from Tacoma to New Jersey and released. His release was the direct result of the church's intervention and its willingness to make a public spectacle of the abusive system.

Ideas for Leaders

1. Do you believe that the church is powerful enough to disrupt the systems of this world?

2. Are you willing to be a thorn in the side of the government or oppressive agencies for the sake of immigrants? This question only became an affirmative for our church once we got to *know* immigrants and their plights.

3. Are you willing to ask congregants to "go the distance" in terms of supporting the neediest members in your church?

Getting within Earshot of Undocumented Immigrants

Our behavior, as a congregation, has meant that more and more people come to us when they are struggling with immigration matters. They come to me, personally, and they come to others in the church. We haven't, however, waited for people to come to us.

Leadership around immigration has been about encouraging the church to move within earshot of those who are suffering due to our broken immigration policies and practices that are often strangely tied to security and economic policies. Harry's detention opened our eyes to the thousands who suffer in a warehouse in our region each year— awaiting deportation or resolution of their cases.

Now, each Monday night, a small group of faithful visitors go to the Elizabeth Detention Center to visit with people we know are locked up. Then, throughout the week, calls are made to family members of those who were visited (calls of encouragement, calls to offer occasional financial support). Calls are also made to ICE field office directors, as we try to make a humanitarian argument for why a particular person should be released.

Congregants who do these visits and congregants who are within earshot of other undocumented immigrants pick up on trends and listen for patterns. Through the work of visitation, we have now become very involved in helping asylum seekers to be released from detention and involved in assisting victims of human trafficking.

Ideas for Leaders

1. In many ways, "getting within earshot of undocumented immigrants" is similar to "getting to know undocumented immigrants." However, the difference is that some people won't be "knowable" unless you go to extreme measures to draw near to them. Can you think of places where you can go to get within earshot?

2. Try teaming up with social justice organizations who have the beat on where human trafficking occurs. Talk to school

social workers to see if there are children in your district with detained or deported fathers or mothers. Call an immigration attorney to get a list of the nonprofit groups that advocate for undocumented persons, and reach out to see if you can assist them with any desperate case.

Expanding the Scope of the Church's Significance to Influence Governmental Policies

Jesus modeled a form of leadership that started by caring for individuals and groups of people and then expanded into governmental confrontation. The church leads in this way, too.

While our efforts started in personal ways and, to some degree, continue in that way, there is another side to our efforts around immigration. We spend much of our time (though not all of it) moving from the micro to the macro.

Collecting Stories

After Harry Pangemanan was released in April 2009, our church started collecting stories of undocumented immigrants in America. We wrote the stories of some fifty people we had gotten to know. Some of these were other detainees that Harry asked us to visit; others were undocumented persons living in fear in our community. We compiled the stories and shared them with an administrative person at ICE in Washington, actually driving a group from the church down to present the package in person.

The Children's Vigil

We joined immigrant advocates in planning a children's vigil, which shared the reality of children losing their parents to deportation. Children shared, on the steps of the church, about the day their fathers were sent away.

Orders of Supervision Program

The day after the children's vigil, four Indonesian men were arrested. Two were arrested just after dropping off their children for elementary school. With the children's vigil deeply etched in my mind, I engaged again in rigorous phone advocacy to Washington, DC, and to Newark.

Eventually, after seemingly endless phone calls, the ICE field office director made an incredible offer. They offered to release all Indonesians in detention in New Jersey and to offer Indonesians living in fear of deportation (with final orders of deportation) a chance to stay in this country for at least two years—while new policies were considered. The church convinced the Indonesian community that ICE was playing fair, and we accompanied them to the ICE office to receive this benefit. This program was a unique and amazing one—and it was covered by Nina Bernstein of the *New York Times*.

Asylum Seeker Temporary Housing

For the past year and a half our congregation has been offering beds to ICE for any asylum seeker who came to this country under duress and is now locked up in detention. On four occasions, individuals from four different countries have been released to our custody. The church works together to raise a small stipend to help with food and to thank "host congregants" for providing a spare bedroom in their homes. The church helps the asylum seeker get medical attention, legal aid, transportation, and any other service needed.

The Indonesian Refugee Family Protection Act

It has been almost two years since the Orders of Supervision Program was put into place, and the immigration policies of this nation have hardly changed. The temporary amnesty gained through the Orders of Supervision will not last forever. So, the Reformed Church of Highland Park (RCHP) Immigration Committee has written a bill. This bill explains why Indonesians came to this country when they did, and it asks for them to be given another chance to apply for asylum. Church leaders have crafted the bill, worked closely with a US House member, and laid the groundwork for a massive calling campaign to push for this bill's introduction and potential passage.

Dreaming the Kingdom of God into the Reality of Today's Government: The Kingdom of God Taking over the World of Caesar

The vast majority of our actions have been around the Indonesian community, for that is the community that God has put before us, but the longer you serve one community, the more you see how the whole system needs to be repaired. Jesus's involvement with the government ended with his table flipping in the Temple; his life was taken before he could demonstrate what would have been next. But it seems likely, I think, that Jesus would have gone from destructive ministry of cleansing to productive ministry of re-creating government, even as he'd re-created community in Galilee.

Faith communities can have a hand in re-creating governmental policy and practice in ways that serve all people.

A Home-Based Detention Center

The RCHP Immigration Committee has floated an idea for a home-based detention center as an alternative to locking up detainees. This "detention center" is a way for the government to track those who are here without proper documentation but whose lives are complicated (e.g., they have American children, they employ people in their business) and who should not be a deportation priority. The church committee has put together a $1 million proposal that would have the church overseeing fifteen hundred people at a time. This proposal has been received by the highest immigration officials in the land.

Speaking Out against a New Private Detention Center

Even while working with the government to be considered for a new proposal, our church has continued to speak out boldly against a new detention center. "Speaking out" has meant preaching against it, speaking out at street corner rallies, and participating in research about why the center is, pragmatically, a bad idea.

You Are God's People—
Believe That You Are Powerful!

Our nation desperately needs leadership around the issue of immigration. Congress cannot seem to make anything happen. Undocumented immigrants can't vote, and the people all around them seem to be anti-immigrant (on the whole). Communities of God should be a fresh voice for justice. We have nothing to lose, and everything to gain, by making the undocumented-last first, for they are first to God.

Amen.

About the Contributor

Rev. Seth Kaper-Dale, MDiv, has co-pastored the Reformed Church of Highland Park with his wife Stephanie for the past ten years. Together they are raising three little girls and raising a growing church. In addition to general pastoral ministry, Seth specializes in creating special needs housing and helping undocumented immigrants get released from detention as well as coming up with creative arrangements with Immigration Customs and Enforcement to stop deportation.

18

Why Are People Poor?

Rev. David Billings, MDiv, DMin

The People's Institute for Survival and Beyond (PISAB), in their highly influential "Undoing Racism/Community Organizing" workshops, starts its workshop with a seemingly easy question and one that on the surface has nothing to do with racism or its "undoing." The question is "Why are people poor?"[1]

Why does the People's Institute start the workshop on racism with what seems to be a question about class? It took me a while as a longtime organizer and trainer with PISAB to answer the question for myself. Even more important for me was to appreciate how much our own (or in this case the group's) answer to the question dictates organizing strategy. In large measure the answers we receive from persons in the workshop have remained remarkably similar for more than thirty years. Depending on how politically active most members of the group are or how progressive in their thinking, the responses on the one hand are systemic in nature: People are poor because, among other reasons:

- They do not have adequate access to the economic system.
- They lack sufficient opportunities.
- They are uneducated or miseducated.
- They are people of color.
- There are too few jobs.

If the group is made up of people who are not as politicized or who are more conservative in nature and thus more individualistic in their outlook, the responses on the other hand tend to be more personal and even judgmental. People are poor because, among other reasons:

- They lack a work ethic.
- They don't want to work.
- They are lazy.
- They like living off the system.
- They don't know how to manage their money.

What do these two lists tell us? Many things, of course, but from an organizing perspective, the lists give us a starting point. The responses root us in an analysis of sorts—one that tells us where to begin and how as organizers in leadership positions we might move a group to some type of concerted action and to work together more cohesively. If we don't know who is in the room, our strategies are likely to be fragmented and disjointed. The question is provocative. It is not as easily answered as we might assume. Again, in the "Undoing Racism" workshop, most people attending will not be poor themselves. They are more likely to work with poor people than to be poor. Most will have biases of one sort or another, admitted or not, about poor people. Some of us will likely answer from a standpoint of what we have been taught in a college classroom or an in-service training on the job. Others of us might have strong feelings about poor people that we are afraid to voice lest we be perceived as uncaring or insensitive. In both instances, our answers are more emotive than analytical, based more on personal experience than on the context of race and class as the two intersect. Our answers are likelier to be based on our own opinion than on our determined study of what causes some people to have wealth and other people to be poor in the United States.

There are myriad reasons for people's poverty. There is a generational factor at work that can become circular in nature. Poverty has a way of being handed down from one generation to the next. It can be the region in which a person is raised. Some parts of this country have been historically underdeveloped economically, affecting people's opportunities for wealth accumulation. Some people are poor because of natural disaster or calamity. The Gulf Coast of the United States is a case in point. Hurricanes Katrina and Rita devastated the Gulf Coast in August and September 2005 from Houston, Texas, to Mobile, Alabama. In some ways, no one saw it coming. In other ways, the region had long been in denial of what would be required in terms of infrastructure and flood control preparedness. Katrina and Rita (with hurricanes, one is quickly on a first-name basis) were great levelers in more ways than one. It is common to hear that Katrina or Rita, depending on where you lived at the time, was "an equal opportunity disaster"; it saw neither race nor class. Rich people got flooded and blown away just as poor people did. Everybody suffered and many lost everything.

With the perspective of time, we now know that the disaster did not hit everyone with the same force and especially the same results. Certain historical factors held sway. Rich people were less likely to have been wiped out, home and hearth. Rich people were more likely to have lived on the high ground than in the flood plain. Rich people were more likely to have had the right type and amount of insurance, a place to run to, and a car to get them there. Poor people were less likely to have had insurance of any amount; many did not have a car and had nowhere to go. The list goes on.[2] Nothing hits everyone the same in the United States. Much depends on economics and how one's economics are intertwined with both race and class dynamics.

In the case of the hurricanes of 2005, this was certainly the case. Katrina and Rita tore across the coastal landscape with both vicious wind shears and floodwaters to the rooftops in New Orleans, Biloxi, and small towns in between. Houston had floods that overwhelmed the city's capacity to respond. Fleeing residents literally bolted. They had little or no warning, and many left with nowhere to go in mind. Six years later, the destruction can still be seen all along the Gulf Coast. Thousands of poor New Orleanians have not been able to return.

What did these calamities teach us about why people are poor? In hard times, the poor get hit harder every time. That is one thing we learned. Not for the first time, either. They lose more. Recoup less.

Then there is race. Back to New Orleans and the Gulf Coast. Few white people, rich or poor, were forced to take refuge in the New Orleans Superdome, for example. Some did, but not many. Thousands of poor black people were forced to take sanctuary there. Try as the city might, it was not prepared to handle it.

In a race-constructed country, poverty is not equally distributed. Neither is wealth. Race is also not equal in this country. Whites do better. This is fact. So, why are people poor? Diana Dunn, one of the trainers with the People's Institute, has said this: "There are millions of poor white people in this country, but not one of us is poor because we are white." Ron Chisom, the co-founder of the People's Institute, says, "People are poor, not because they lack services, but because they lack organized power."[3] Both Dunn and Chisom are saying something profound on this question as to why people are poor. Race and class have much to do with it. But, in addition to these factors, so does the lack of an organized constituency of poor people. Poor people, as a collective, must address the power of the various systems that impact poor people's lives in this country. It is about power. Individual poor people do not have the power to confront their situation by themselves. People are not poor due to just personal faults or failings. Rich people have personal failings, too. But, unlike rich people, the poor lack systemic support. There is an abundance of systemic support for the rich, from the tax system to the health care system. Thus, the gulf between rich and poor in this country is not something that just happens. It is structural in nature. The chasm between rich and poor continues.

In the United States, racism must be addressed. It is the backdrop of any community organizing meant to address poverty and its root causes. Race, in fact, was "invented" to make sure class-based challenges to the economic realities of this nation never occur. This is not for lack of trying. There have been numerous attempts historically to transcend the racial divide and build movements that represent the interests of poor people. Most often, these efforts have failed. The failure of such movements is tied to racism. When organizing is white-led, people of color's voices and day-to-day realities are usually silenced or minimized. The concerns of white people dominate. This is not necessarily intentional. It is how the arrangement works. Without an understanding of these dynamics, organizing efforts will fail. Race still divides us, as was its intent. This is why the People's Institute's "Undoing Racism" workshop begins its sessions with the question "Why are people poor?"

Professor Y. N. Kly, a widely recognized expert in international law especially concerning minority rights, speaks to this in what he calls the nation's "anti-social contract."[4] Kly spells out how, in the founding era of the United States, the anti-social contract developed alongside the nation's "social contract." The nation's social contract was with white people and those who would become white. Not just rich white people and not just white men. All white people benefit from it and are a part of it. In Kly's analysis, persons of color were never intended to be a part of the arrangement and were excluded from both the body politic and its founding culture. He says, "The anti-social contract is an unwritten, unspoken and unofficial agreement between the U.S. ruling elites and the remainder of the white ethny to maintain the minorities, especially the African and Native American minorities, in a position inferior to that of the white ethny."[5] This would be enacted into law for the first 360 years of nation building of the new American racial state. From the introduction of the first "Negars" into Jamestown, Virginia, in 1619 until the passage of the Civil Rights Acts of the 1960s, racism was the legalized foundation of the nation. Every system in the United States, from education to transportation, was created when racism and white supremacy were the laws of the land. This has not changed even as the laws were changed. Racism has not obeyed the law.

So, why are people poor? In large measure, it is because "white people" have bought into the racial arrangement rather than pursue their own class or even human self-interest. Likewise, "people of color" have internalized the racial arrangement as normative. It is just how it is. The poorest white person has historically based his or her future on allegiance to white supremacy rather than a multiracial movement aimed at addressing poverty. This has been true and continues to be true today. Lyndon Johnson told his biographer, Robert Cano, "Convince the lowliest white person he is better than the most accomplished colored person and he will never know he is having his pocket picked."[6]

Today, white people have, according to research by the Pew Research Center, twenty times the wealth of African Americans.[7] This is higher than at any time in our nation's history since the Thirteenth Amendment abolished slavery in 1865. This means that even as we have made great strides in "race relations" since the civil rights movement in all phases of American life, we have failed to bridge the great racial divide structurally. This is true even as we have an African American president. The United States is not a post-racial nation. For every indicator that measures institutional outcomes and quality of life standards of comparisons, white people still win out, whether it is wealth, health, longevity, educational access, or home ownership. Race is still with us.

So, what must we do? There is no panacea out there to racism's destructive impact.

Thus:

- We must understand racism, what it is and how it works, in our various collectives.
- We must organize with an understanding of racism, culture, and history.
- We must do a power analysis, again in our organizing collectives.
- We must understand the process of leadership development and develop new leadership as we organize.
- We must have a sense of our own power as a people.[8]

Why are people poor? One answer is "Because poor people have no voice in this nation." The poor are not organized and thus largely ignored when policy is made and priorities set. People are poor because the poor remain divided and fragmented.

It is not easy for the poor in this country to get a seat at the table. Yet, that is what it will take, and the only way to get an invitation is to be strong enough as a collective to demand one. Frederick Douglass's oft-quoted statement is always true: "Power concedes nothing without a demand. It never has and never will."[9]

Notes

1. Ronald Chisom and Michael Washington, *Undoing Racism: A Philosophy of International Social Change*, vol. 1 (New Orleans: People's Institute Press, 1996).
2. Jordan Flaherty, *Floodlines: Community and Resistance from Katrina to the Jena Six* (Chicago: Haymarket Books, 2010).
3. Chisom and Washington, *Undoing Racism*.
4. Y. N. Kly, *The Anti-Social Contract* (Atlanta: Clarity Press, 1986).
5. Ibid, 30.

6. Robert A. Cano, *The Years of Lyndon Johnson: The Path to Power* (New York: Vintage Books, 1983).

7. Pew Research Center data release, summer 2011.

8. People's Institute for Survival and Beyond.

9. The Speeches of Frederick Douglas, compiled, "The History of African Americans, Schomberg," 1988.

About the Contributor

Rev. David Billings, MDiv, DMin, is a writer, an antiracist historian, and an organizer associated with the People's Institute for Survival and Beyond. He is a minister in the United Methodist Church. He currently resides in McComb, Mississippi, where he was born. Throughout his career he has been a teacher and is currently an adjunct professor at the New York University Silver School of Social Work in New York City. He is author of many articles and a forthcoming book, *Deep Denial: The Persistence of White Supremacy in American History and Life.*

19

Contextual Leadership

An Urban Case Study

Rev. Anthony Miranda

A Note from the Editor

Leadership is not one size fits all: leaders come in all different shapes and sizes. Leaders do not require a PhD or an MBA degree to be effective. This chapter chronicles a practical leader who overcame his own struggles to help a struggling urban community.

Rev. Anthony Miranda seemed to have so much working against him. He was a dyslexic Hispanic male from another country growing up in an economically challenged neighborhood. Rev. Miranda formed a gang during his teenage years and was nearly stabbed to death. Post-September 11, 2001, he took the sum total of all his experiences and developed the second largest food pantry in New York City. As the executive director of Elohim Community Development and Outreach, Inc., Rev. Miranda offers support for women in prison and oversees volunteers who provide groceries for eleven hundred families and individuals per week.

This is an amazing story of how one person saw a need, and did whatever he could to make sure that that need was met. It is my hope that reading Rev. Miranda's story will inspire you and offer hope for your own leadership journey.

It's hard to believe that eleven years have passed since I graduated from the Blanton Peale Pastoral Care Studies program. The skills that I learned and incorporated into my daily life have helped me navigate through a host of life's ups and downs, and a past that, at times, crippled me.

My family and I were going through a very hard time in the church we were attending in Brooklyn, New York. A new pastor, who felt that we were trying to undermine his ministry, launched a sequence of attacks from the pulpit aimed to identify "the wolf" in the church. In one such attack, he spoke about how "the wolf" comes to steal the joy of the church. During one of his sermons, he described how the wolf can be identified: the wolf can be active in church matters so he can undermine and sabotage church projects; he can be a teacher so he can spread his poison, and he can also drive the church van to spread the poison as well. All the heads in the church turned and looked at me because these were positions I was involved in. Although the congregants love me and we still keep in touch, they would jokingly call me "El Lobo" and make the sounds that a wolf makes. My wife, Marilyn, was born into the Pentecostal (Protestant) faith and is the daughter and granddaughter of two well-known ministers. When we first met, she was a divorced mother of two, a New York City schoolteacher, and the church's secretary. I was a forty-five-year-old alcoholic, pill-popping (acid), atheist interstate trucker, whose citizens band (CB) radio transmitter code handle was "Wrong Way." That's how I lived my life, always doing things the wrong way. With an introduction like that, you can imagine why so many members of the church community were opposed to Marilyn and me dating and later, to our marriage.

I was born in the Dominican Republic and grew up in a rough part of New York: Williamsburg, Brooklyn. Growing up there as a Hispanic in the 1940s was not easy. You learned quickly that when you heard the words "Hey, spic," that was your signal to run, and you never looked to see where the words were coming from. If you stayed to fight, you fought not only the one who called you out but also the entire neighborhood. If and when the police got there during the commotion, whatever size shoe the police wore would be so far up your backside that you would have trouble walking and sitting for a week. Saying that growing up in Brooklyn was tough is an understatement.

I was among the first Hispanics to attend PS 145. Every day, on my way to school, I had to walk through what was known as the Rheingold Brewery, where grown men would see a skinny Hispanic kid walking to school and shout out, "Hey, spic, go back to where you came from." If that wasn't bad enough, a group of white kids would wait for me almost every morning at the corner of Stanwick and Noll Streets in order to prevent me from going to what they called "their school." My fourth grade teacher, Mr. Foreman, was tired of seeing me come to school with dirty clothing, so he asked that my mother come to school to speak to him; I was the translator. I still remember what he told my mother: "Is this the way you people send your children to school?" I tried to tell him that I had to fight my way to school almost every day, but he would not believe anything I had to say. My years at PS 145 were not just a physical battle; they were also a mental struggle. From fourth to sixth grade, the chair that I sat on most of the time was a high stool with a "dunce cap" that I had to wear in front of the class. By the time I reached seventh grade, the practice was prohibited because it was considered to be corporal punishment, cruel, and mentally damaging. At the time, I could not understand why I couldn't learn like everyone else, especially since my sister was a straight-A student. Both of my grandparents were well educated; one was a veterinary doctor, and the other was a teacher. My father was the only one on his side of the family that did not have a degree. As you can see, PS 145 holds some very heartfelt memories for me as a young child new to this country, and all that I ever wanted was to fit in. However, the white kids who were part of a gang called "the Tiny Tims" opposed me at every turn. All of that would soon change with a growing Latino population.

A short time later, as we Hispanics grew in numbers, we formed a group and called ourselves "the Shadows." We had to do this to protect ourselves. We were not allowed more than a few blocks in either direction of Bushwick and Flushing Avenues. The Shadows later became a baseball team, and we started a gang called "the PROs" (Puerto Rican Outlaws). One month short of my fifteenth birthday in a schoolyard on Ellery Street, a local gang beat and stabbed me several times, and they left me for dead. By the end of the summer of 1956, a fifteen-year-old kid would lose his life in ongoing gang warfare, and that really hit close to home.

I must have been about seventeen when I saw the front-page head-line of the *Daily News* that read, "Governor Rockefeller Dyslexic." I had been diagnosed as dyslexic in the summer of 1958. After seeing that headline, I was able to tell myself, "I am *not stupid*. I am smart, and I am in good company with some of the greatest minds in the world who are dyslexic." It was as if a new door opened for me; I moved from a job working in a grocery store to a sales position with Brown and Williamson Tobacco Corporation in mid-January of 1961. Again, I was the first at something, this time the first Latino salesper-son for any tobacco company in the United States.

The reason I mention these events in my life is they helped form who I am today. God has taken every event in my life—both good and bad—to produce positive and long-lasting changes. It is my belief that when God is preparing to use us, God allows things to happen in our lives so that the Divine will be glorified. 1 Corinthians 1:27 teaches us that "God chose the foolish things of the world to shame the wise." Entirely out of my own control, God chose me (I could not think of anyone more foolish) on an interstate outside of Nashville, Tennessee. I pulled my eighteen-wheeler big truck to the side of the road, ran to the rear tandems, and did something I had said I would never do. I had told God, "I don't care what You do to me, just keep Your hands off my kids; You will never make me kneel before You." Now I threw myself to the ground and cried out, asking God to forgive me and to enter into the wrecked life that I was living. Two days later, I had what I called a "Damascus road experience" that changed my life—no more drugs or alcohol. I changed my CB code handle from "Wrong Way" to "Deacon."

And as the days grew into weeks and the weeks into months, God was doing something in my life that, at the time, I did not understand. God was mending bridges and relationships that I had destroyed and, most important of all, the relationship with my children. It's very sad to reach a time in your life when you can say to yourself, "If I die this very minute, there is no one who would shed a tear for me." That in and of itself is heartbreaking. During my first year with God, I mended my relationship with my children and grandchildren, and I can truly say that if I died today there would be many people who would cry.

My family and I moved to Puerto Rico in 1964, where I worked for 3M Company, a Fortune 500 company known for the "Scotch" brand of tape and hundreds of other retail products. While working for 3M, I was able to specialize in the field of ribbons and gift wrap products. As a gift wrap consultant, I had the opportunity to set up and train the gift wrap personnel at Sears, JCPenney, and many other larger local department stores. 3M also lent me out to the Puerto Rico Department of Consumer Affairs to give demonstrations in different towns on how to properly gift wrap for the holidays. One of the demonstrations was videotaped and seen on channel 4, which at the time was the most watched channel in Puerto Rico.

The battles that I fought as a child did not make me bitter or antagonistic, but rather made me tougher, more determined, and stubborn in a way that drove me to never give up on things easily.

I hear people say, "I want to make a difference in someone else's life or to serve God, but I don't know where to start." I always ask them, "What do you like to do or what skills do you have?" Use the skills you have and see where you can put them to work for the Kingdom of God! God asked Moses, "What is that in your hand?" (Exodus 4:2). We, like Moses, voice complaints about assignments because of our sense of personal inadequacy. When God asked Moses, "What is that in your hand?" it's not that God did not know what was in his hands. Sometimes God asks questions like that. God asked Adam, "Where are you?"(Genesis 3:9), knowing where he was. We are the ones who should know where we are and what know-how we have. You will never be asked to do anything outside of your area of expertise.

In my life I was able to see how God used the good, the bad, my interests, and my skills to help myself and others. Today, I am the executive director of Elohim Community Development and Outreach, Inc., one of New York City's largest multiservice food pantries. We provide free food to more than eleven hundred families every week. Founded in 1999, the food pantry at Elohim Christian Church opened its doors to forty-eight families. By August of 2001, we had grown to serving more than 250 families. In November of 2001 (post-9/11), the number of people seeking help more than doubled, and a new demand for essential services was born, including pastoral care, ESL classes, support groups, referrals to hundreds of services offered by government and nongovernment agencies, and services that helped families rebuild their lives that were torn apart by the shocking events of 9/11. In 2003, Elohim Community Development was born as part of an expansion program to meet the unprecedented demands for help. By 2009, Elohim completed its tenth year and had grown to be one of the largest food pantries in New York City. Through our partnerships with the New York City Office of Adult and Continuing Education, we are able to provide teachers and classrooms for four ESL classes, referrals to GED programs, and job training throughout schools in New York City. We also partner with other worldwide organizations, one of which assists women who are getting back into the workplace by providing job training, clothing, accessories, and continued help for up to one year after they get the job. The bigger picture is that we don't just get these women jobs; we also help them keep those jobs. We don't want to reinvent the wheel; we want to connect with organizations that are out there helping people to become self-sufficient.

Sometime later and after being grounded in the Word, God opened doors for me to minister at the Taconic State Correctional Facility for Women, in Bedford Hill, New York, where my wife and I spent seven years helping many inmates find their way back to God and experience a drug-free life.

At the same time, God was stirring a fire within me. This is when a small group of individuals from the drug and alcohol culture came together, desiring to let others know that there is a better way than just getting high. We received a permit to close off what was at the time the worst street in the city, Troutman Street in Brooklyn, New York, and cater to the need that was evident there. We all had something to do—worship, preach, give out tracks—and I had the kitchen. Coming from that culture, we knew if stomachs were full, ears would be open and they would be more receptive to hearing the Word of God. Something happened to me that day. I saw myself in their faces and said to myself, "That would be me if not for the grace of God in my life."

It's hard to explain the feeling that comes over you when things start to fall into place and everything makes sense. As a child and young man, I had no idea what God had in store for me.

Final Words

My hope is that, after reading my story, you take away the following lessons:

- Difficult starts in life do not doom us to a lifetime of failure or hardship.
- Effective leaders learn from their mistakes and keep trying until they succeed.
- "No" to a leader simply means, "We have to try another way."
- You can write your own script in life if you put your mind to it.
- Every experience—good or bad—grooms us for leadership.
- "Bad kids" are sometimes diamonds in the rough—help children find the leader in themselves.

About the Contributor

Rev. Anthony Miranda is the executive director of Elohim Community Development and Outreach, Inc., located in the Richmond Hill section of Queens, New York. It is the second largest food pantry in New York City. Each week, Elohim provides eleven hundred families and individuals with enough food to prepare three complete meals a day for the week for a family of four. Miranda is a graduate of the Blanton Peale Pastoral Care Studies program.

PART IV

How Do You Collaborate with
Specific Spiritual Leaders?

20

Kin'dom Come

Houses of Worship and Gender Justice in the Twenty-First Century

Rev. Sally N. MacNichol, MDiv, PhD

I am persuaded that the path to follow is to seek personal and institutional honesty rooted in the here and now. Such honesty involves recognizing that there is a sickness in our social relationships and that we are all, men and women alike, victims of its contagion and spreaders of this same disease.[1]

Women and men seem to function well enough together from day to day—in families, workplaces, and places of worship. However, if you are very still, listen intently, and allow yourself to look closely, you will hear and see and feel the profound subterranean uneasiness—the mistrust, the brokenheartedness, the anger and resentment, the bewildered and anguished longing for communion and mutual respect—that exists between women and men in our communities and congregations.

Nothing speaks to the paucity of relational reverence that exists in our society more concretely than the problem of violence against women. The statistics are alarming—an average of three women are killed every day by an intimate or once intimate partner; violence is the leading cause of injury to women aged fifteen to forty-four and responsible for 25 percent of all women's visits to emergency rooms; and one in four are women raped before the age of eighteen—and yet these statistics tell only a fraction of the story.[2] The vast majority of women of all ages, races/ethnicities, nationalities, and socioeconomic levels suffer in silence. Isolated, blamed, shamed, threatened, and betrayed, not only by someone they once loved and trusted, but by the very families, communities, congregations, and systems that were meant to protect them, most victim-survivors and most perpetrators never show up in the statistics.

Furthermore, these statistics do not capture the realities of rampant verbal, emotional, psychological, and spiritual abuse that does not rise to the level of a criminal offense but may, ultimately, cause more profound harm, creating wounds of the soul that take far longer to heal. The silence of our communities and congregations about intimate violence and abuse sends the message that women don't matter, that women's suffering does not matter, and that those who choose to use violence and abuse to maintain power and control over their intimate partners will not be held accountable. The refusal to name and address this reality and to recognize its roots in a social arrangement that is "geared to degrade one pole of humanity and exalt another" is collusion with evil.[3]

Intimate violence is about gender, and when we talk about gender, we are talking about issues of power. "Gender" as I am using it here, refers to what it means to be "man" and what it means to be "woman" as we *learn* it from our families, communities, and our political, cultural, and religious institutions.[4] Gender is one of the fundamental ways in which our world is organized (along with race and class), a sociocultural construct—a way of being in the world, a way of perceiving and being perceived. Of course, there are many different ways to be a woman and many different ways to be a man. Our gender identity and experience are intertwined with and radically shaped by the dynamics of our social location. Our race/ethnicity, class, culture, religion, sexuality, and age, to name a few of the most significant variables, and the history that informs our community in the present make a difference. Gender norms that assign different roles, responsibilities, expectations, and special entitlements vary from community to community, as do the rules and regulations of gender relations—how we relate to one another as women and men, as mothers and fathers, sisters and brothers, friends, coworkers, lovers, and life partners.[5]

However, one thing is common across all differences: we learn what it means to be "man" and learn what it means to be "woman" in relation to self, other, and God in a patriarchal society where gender inequity, injustice, and gender oppression are the norm—so normalized that the idea of gender injustice is foreign for many, so normative that even "prophetic" congregations committed to the struggle for justice, be it racial, environmental, or economic justice, rarely include gender justice as part of their agenda for change.[6]

A Deep Spiritual Ordering

A commitment to gender justice in our faith communities must start with acknowledging and naming sexism, misogyny, and patriarchy as sin and confronting the tremendous suffering and harm that patriarchy does to each and all of us, as women, as men, as communities.

As Allan G. Johnson explains in his excellent book *The Gender Knot: Unraveling Our Patriarchal Legacy*, patriarchal societies promote male privilege by being:

- **Male-dominated**, in that positions of authority—political, economic, religious, educational, military—are generally reserved for men.

- **Male-identified**, in that core cultural ideas about what is considered good, desirable, preferable, or normal are associated with how we think about men and masculinity.

- **Male-centered**, in that the focus of attention is primarily on men and what they do.[7]

An obsession with control and the devaluation of women (sexism) are the modus operandi of a patriarchal society.

The patriarchal practices of male supremacy hurt men as well as women. To call for the deep examination and transformation of patriarchy is not an attack on men individually or collectively. Patriarchy is a kind of society, a *system* of domination in which we all participate. It is a pervasive social, political, and economic phenomenon, expressed in personal, interpersonal, institutional, and cultural ways. It is not only a personal ideology based on the belief that men are superior to women, but it is also a system that involves complex and insidious cultural messages, institutional policies and practices, and the beliefs and actions of individuals. As theologian Rebecca Chopp writes:

> Patriarchy is revealed not simply as a social arrangement nor as individual acts of cruelty towards women on the part of men but *as a deep spiritual ordering* [italics mine] that invades and spreads across the social order—through individual identity, to social practices, to lines of authority in institutions, to cultural images and representations.[8]

Tragically, this "deep spiritual ordering" is alive and well in a majority of the houses of worship, seminaries, and faith institutions. My individual experience working with churches on domestic violence as well as counseling hundreds of Christian victim-survivors for the past two and a half decades confirms what many womanist and feminist theologians, ethicists, biblical scholars, and church/faith historians have illuminated: the practices of patriarchy and the sin of sexism are a central moral and ethical contradiction in the life of the church, synagogue, mosque, temple, and so forth. Without addressing these contradictions, the illness afflicting so many of our faith communities will deepen. There are so many women and men who have been exiled or had to flee from their faith communities because of the refusal or inability of their congregation to understand itself as a sanctuary of healing and justice committed to upholding nonviolence, mutuality, and the human dignity of each individual.

As Common as Breathing

> *In my conversations with women, I am finding that abuse is as common as breathing.*
>
> PASTOR MARGUERITE LEE

I often find myself sitting in a room with between fifteen and twenty-five women, usually the women's ministry of a Baptist, Pentecostal, sometimes AME, or nondenominational Christian church, who want "a workshop" on domestic violence. Usually they have reached out because something has happened in the news or to someone they may have come across outside the church. A recent example was a group who had been upset with their inability to help a young mother of two, fleeing an abusive boyfriend, who had been sent by the local police precinct to wait in their sanctuary while the officers were changing shifts.

They were bewildered by this (as well they should have been—a message that women's safety is not a priority for the police) and frightened for the young woman and her children. She stayed all afternoon and then returned reluctantly to the precinct. They never saw her again.

We met for a workshop after church a few Sundays later. As we talked about the realities of domestic violence and our alarm at the recent spike in domestic violence femicides in our city, an older woman in the back of the room spoke up. She spoke softly but steadily with strong emotion: "You all remember Joe, my husband, who passed a few years ago?" Everyone nodded their heads. "He seemed like a nice man right? ... Well, you know, he was a nice man, but he could be a mean man, too. When we were at home, he called me names, told me what to do, cheated on me too, and sometimes he would smack me" (a long pause) "and other stuff ..." There was a long silence. Someone whispered, "We didn't know."

And then, it started. The stories poured out—the controlling husbands, the childhood experiences of family violence, the sexual assaults and childhood sexual abuse, the teenage niece who is being battered right now, the sister whose philandering boyfriend infected her with HIV and won't let her get further medical attention—the list goes on. And then there were the women who wanted to tell their stories in private.... Later, the associate pastor, who had stayed for the workshop and listened with furrowed brow, said, "I never knew any of those stories and I have been here for seven years!"

This happens time after time, and time after time. I am stunned by the blatant lack of attention to and care for women's suffering and empowerment by leaders of faith communities, especially male leaders. When this kind of callousness prevails, women's pain is trivialized and so is women's spiritual power. Disclosing what has been hidden, naming soul wounds and injustice, releases enormous amounts of women's creative spiritual energy. Leaders committed to healing, justice making, and kin'dom building must find ways to facilitate the liberation of this energy, rather than exploit, suppress, and repress it. To quote the writer Ursula K. Le Guin, "When women offer our experience as our truth, our human truth, all the maps change."[9]

The consequences of intimate violence are far-reaching. Even if a woman has not been directly victimized by physical abuse or sexual assault, she has experienced the anguish, fear, sorrow, and broken-heartedness of friends and family who have. The spiritual wounds of abuse cascade through a woman's life cycle, into the next generation and the next. If we refuse to see the pervasive reality of intimate violence and the unresolved trauma afflicting the lives of the people in our congregations, our praxis will remain incomplete. Opportunities for justice and healing the broken body of Christ (or in the Jewish tradition, *tikkun olam*, "repairing the broken world"), will endlessly elude us.

Sexism—like racism, heterosexism, and classism—is a powerful and inescapable force in the lives of women and men. It's important to acknowledge what activist scholar of masculinity Michael Kaufman has called "the triad of men's violence"—the reality that men's violence against women "is linked to men's violence against other men and to the internalization of violence, that is, a man's violence against himself."[11] Each form of violence helps create the others. Male-dominated societies are based not only on a hierarchy of men over women but also on men over men. While male privilege offers men a variety of benefits and unearned advantages in relationship to women, privilege has its costs. The demands of masculinity can be as oppressive and constricting for men as the demands of femininity are for women.

Like women, many men live with the persistent threat of violence from other men. Obviously, patriarchy manifests in different ways according to one's social and geographical location, but boys from many different communities grow up exposed to violence in their families and experience it at school and in the streets. Furthermore, most men are socialized to ignore pain and suppress fear. A whole range of emotions is off-limits or channeled into anger, the acceptable male emotion. Many men develop a kind of psychic armor for protection and distance from self and others that seems to decrease their capacity for empathy and increase their capacity for abuse. Because what is masculine is defined by what is not feminine, qualities ascribed to women, like nurture, care, and vulnerability, are disallowed. Most masculinities, regardless of race, ethnicity, socioeconomic status, and so on, have at their core the idea that a real man has power and control. Thus, not having power and control means you are not a real man. Violence becomes the means to prove your manhood to yourself and others.

Working with men and women, honestly, with healing, wholeness, and justice in mind, requires (individually and collectively) ongoing inquiry and self-critique, truth telling, and a "fearless moral inventory" concerning the organization of power and the commitment to gender justice in your congregation. If your understanding of the appropriate relationship between men and women is one of rule and obedience, domination and subordination, then the possibility of a whole and healthy congregation will be impossible.

At the heart of leadership around gender is a commitment to gender justice and a paradigm of partnership and mutual respect, fostering safe spaces and facilitating an environment that supports the free expression of each individual in the congregation.

What You Can Do

- Acknowledge and name sexism, misogyny, and patriarchy as sin. Preach it. Teach it. Pray it.

- Engage in ongoing self-examination. Reflect on your own gender socialization. How does your understanding of gender shape your theology and your leadership style, and vice versa? Continuously develop critical consciousness as you support others to do the same.

- Listen to the voices of women. Encourage the creation of ongoing safe spaces for truth telling.

- Support explicit biblical, theological, and spiritual reflection on what it means to be a woman and a woman of faith in "a rape culture" that condones physical and emotional violence against women as the norm.[11] Pay special attention to theological themes of suffering, sacrifice, obedience, and forgiveness.

- Facilitate safe spaces of accountability and vulnerability for men where patriarchal assumptions and privileges can be challenged and transformed with respect and compassion.

- Support explicit biblical, theological, and spiritual reflection on what it means to be a man and a man of faith in "a rape culture" that condones physical and emotional violence against women as the norm.[12] Pay special attention to the way Jesus lived out his ministry in the patriarchal world he was challenging.

- Organize ongoing dialogues on gender where men and women come together to listen, share, and learn about each other's experience, and develop ways they can struggle for gender justice together.

- Pay attention to the balance of power in your congregation. Be aware of how roles and responsibilities are organized.

- Educate yourself and the congregation about intimate violence (domestic violence, sexual assault, child sexual abuse). Invite facilitators of local domestic violence programs and batterers' intervention programs to do workshops and presentations on a yearly basis.

- Know your local resources. Put information, telephone numbers, and resources in weekly bulletins, brochures, etc., and make them available to congregations at all times.

- Make connections between men's violence against women and other issues (e.g., racism, HIV/AIDS, poverty, prison reform). Make sure that social justice ministries address the gendered dimension of their work.

Notes

1. Ivone Gebara, *Out of the Depths: Women's Experience of Evil and Salvation* (Minneapolis: Fortress Press, 2002), 81.
2. See Futures without Violence, www.futureswithoutviolence.org. It should also be noted that while women abuse men and other women, men commit the majority of intimate violence in the US.
3. Gebara, *Out of the Depths*, 81.
4. "Gender" and "sex" are often confused. "Sex" refers to biological characteristics that define humans as male or female. One's sexual identity, defined as who one is attracted to, can be different from one's gender identity.
5. It is important to note that there are a growing number of people who are resisting the gender binary of male and female, and they are often referred to as genderqueer, a catchall term for gender identities other than man and woman, thus outside of the gender binary and heteronormativity model. See Raven Usher, *North American Lexicon of Transgender Terms* (San Francisco: GLB Publishers, 2006). This is also an important gender issue for the church but, because of space, is out of the scope of this paper.
6. Recently, a church known for its commitments to social justice rejected congregants' proposal for an intimate justice working group.
7. Allan G. Johnson, *The Gender Knot: Unraveling Our Patriarchal Legacy* (Philadelphia: Temple University Press, 2005), 5–10.

8. Rebecca Chopp, *Saving Work: Feminist Practices of Theological Education* (Louisville: Westminster/John Knox Press, 1995), 56.

9. Ursula K. LeGuin, 1986 commencement address at Bryn Mawr College. Reprinted in *Dancing at the Edge of the World: Thoughts on Words, Women, Places* (New York: HarperRow, 1989), 147–160.

10. Michael Kaufman, "The Construction of Masculinity and the Triad of Men's Violence," in *Beyond Patriarchy: Essays by Men on Pleasure, Power, and Change*, ed. Michael Kaufman (Toronto: Oxford University Press, 1985).

11. Emile Buchwald, Pamela R. Fletcher, and Martha Roth, eds., *Transforming a Rape Culture* (Minneapolis: Milkweed Editions, 1993).

12. Ibid.

Further Reading

Adams, Carol J., and Marie Fortune, eds. *Violence against Women and Children: A Christian Theological Handbook*. New York: Continuum, 1995.

Adams, Carol J. *Woman-Battering*. Minneapolis: Fortress Press, 1994.

Boyd, Stephen. *The Men We Long to Be: Beyond Domination to a New Christian Understanding of Manhood*. New York: HarperCollins, 1995.

Boyd, Stephen, W. Merle Longwood, and Mark W. Muesse, eds. *Redeeming Men: Religion and Masculinity*. Philadelphia: Westminister/John Knox, 1994.

Brock, Rita Nakashima, and Rebecca Ann Parker. *Proverbs of Ashes: Violence, Redemptive Suffering and the Search for What Saves Us*. Boston: Beacon Press, 2001.

Cooper-White, Pamela. *The Cry of Tamar: Violence against Women and the Church's Response*. Minneapolis: Fortress Press, 1995.

Fortune, Marie. *Keeping the Faith: Questions and Answers for the Abused Woman*. San Francisco: HarperRow, 1987.

Hooks, Bell. *The Will to Change: Men, Masculinity, and Love*. New York: Atria Books, 2004.

Kivel, Paul. *Men's Work: How to Stop the Violence that Tears Our Lives Apart*. Center City, MN: Hazelden, 1992.

McLure, John S., and Nancy J. Ramsay, eds. *Telling the Truth: Preaching about Sexual and Domestic Violence*. Cleveland: United Church Press, 1998.

Neuger, Christie Cozad, and James Newton Poling, eds. *The Care of Men*. Nashville: Abingdon Press, 1997.

———. *Men's Work in Preventing Violence against Women*. Binghamton, NY: The Haworth Pastoral Press, 2002.

Neuger, Christie Cozad. *Counseling Women: A Narrative Pastoral Approach*. Minneapolis: Fortress Press, 2001.

Schmidt, K. Louise. *Transforming Abuse: Nonviolent Recovery and Resistance*. Philadelphia: New Society Publishers, 1995.

Sokoloff, Natalie J., ed. *Domestic Violence at the Margins: Readings on Race, Class, Gender and Culture*. New Brunswick, NJ: Rutgers University Press, 2005.

West, Traci C. *Wounds of the Spirit: Black Women, Violence and Resistance.* New York: NYU Press, 1999.

Educational Documentaries

Broken Vows: Religious Perspectives on Domestic Violence. Directed and produced by the FaithTrust Institute. Seattle: FaithTrust Institute, 1994.

Hip Hop: Beyond Beats and Rhymes. Directed and produced by Byron Hurt, 2006.

I Believe You: Faiths' Response to Intimate Partner Violence. Directed by David Vinik. Written and produced by Debra Gonsher Vinik. New York: Diva Productions, 2011.

Killing Her Softly 4: Advertising's Image of Women. Directed by Sut Jhally. Northampton, MA: Media Educational Foundation, 2010.

Tough Guise: Violence Media and the Crisis in Masculinity. Jackson Katz and Jeremy Earp. Directed by Sut Jhally. Northampton, MA: Media Educational Foundation, 2000.

Websites

CONNECT: Safe Families, Peaceful Communities: www.connectnyc.org/program/connect-faith.

Faith Trust Institute: Working Together to End Sexual and Domestic Violence: http://faithtrustinstitute.org.

Futures without Violence: www.futureswithoutviolence.org.

Michael Kaufman: www.michaelkaufman.com.

Paul Kivel: www.paulkivel.com.

Rave: Religion and Violence e-Learning: http://theraveproject.org.

SAIV: The Spiritual Alliance to Stop Intimate Violence: http://saiv.net.

About the Contributor

Rev. Sally N. MacNichol, MDiv, PhD, has been an antiviolence activist, advocate for survivors of domestic violence, and educator for more than twenty-five years. She has counseled victim-survivors of domestic violence, run empowerment groups for survivors, worked with abusive men, and trained hundreds of staff from child welfare programs and community and faith-based organizations across New York City's five boroughs. She is currently the co-executive director at CONNECT, a nonprofit organization committed to eliminating gender and family violence in New York City, where she also developed and directs CONNECT Faith, a program dedicated to helping communities of faith address and prevent family violence. She received her master of divinity and PhD in systematic theology from Union Theological Seminary.

21

Working with the Black Diaspora

Antoinette Ellis-Williams, PhD, MPA

This chapter will explore the challenges and opportunities of the black diaspora and offer ways for community faith leaders to work across boundaries. If we are to build truly beloved communities based on social justice, equity, mutual respect, and faith-based values, we must be vested in understanding the most basic knowledge and history of black communities. Often stakeholders are moved by their hearts and find themselves trying to repair broken relationships or are left with hurt feelings due in part to misunderstandings, power dynamics, stereotypes, and/or ignorance.

This chapter attempts to build historical and sociological content for leaders across the sociopolitical and cultural boundaries of religion and race. It will (1) define the significant demographic shifts within the black diaspora in the United States over the past forty years; (2) explore a few of the current issues facing the black diaspora (post-racial syndrome, class divide, diminishing male leadership, reactivating the imagination of our youth, and individualism versus collective values clash); (3) examine shared challenges and cultural ties; (4) examine questions stakeholders need to ask when working with the black diaspora; and (5) provide practical tools to help move to better understanding among all groups.

Shifting Identity within the Black Community

Blackness is more than color. Within the African American diaspora, increased diversity exists due in part to several interconnected and

249

complex demographic reasons, including immigration, migration, integration, nationality, culture, region/geography, education, class, and growing biracial population. Journalist Eugene Robinson argues:

> Instead of one black America, now there are four: (1) a Mainstream middle-class majority with a full ownership stake in American society; (2) a large, Abandoned minority with less hope of escaping poverty and dysfunction than at any time since Reconstruction's crushing end; (3) a small Transcendent elite with such enormous wealth, power, and influence that even white folks have to genuflect; and (4) two newly Emergent groups—individuals of mixed-race heritage and communities of recent black immigrants—that make us wonder what "black" is even supposed to mean.[1]

Robinson asserts that these distinct categories have "different profiles, different mind-sets, different hopes, fears, and dreams."[2]

Since the 1960s, we have witnessed significant shifts within black communities as a result of the civil rights movement. Integration provided increased access to the resources and cultural nuances of white communities. Educated African Americans were able to leave growing urban "ghettos." Black flight from urban communities further isolated poorer communities. While Robinson argues that the majority of middle-class black people have had more opportunities, "with a full ownership stake in American society," I would disagree with this assertion. Data suggests that African Americans still lag behind their white counterparts in achieving the American dream (e.g., home ownership, employment, education).

This is not to suggest that the elite black communities have not flourished in newly integrated suburbs and exclusive black havens, with growing access to capital and resources.

In an interview for *Martha's Vineyard Magazine*, Professor Henry "Skip" Gates agrees with Robinson's assertions, arguing for familiar and safe spaces for the black elite:

> There are a few things that are special about race relations on Martha's Vineyard. First of all, the Island must have the highest concentration in the world of successful, middle- and upper-class black people. If you're a successful black person, chances are you've raised your children in predominantly white neighborhoods, and they've attended predominantly white schools.

Martha's Vineyard allows the black upper-middle class to get to know each other, and it allows our children to socialize every day with other black children—and white children—of their same educational and economic backgrounds. This is particularly valuable for mixed-race children: They don't feel abnormal for being smart and the children of successful people. This performs a very important function within the African American community.[3]

The idea that the black elite has to escape poorer urban neighborhoods to find a "safe space" because they feel "abnormal" only underscores the divide and idiomatic identities within the black diaspora around education, class, and color identity. Many successful black children have been raised with other equally as smart black children in poorer communities. We may wonder if Gates's notion of "normal" negates his full understanding of institutional racism and the fact that biracial children are at all economic levels within black communities. Class differentiation is ever more present, palpable, and painful—a secret divide that many in African American communities are afraid to recognize or publicly expose. Few have made it to the White House, while many others still use "outhouses."

During the past forty years, the population of immigrants from Caribbean and African countries significantly increased in predominant African American neighborhoods. The food, culture, language, music, and foods from Haiti, Jamaican, Ghana, Nigeria, Ethiopia, and Liberia, among other countries, have created a new cultural depth and fusion but also shifted the power dynamics in these communities. According to Aaron Terrazas from the Migration Policy Institute, "The number of African immigrants in the United States grew 40-fold between 1960 and 2007, from 35,355 to 1.4 million. Most of this growth has taken place since 1990."[4] When compared to other immigrants, African immigrants tend to be highly educated, but they also tend to lack citizenship. Eugene Robinson additionally argues that the Abandoned accuse the Emergent— "the immigrant segment, at least—of moving into Abandoned neighborhoods and using the locals as mere stepping-stones. The immigrant Emergent, with their intact families and long-range mind-set, ridicule the Abandoned for being their own worst enemies,"[5] thus creating nationality tensions and competition within the communities between US citizens and undocumented immigrants over scarce resources.

Southern African Americans who migrated to Northern cities with the rise of industrialization and urbanization from the 1920s through the 1960s began to feel the changing landscape of intact neighborhoods in the late 1960s. The decline of manufacturing jobs and civil rights rebellions in the 1960s left less educated Southern laborers at a disadvantage. The decline of urban communities was fast and intense; violent crime increased, and the drug culture replaced the legitimate labor market. White/black plight, a growing educated middle and upper-middle class, and shifting labor markets resulted in lack of employment opportunities for Southern labor migrants. The growth of the service and technological industries also added to the disenfranchisement of manufacturing workers.

The depth and precipitous changing black diaspora may seem far too complex and elusive for leaders to build bridges among different communities. But we cannot minimize or overlook these trends of a growing middle class at large; an abandoned urban minority; a growing black elite, with its wealth, power, and network; and lastly, emergent groups, mixed-race heritage and immigrant communities. Arguably, understanding the specifics associated with each group will enable a healthy exchange of ideas and hopefully yield more productive collaborations, regardless of race or religion/spirituality.

Common Challenges and Shared Culture of the Black Diaspora

Understanding the intersecting shared cultural values and challenges can serve to develop a framework for our collective work. Racism and freedom music unite all the groups within the black diaspora. The stories and memories including the Exodus experiences from the grips of "Jim Crow Pharaoh," the fight for inclusion in the American sociopolitical economic systems, and the reliance on cultural musical traditions serve to draw a powerful binding narrative for all black folks.

Common Challenges

Lingering effects of racism at both conscious and unconscious levels still exist. Undoubtedly, the African American diaspora has made strides in American race relations. However, refusing to honestly explore the polarizing reality that racism is alive and thriving (perhaps in a more insidious and hidden manner) in our country is at best naive and at worst indifferent or dishonest. The election of President Barack Obama did not create a post-racial America. We had a "we are the world" moment on November 4, 2008; some might have even felt a seismic racial shift, in part as a result of the powerful visual images of our new first family. The stunningly attractive presidential Obama family, complete with various shades of black skins and two darling daughters, enthralled us. The "feel good" moment was just that, a moment; this was the birth of the "post-racial syndrome." America's ability to elect a black man to the highest office spoke of a collective American ideal of "one nation."

Caution ought to remain before we shut down the NAACP or other groups committed to addressing racial inequities. Yes, we have come far, but regardless of social class, as Professor Gates discovered, race still matters. His desire to find solace in Martha's Vineyard and his Ivy League education did not insulate him from the Cambridge police who arrested him for breaking into his own home. Racism touches every group within the black diaspora, especially young men.

The 2009 Census Bureau report "showed increases in poverty for whites, blacks and Hispanic Americans, with historic disparities continuing. The poverty rate for non-Hispanic whites was 9.4 percent, for blacks 25.8 percent and for Hispanics 25.3 percent. The rate for Asians was unchanged at 12.5 percent."[6] The disproportionate employment data suggest that there is an intractable nature of racial disparities. The black workforce is younger than the white workforce, with fewer African Americans with college degrees, more female-headed households, and many more living in urban communities.[7]

There is a diminishing number in formal male leadership inside and outside black churches. The rise in female leadership is a positive note in the fight against sexism. However, patriarchy is still the order of the day. An unintentional drawback to the gains in female leadership is the perceived lack of male power in primary community organizations and private-sector positions. Further complicated by the male incarceration rate, illegal options to reclaim manhood in an unfair justice system become a quick fix to manhood. Additionally, unemployment, underemployment, and the lack of jobs have a direct consequence on black male identity. Men are required to protect and provide for their family.

Left with a sense of failure or inadequacy, some resort to violence to prove their manhood. However, many positive and negative informal male leaders fill the gaps: deacons, ministers, uncles, brothers, fathers, teachers, coaches, mentors, cousins, friends, and gang members. These men play a vital active role in their communities and are often overlooked as legitimate leaders. They help protect, parent, and provide for the entire community.

Individualism versus Collective Values Clash

With the growing access to white systems of power over the past forty years, the collective black diaspora struggle was been replaced with individual modes and measures of success. Measures of success are primarily determined by personal income, assets, and power networks. Integration was a singular defining moment for those who were able to have personal freedoms. Voting rights and civil rights were central collective struggles with an aim for "justice for all," but when individuals became "part" of the system, the collective voice became less important.

Shared Connection within the Black Diaspora

On a more positive point of cultural identity, the black diaspora shares a rich spirit-filled culture and history, regardless of location. Traditional families, divorced families, single-headed families, extended families, and alternative families have their specific challenges and idiosyncrasies. However, regardless of income, education, or nationality, the black diaspora is a family-centered community, with long-standing traditions filled with music and food. The ability to encourage one another through spirituals and the blues is special and deeply felt, regardless of shifting trends. James H. Cone, in *The Spirituals and the Blues*, states, "The power of song in the struggle for black survival—that is what the spirituals and blues are about."[8] There is affirmation, release, hope, inspiration, liberation, and memory in those songs. The beat, moans, syncopation, and coded messages serve as a reminder of the collective identity as African people and reinforce the necessity for freedom. Spirituals and the blues are sacred, personal, and direct messages to God and community:

> Do Lord, O do Lord, do remember me.
> Do Lord, O do Lord, do remember me.

As a plea to God to "come by," to not forget about us, spirituals and the blues illustrate an aching need for power and grace:

> Come by here, my Lord, come by here
> Come by here, my Lord, come by here
> Come by here, my Lord, come by here
> Somebody needs You Lord, come by here
> Somebody needs You Lord, come by here
> Somebody needs You Lord, come by here
> O, Lord, come by here.

Avoiding Biases and Stereotypes

Once we understand that there is difference within the black diaspora, including different forms of worship, our expectations can shift accordingly. In any urban community you will find dozens of black churches with very different forms of worship, usually based on social class, culture/ethnicity, and/or nationality. African Methodist Episcopal, Baptist, Evangelical, Pentecostal, Lutheran, and Church of God in Christ (COGIC), all offer the African diaspora choice. Some are more spirited, some do not use instruments, some are more formal, some are more emotionally free, some use hymnals, still others line the hymns along with anthems, and many enjoy contemporary Christian or Southern Gospel.

Questions We Need to Ask Other Stakeholders

Prior to engaging in the hard work of building coalitions with the black diaspora, there are several questions leaders must ask themselves before engaging in the work:

1. Why are you engaged in this relationship? Check your motivations. Are you guided by spiritual conviction, a political agenda, a sense of responsibility, or a need to save the community?

2. What do you bring to the table (positive and negative)? Delineate exactly what you bring to the table (e.g., networking, financial capital, specific expertise, basic resources, regrets, guilt). Separate the list into positives and negatives, and honestly assess how each will help and/or hurt the community.

This list is not intended to prevent any leader from moving forward with working with the black diaspora; rather, it will help gauge personal assets and deficits.

3. What do you want? Selfless leadership is rare and perhaps not completely selfless. It is human nature to want even a small thank you. Indicate your expectations up front.

Working with the Black Diaspora: Cultural Proficiency 101 (Dos and Don'ts Checklist)

- **Don't assume to know.** You cannot apply your limited understanding of some African Americans to all groups, "even if your best friend is black" or even if you are black.

- **Don't fake the funk.** Do not try to act, talk, sound, or think "black." The community resents when "do-gooders" try to put on airs. While this is often an unconscious desire by those working in mixed coalitions to feel a part of the group, it is often viewed as offensive.

- **Do be yourself.** Authenticity is respected and appreciated. Leaders such as John Brown (abolitionist), Bob Zellner (Student Nonviolent Coordinating Committee, aka SNCC), Tom Hayden (SDS), and Morris Dees and Joseph Levin Jr. (founders of the Southern Poverty Law Center) have all been effective in part because of their willingness to cross boundaries in a manner that maintained their identity without an air of arrogance or privilege.

- **Don't gift and dump.** Do not simply give a gift without sufficient knowledge of the infrastructure or capacity of the community. Do not expect that because you give a big check you deserve more respect or attention than community leaders. You cannot buy trust. Bill Gates was criticized by some for donating computers to schools without the necessary electrical wiring within dilapidated public schools. While there is good intent behind donors, the lack of knowledge about the needs may nullify the gift. Another problem with writing a check is the assumption that as a donor you have the right to dictate policy or make changes with minimal consultation with grassroots constituents.

- **Don't start if you can't stay.** Working with a new group is labor-intensive and a long journey. If you are not prepared to stay for the long haul, reconsider your role as a leader. Change will take time. Many are moved to get involved as an emotional reaction. However, community work takes time; it is painful and involves long-term commitment.

- **Do prepare.** Read great works, novels, and writings by and about black people, history, and culture. Include political biographies, memories, historical nonfiction, and sacred writings and teachings. Learn about folklore, myths, and fables.

- **Do resist the "savior syndrome."** View the community from an asset-rich perspective rather than a deficit model. Unconscious paternalistic attitudes and behavior will prevent different groups from working together if outsiders believe their role is to "save" the community. Find the richness of the community by asking questions and listening.

- **Don't assume it's all bad or tragic.** The ghetto single-parent, daddy-in-jail rapper is one the media perpetuates. Tragedy becomes the norm, and many feel sorry.

- **Do ask questions in a respectful manner.** No one person has all the answers. Lifelong learners are the best leaders. There is ever present a joy in the exchange between those who are unfamiliar with one another. A humble word goes very far in all communities.

Key Things to Remember

- History frames today but doesn't limit today. We all have important histories that frame our present identity. However, we should never permit the past to limit the possibilities of new *shalom* moments.

- There are opportunities in partnership. People of faith know the importance of service, love, and forgiveness. This is how we can share in our work of knowing our better selves. We are called to love, without exceptions, without boundaries, and without judgments. Until all men and women are free from oppression, poverty, and bigotry, our work requires us to unite.

- It's not all bad. Resist the naysayers who say there is not hope. While there is suffering in some parts of the black diaspora, it's not all bad. Look for those moments where a brother pushes his little sister on the swing set, or a teacher stays late every day to review math problems, or a dad goes to the supermarket. There are glimpses of God's loving-kindness, grace, and mercy in every home and every situation. Leaders should pause to observe these moments. There is always "Good News."

Notes

1. Adapted from Eugene Robinson, *Disintegration: The Splintering of Black America* (New York: Doubleday, 2010), 5.
2. Ibid.
3. Laura D. Roosevelt, "A Conversation with Skip Gates," *Martha's Vineyard Magazine*, August 2008, www.mvmagazine.com/article.php?17721.
4. Aaron Terrazas, "African Immigrants in the United States," US in Focus, *Migration Information Source*, February 2009, www.migrationinformation.org/usfocus/display.cfm?ID=719.
5. Robinson, *Disintegration*, 6.
6. Erik Eckholm, "Recession Raises Poverty Rate to a 15-Year High," *New York Times*, September 16, 2010, www.nytimes.com/2010/09/17/us/17poverty.html.
7. Annalyn Censky, "Black Unemployment: Highest in 27 Years," *CNN Money*, September 2, 2011, http://money.cnn.com/2011/09/02/news/economy/black_unemployment_rate/index.htm.
8. James H. Cone, *The Spirituals and the Blues: An Interpretation* (Maryknoll, NY: Orbis Books, 1991), 1.

Further Reading

Achebe, Chinua. *Things Fall Apart*. New York: Fawcett Crest, 1959.
Cone, James H. *A Black Theology of Liberation: 20th Anniversary Edition*. New York: Orbis Books, 1990.
Franklin, John Hope. *Mirror to America: The Autobiography of John Hope Franklin*. New York: Farrar, Straus and Giroux, 2005.

Gates, Henry Louis Jr., ed. *Bearing Witness: Selections from African-American Autobiography in the Twenty-First Century.* New York: Pantheon Books, 1991.

Glaude, Eddie. *Exodus! Religion, Race and Nation in Early Nineteenth-Century Black America.* Chicago: University of Chicago Press, 2000.

Height, Dorothy. *Open Wide the Freedom Gates: A Memoir.* New York: Public Affairs, 2003.

Lusane, Clarence. *African American at the Crossroads: The Restructuring of Black Leadership and the 1992 Elections.* Boston: South End Press, 1994.

Robinson, Eugene. *Disintegration: The Splintering of Black America.* New York: Doubleday, 2010.

Sanchez, Sonia. *Wounded in the House of a Friend.* Boston: Beacon Press, 1995.

Schomburg Center for Research in Black Culture, the New York Public Library. *Standing in the Need of Prayer: A Celebration of Black Prayer.* Foreword by Coretta Scott King. New York: Free Press, 2003.

Tutu, Desmond. *Hope and Suffering: Sermons and Speeches.* Grand Rapids, MI: Wm. B. Eerdmans, 1984.

About the Contributor

Antoinette Ellis-Williams, PhD, MPA, graduated from the University of Pittsburgh, Graduate School of Public and International Affairs with a master of Public Administration and earned her PhD from Cornell University, School of Human Ecology. Dr. Ellis-Williams is currently the director of the Lee Hagan Africana Studies Center and professor of women's and gender studies at New Jersey City University (NJCU). She is also a minister at Bethany Baptist Church in Newark, New Jersey. Some of her recent publications include "Discovering the Possibilities: A Study of African American Youth Resistance and Activism" and the poem "Letter from Mama Olewagi." Dr. Ellis-Williams is executive producer, director, research methodologist, writer, assistant editor, and narrator for the documentary *Connecting Generations: The Lee Hagan's Legacy.* She is an active member in the community, serving on several boards including as immediate past president of the board of trustees for East Orange, New Jersey, Hospital Association Governance Committee; the regional policy board for the American Hospital Association (AHA); New Jersey Hospital Association board of trustees; board of directors for the Coretta Scott King Humanitarian Group; and the board of the New Jersey Institute of Social Justice.

22

Afro-Caribbean, Afro-Latino/a Spirituality

Hiding Religious Beliefs Out in the Open

Rev. Carlos Alejandro, MS, MDiv, BCC

It was 3 p.m. and a phone call came into the pastoral care office at a New York City hospital to request that a chaplain visit a patient who was dying. Though the patient had been listed by a staff chaplain as having "no religion," another chaplain, a clinical pastoral education student who had visited with the same patient, wondered about the patient's barely audible insistence that he practiced a different religion. With further exploration it became clear that the patient not only practiced a different religion but was also a fully initiated priest. The patient, a man in his seventies from Trinidad, had traveled decades ago to Ile Ife in Nigeria to be initiated as a priest of Sango in the religion of Ifa—the African traditional religion of the Yoruba people. Once this was clarified, a priest from the same religion who lived nearby was contacted, visited with the dying patient, and performed libations at the request of the patient. The patient died a day later. The admitting chaplain later mentioned that he was aware of the religion of the patient but considered it a "non-religion" and dismissed it as idolatry.

How can this happen in a field that rightfully celebrates its ability to embrace multicultural, interfaith dialogue? How many persons have been harmed due not just to ignorance, but also to the intolerance of religious persons charged with providing community and support to the stranger? The behavior of this chaplain was unacceptable, perhaps more so because he had some clinical training. He had training in walking alongside those who are suffering, yet he violated the basics of the right of patients to embrace spiritualities of their own choosing.

African Traditional Religions lay the foundation of many of the Afro-Caribbean, Afro-Latina/o religious practices in the Americas. Some of these religious practices and worldviews include Santeria (Regla de Ocha) in Cuba and Puerto Rico, Vodun in Haiti, Candomble in Brazil, Obeah and Kumina in Jamaica and some of the islands, and Ga Ga in the Dominican Republic, among others. There are also other traditions such as Spiritism, with French roots, and Palo Mayombe, with Central African roots, found throughout the African diaspora and also present within the worldview of our patients, clients, and neighbors. It is important to point out that these traditions continue to evolve and flourish in new contexts, where they meet, embrace, and dance with new cultures and new religious practices.

Historical Background

During the Middle Passage, enslaved Africans were torn away from villages with unique religious and spiritual practices. These enslaved Africans came from various parts of Africa, including West and Central Africa. Those who were brought to the Americas were forcibly baptized as Christians by their "slave owners." With their indigenous traditions demonized, they were forced to seek creative ways of maintaining their religious traditions hidden from the eyes of the slave owners. They were baptized Christians but remained committed to the traditions and worldviews of their ancestors. As they intermingled with people from other African cultures, they also integrated some of their religious traditions into their faith practices. This is clearly seen in Cuba and other countries where a Yoruba worldview is integrated with a Central African or Congo worldview.

From Where I Sit

I am Puerto Rican raised in an inner-city neighborhood of Brooklyn. Both sides of my family trace their roots in Puerto Rico to Loiza, a strongly African community. Though my family never worshipped in any church, we were taught to self-identify as Roman Catholic. (All of us were baptized into the Roman Catholic Church by the age of two.) I do, however, have early childhood memories of attending what I later learned were séances and African-influenced rituals. These were very intense spiritual/ emotional and physical experiences within a strong community context. There was a clear belief in a world where the physical and the spiritual interacted freely. There were spirits manifesting, sending messages through mediums who channeled the messages, to guide the lives of the living. There were also cases of spirits who themselves needed help transitioning fully from this world to the next. Ritual herbal baths, prayer, and faith all came together to help the community make meaning of any crisis that may have emerged. I was initiated as a priest in Congo-based diasporal religions more than thirty-five years ago. Family members were also involved on different levels with Santeria (Regla de Ocha). In my late twenties I converted to Christianity, went to seminary, and was ordained a Christian minister. Soon after the 9/11 attacks in 2001, in search of a deeper connection to nature and healing, I traveled to Nigeria to study and experience the religion of Ifa. I am a certified Association for Clinical Pastoral Education (ACPE) supervisor, and I have served as a clinical pastoral education (CPE) supervisor in Harlem, in Puerto Rico, and at a northern New Jersey hospital with a largely Cuban and Central American population. I also served as a chaplain at Rikers Island's Central Punitive Segregation Unit, with a large African American, Caribbean, and Latino inmate population. All of these experiences impact how I view transformative community, healing, interfaith, and multicultural dialogue.

To work with Afro-Latina/o persons in any setting, it is required that we explore the person's unique view of the world. How is suffering defined and experienced not only through religious metaphor but also through the deep spirituality that speaks louder than drums during a wedding in a West African village? This worldview is held in community, with obvious individual expressions. This rich diversity may be found in a therapist's office, Christian church, hospital, prison, neighborhood, or New York City subway train. What kinds of paradigms are to be created in order to address the spiritual care needs of persons who almost instinctively hide their religious beliefs "out in the open"? Are we able to see what the client, patient, and/ or inmate is presenting as they seek to understand their loss of emotional/ spiritual and physical health? Are we able to hear and embrace the impact of incarceration on people and their loved ones? In the inner cities of New York City, there exist a multitude of people who have integrated, and will continue to integrate, various religious traditions and spiritualities. While there are those who may claim devotion to one particular path, many live and embrace multiple expressions privately. I should point out here that while many of these traditions have been practiced for generations in a specific cultural context or community, there are increasing numbers of people from other cultures, ethnic groups, and racial groups who have been drawn to and initiated into one or more of these traditions. Those being initiated into Vodun, for example, may be black, white, or Asian, from around the world, and they may be from all walks of life, from physicians and attorneys, to teachers, professional athletes, and government officials.

But there are other challenges as well. There are moments when the integration of multiple religiosities creates conflicts in the lives of the persons in the community. This is further complicated when a religious leader from a different religion preaches that Afro-Caribbean and Afro-Latina/o disaporal religious expressions are manifestations of evil. The reality of slavery in the West created a context where these traditions had to be hidden or severe consequences could follow, and a religious leader who has yet to explore the richness in these traditions pushes practitioners and believers away into a place of silence. The "demonization" of indigenous religious traditions can at times occur even among persons who come with some kind of clinical training. They wrestle with issues of diversity, some more effectively than others. So when these patients or clients are in need of our help, they keep valuable insights invisible for fear of being judged and condemned by others.

It is foundational to effective religious leadership and competent pastoral care to remain sensitive to the worldviews that continue to present in patients/clients/congregants as they sit in therapists' offices, hospital rooms, and hospices. It is a worldview that if left unexplored will interfere with the adequate care of patients and clients. Patients and clients arriving in emergency rooms are too often identified as Roman Catholic, especially if they are Latinos/as, when in reality they are practitioners of Santeria or have been influenced by the traditions in some way. To understand the worldview of these patients, religious leaders, professional caregivers, and religious communities must listen deeply to what is being communicated. Perhaps the first thing they must listen to is their own voices, their own prejudices and fears. The more that this kind of internal work is done, the more the voices of this diverse community may be heard.

It Takes a Village That Is Radically Hospitable

As I write, I am very much aware of the concept of "radical hospitality," where spiritual and pastoral care providers create a context where people and their loved ones may freely share their understanding of their lived experience. It means that we learn to embrace "the other" whose spiritual religious traditions may predate our own or those of the religious practices more familiar to us. We should remain attentive to how persons make meaning of their suffering—how they understand the why and the "what now?" of what is happening. Our nation's hospitals, prisons, military services, and psychiatric facilities are filled with African diasporal believers and/or practitioners, just as they are filled with Pentecostals, Roman Catholics, Muslims, Jews, and so on. The challenge comes when religious leaders and pastoral care professionals remain oblivious to the real existence of persons whose worldviews are radically different.

As we enter into relationship with Afro-Caribbean or Afro-Latina/o persons, which includes the English- and Spanish-speaking Caribbean, it becomes clear that there are biases within some religious communities that dismiss their traditions and worldviews as evil, denying the existence of the Divine. The fears are real, the threat perhaps just as real. I remember hearing a clinically trained chaplain make a flippant remark about Santeria, saying, "Santeria? Yes, those are the people who sacrifice chickens?" as he walked away with a slight smirk on his face. The ignorance remains. And this from a chaplain whose own religious practices involve the regular, but perhaps not too popularly known, use of animal sacrifices.

The Experience of Healing Traditions

Among those we may find in our communities are people who visit both physicians and faith healers, both *Babalawos* (Orisha priests) and Paleros/as, an Afro-Caribbean religion with roots in Central Africa. Cleansing rituals such as *ebbos*, offerings to appease the Orisha for healing, may be found in patients' hospital rooms, on the streets, and in parks, rivers, and oceans. There are only rough estimates as to how many persons are formally initiated into these traditions. Perhaps what is more important to note is that there are no initiations into the world-view, which remains relevant and prevalent even among the many who are not formally initiated into any of these traditions. Worldviews are passed on as soon as a child is born.

The Experience of Fear and Chaos

The concept of fear and chaos is prevalent among some believers and practitioners of these traditions. For some, the world is a place where danger lurks around each corner; for others, God created a world where people may live their lives fearlessly and boldly. Within the diasporal expressions of some of these traditions are persons who live free of some of the fear and chaos that impact the lives of others. There is a certain "fearlessness" that comes when a person feels connected to the Meta-intellect: the energy of the spirit world, Orishas, Orunmila (the prophet of God), and Olodumare (God). There are still others whose lives are fear-based. They believe that the world is an unsafe place, in both its physical and its spiritual realms, and constant vigilance is required. Caregivers with this population must be able to tune in to the signals as they emerge. An illness may be perceived as being caused by a spiritual entity who is angry with the client or patient. This is not too distant from the belief in some Christian circles that illness is caused by God to punish or correct inappropriate behavior.

To work with Latinos/as within the context of New York City requires the ability to listen for myriad racial, cultural, religious, and spiritual voices. Hailing from Puerto Rico, Cuba, Dominican Republic, Mexico, Ecuador, and other countries, our communities are living communities of diversity. Let's look at Joaquin, a forty-year-old man who arrived in the United States by crossing the waters from Cuba to Florida on a raft under cover of darkness. He was diagnosed as bipolar and has been in and out of hospitals and jails for years. When visited by a chaplain for the first time, he had been at a local psychiatric facility for almost four months. A psychiatrist made a referral for pastoral care. Dark-complexioned and portly, the patient spoke in measured cadences. The patient welcomed the chaplain's visit and spoke of having been incarcerated and hospitalized off and on for many years. When Joaquin spoke of life in Cuba and his dream of living in the United States, the chaplain wondered how he had prepared for the trip. The patient smiled and remained silent for several moments, studying the face of the chaplain as if looking for something.

Joaquin then spoke of making offerings to Yemonja, the Orisha of the ocean, for safe passage. He also shared that he was a fully initiated Santeria priest who was forced to leave all of his Orisha icons in Cuba. The patient believed that his emotional/spiritual problems may be traced to his having left his Orisha in another country. No one on the team had explored the how and meaning of Joaquin's physical (spiritual) journey.

Syncretism versus Integration

"Syncretism" is at times a disturbing term because it challenges us to somehow reduce someone's religious faith and doctrines to simple additions and subtractions. In the lives of our patients, clients, and congregants, we have to remain open to the integration that has already taken place before they enter our communities of faith, clinics, hospitals, offices, and prisons. In deeply listening, we honor as sacred the traditions that are being shared with us. Leadership requires that we remain curious about "the other" who may seem to be exactly like us on one level but quite different on other levels. It requires that we not only explore the feelings and thoughts that may emerge for us when the words of the "other" are confusing, but that we also pay attention to what may have been left unsaid.

Many of the indigenous diasporal religious traditions are oral traditions that have yet to be formally codified. This remains an ongoing discussion in religious communities, with some who support it, while others remain concerned about sharing secrets of the faith and the possible strangulation of the freedom that is inherent in oral traditions. What do you do when someone says, "Well, God told me this is the truth," or "The Spirits revealed the way we should go with this problem"? Each community interprets every situation in the same way dreams are interpreted; it is a profound process that honors the symbols and meanings of the community.

The resilience in these traditions often defies belief. Have we wondered about the indigenous person's or communities' ways of knowing? This is then further expanded in the cities of the United States, not only where large number of Afro-Caribbean people may be found, but where Afro-Latino/as may be found as well. The roots of these traditions may be traced to Africa during the enslavement and transport of enslaved Africans to the Americas. It is a story of the resilience and the ability of religious traditions, spiritualities, and worldviews to attempt to create new realities.

Key Things to Remember

- Just as there are many diverse ways of worshipping God in other religions, so too with indigenous religious traditions in the diaspora.

- There is *no one way* of practicing these traditions. In other words these are primarily oral traditions with no formal scriptures or one "Pope" recognized by all. They come close to the primitive church, yet the traditions predate Christianity.

- The worship community in Ifa is called Ile, and in Palo Mayombe, the Munanso—literally communities that gather for worship in people's homes. Just as in other religious communities, there is diversity in practices, customs, expressions, and so on.

How do these worldviews challenge members of the "mainline" religious traditions to engage and move forward? The challenges stem from various places. It is an essential truth that a new relationship within a new context is created each time we meet the other. Equally important is the realization that all of what we have lived, integrated, embraced, and rejected in our lives emerges at the point we meet with persons from diverse backgrounds. This holds true for the staunch, dedicated, and mature Christians, in whom we may still see glimpses of different cultures or worldviews.

Lessons from the Field of Pastoral Care

In the clinical pastoral care formation process, trainees are encouraged to explore their own lives as they explore the lives of others in crisis. We intentionally place them in situations where they must be fully present to "the other." We train them within a group, a village, where they learn how their own personal narratives may impact the patient's unfolding narrative. Yes, during group and individual supervision, they learn the technical side of pastoral care, but they also learn to listen to the rhythm of their own hearts. They listen to the beats and sit in the quiet spaces between the beats.

Working with people from diverse cultural backgrounds requires an ever-expanding sense of "awe"—a sense of the awesomeness of God's creation. It requires a sense of curiosity, the same curiosity that we as chaplains have about our patients and their loved ones. There is a sense of the sacredness of the space created the moment we begin to share time and space. Our patients teach us who they are by inviting us into their world. Persons from Afro-Caribbean and Afro-Latino/a contexts must be allowed to write their own stories, in their own voices. As spiritual leaders, we provide the space and "writing materials."

There is no room for assumptions of any kind. The living human web holds all of the knowledge, wisdom, and information we are called to explore. Earlier today, I received a phone call from a *Babalawo*, an Ifa priest. He wanted to inform me that in a couple of days a patient would arrive who will "self-identify" as a Roman Catholic, but whose adult children are practitioners of what is popularly known as Santeria. He shared that the family was "taking it hard" and needed to know that they would be fully welcomed for who they were.

While there is wide variation in many of these diverse indigenous religions, there may be room to establish as a framework the following doctrinal paradigm:

1. There is one God, called Olodumare.
2. Orunmila, or Orula in Ocha, is God's prophet.
3. There is no devil.
4. Except for the day you were born and the day you are destined to die, there is no single thing that cannot be divined (forecast), and when necessary, changed through *ebbos*, offerings to appease the Orishas.
6. It is your birthright to be happy, successful, and fulfilled.
7. You should grow and obtain wisdom during the process.
8. You are reborn through your blood relatives.
9. Heaven is "home," and earth "the marketplace." We are in constant passage between the two.
10. You are part of the universe in a literal, not figurative, way.
11. You must never initiate harm against another human being.
12. You must never harm the universe of which you are a part.
13. Your temporal and spiritual capacities must work together.
14. You are born with a specific destiny, or life path. It is your goal to travel it. Divination provides your road map.
15. Our ancestors exist and must be honored.

16. Sacrifice guarantees success.

17. The Orishas live within us.

18. You have no need for fear.

In some indigenous African-based diasporal religions, some may also hold to a simple view that there are "three legs of Ifa": ancestral worship, Orisha, and divination, which is essentially spiritual diagnosis using a family systems base to explore the issues impacting a family. Let's take a moment to explore the role that divination plays within some of these traditions. If we are speaking of the religion of Ifa, there are various levels of divination, the highest of which belongs to the *Babalawo*. To the *Babalawo*, or *Iyanifa* (woman), are revealed the secrets of divination through special initiations. Divination is not so much looking into the future, but an exploration of the person's life in a particular context at a particular time. Divination is in essence a spiritual assessment and diagnosis made by a specially trained priest. In the West Indies, we have the *Obeah* man or woman, and in Haiti the *Hougan*. The names of the titles may vary, but their roles center around bringing about healing and restoring balance in the lives of persons, families, or communities. The *Obeah* man or *Obeah* woman tends to work more independently.

The use of animal sacrifices to restore balance in a practitioner's life is neither rare nor common in some of the African diasporal religious traditions. It is perhaps one of the more controversial parts of the religious and spiritual practices. Because of the stigma that is often tied to the use of animals in rituals, practitioners seeking help may be very reluctant to share that they are not only believers but also practitioners of the religion. Animals are used in major initiation ceremonies, where the meat is then consumed in community. At other times, the animal is used as a scapegoat to help cleanse a home or village from negativity. The use of animals as practiced in both Orthodox Judaism and Islam is more acceptable to some than the animal sacrifices made in African diasporal traditions.

In closing, this is a brief overview of some of the dynamics that may emerge when working with persons from Afro-Caribbean and Afro-Latina/o backgrounds. I posit that the embracing of the worldview precedes a person's decision to fully initiate or not.

Further Reading

Ben-Jochannan, Yosef A.A. *African Origins of the Major "Western Religions."* Baltimore, MD: Black Classic Press, 1991.

De La Torre, Miguel A. *Santeria: The Beliefs and Rituals of a Growing Religion in America*. Grand Rapids, MI: William B. Erdmans Publishing Company, 2004.

Fu-Kiau, Kimbwandende Kia Bunseki. *African Cosmology of the Bantu–Kongo: Principles of Life and Living*. New York: Athelia Henrietta Press, 1980.

Idowu, E.Bolaji. *Olodumare: God in Yoruba Belief*. London: Longmans, 1962.

Neimark, Philip John. *The Way of the Orisa: Empowering Your Life through the Ancient African Religion of Ifa*. New York: HarperOne, 1993.

Olmos, Fernandez Margarite, and Lizabeth Parvasini-Gebert. *Creole Religions of the Caribbean: An Introduction from Vodou and Santeria to Obeah and Espiritismo*. New York: New York University Press, 2003.

———, ed. *Sacred Possessions: Vodou, Santeria, Obeah, and the Caribbean*. New Brunswick, NJ: Rutgers University, 2000.

Román, Miriam Jimenéz and Juan Flores, eds. *The Afro-Latin@ Reader: History and Culture in the United States*. London: Duke University Press, 2010.

Thompson, Robert Farris. *Flash of the Spirit: African & Afro-American Art & Philosophy*. New York: Vintage Books, 1984.

Warner-Lewis, Maureen. *Central Africa in the Caribbean: Transcending Time, Transforming Cultures*. Kingston, Jamaica: University of the West Indies Press, 2003.

About the Contributor

Rev. Carlos Alejandro, MS, MDiv, BCC, is the clinical pastoral education supervisor at New York's Calvary Hospital and is certified by the Association for Clinical Pastoral Education (ACPE). He has extensive experience in pastoral care and in clinical pastoral supervision in both traditional and challenging venues. The founding director of North General Hospital's Department of Pastoral Care and Education, Rev. Alejandro also created and led Harlem's Outreach Program for Emergencies (the HOPE team), a faith-based critical incident stress management (CISM) team. He went on to develop the first clinical pastoral education (CPE) supervisory training program in Puerto Rico, which is based in three hospitals and one major university. A board-certified chaplain with the Association of Professional Chaplains, he served as a corrections chaplain at Rikers Island Central Punitive Segregation Unit and at the Manhattan Detention Center, known as "the Tombs." A former journalist, Rev. Alejandro received a master's degree from Columbia University's Graduate School of Journalism and a master of divinity degree from New York Theological Seminary. An ordained minister with the Christian Church (Disciples of Christ), he lectures on Afro-Caribbean spirituality and pastoral care, spirituality and trauma, and cultural issues in end-of-life care.

23

Working with Asians

Miyon Chung, MACSW, MATh, PhD

The overall objective of this chapter is to delineate relevant and applicable insights about working with Asians in the context of Christian ministry in the twenty-first century. As basic and familiar as the name "Asia" is, however, there seems to be something inherently illusive, enigmatic, and complicated about what exactly constitutes Asia or Asians. Perhaps what the world recognizes more clearly is the idea of Asia rather than the specific constituents of Asia. For instance, Asia is generally associated with the terms "East" and "Orient." But precisely what are the geographic, racial, religious, cultural, and political boundaries of the East or Orient? Are the Middle East and Central Asia parts of Asia proper? What is meant by the ancient term "Asia Minor"? Siberia and Turkey are notable examples of the fluidity of Asian boundaries, for they represent both Europe and Asia. Furthermore, Asia also contains a number of offshore, island nations such as Sri Lanka, Malaysia, Indonesia, the Philippines, Taiwan, and Japan, some of which are closely aligned with the Pacific or Oceanic.

The most basic fact about Asia is that it is the world's most capacious and diverse continent, with the highest continental total population. It is also in Asia that the most varied cultural anthropological expressions are found. To learn to work with Asians, therefore, it is imperative to know and appreciate its diversity and complexity. Unlike Europe, Asia was never unified as a whole on ethnic, religious, linguistic, or political ground. As dominant and influential as China and India have been from the earliest days of the continent's settlement history, Asia remains highly pluralistic and heterogeneous.

Moreover, compared to Latin America or Africa, the European colonization of Asia, the Second World War, the Cold War, the contemporary technological revolution, and globalization have engendered more dramatic and diversified impact in Asia. Asia by no means is homogeneous or cohesive. In learning to work with Asians, therefore, one must proceed with caution in order not to make hasty generalizations. Even so, in trying to assist the reader with acquiring an introductory level of cultural literacy about Asia, attention is given to the points of convergence and not necessarily the distinctions.

The Regions of Asia

Stretching from the Pacific Ocean in the east to the Hindu Kush in the west, and from Siberia in the north to the Indian Ocean in the south, Asia covers 30 percent of the Earth's landmass (the eastern four-fifths of the massive Eurasian region).[1] Asia contains both the highest and the lowest points of the Earth's surface and the longest coastline, within which are found highly varied and extreme topographies and climates. Asia's vast and remarkable geophysical composition yields to the world's most variegated forms of environment, vegetation, biodiversity, and human adaptations thereof.

In Asia is found an exceptionally wide range of cultures, religions/spiritualities, political systems, philosophies, technologies, and societies. Asia is home to about 60 percent of the global population. Compared to inhabitants of other continents, Asians are most diversified in racial and ethnic backgrounds. They speak several hundred languages and dialects and worship countless numbers of deities. Therefore, the common practice is to divide the continent into large regions, each of which is composed of a number of countries. Although there are no universally agreed-upon divisions, most geographic literature divides Asia by physiographic characteristics, which also roughly coincide with religious and cultural anthropological affinities. They are North Asia, East Asia, Central Asia, Middle Asia, South Asia, and West or Southwest Asia.

The Face of Contemporary Asia

Asian societies are undergirded by religious, philosophical, and social traditions that have prevailed and evolved from ancient times to today. The postcolonial, post–World War II Asia, however, has been a battleground of polarized ideologies and phenomena—between capitalism and Communism, between nationalism and Westernization, and between the nation-state and globalization.[2] During the past few decades, it became obvious that Western influences have irrevocably and profoundly disturbed and impacted fundamental aspects of Asian life, even contributing to the erosion of traditions and destabilization of social orders and moral norms. Moreover, whereas the West has the shared heritage of Christendom and has chronologically journeyed through the medieval, the Enlightenment, and modern periods before arriving at the postmodern period, Asia is concurrently operating out of the traits of all of these periods. It would not be an exaggeration to say that the whole of Asia is in a state of flux, transience, and confusion and that coherence is difficult to achieve. As such, today's Asia is shaped by the dynamic and intricate interactions among Asia's ancient traditions and circumstances, Westernization, and globalization. In this section, the key aspects or issues of Asia's struggle in carving out its identity are outlined.

First of all, before the arrival of Europeans, Asian nations were ruled by monarchs, oligarchs, or tribal rulers, who were religiously significant figures as well. The postcolonial and post–World War II Asia, however, has been undergoing tumultuous and rapid changes that have resulted in political destabilization and secularization.[3] Although the West's philosophy, religion, education, and culture have infiltrated Asian societies, its political ideologies have affected Asia more acutely and pervasively. The postcolonial Asia faced the enormous challenge of establishing new national governments. Interestingly, no Asian country returned to the precolonial, traditional forms of government. Even Thailand (formerly known as the Kingdom of Siam), which was not colonized, reorganized itself as a constitutional monarchy in 1932. By the middle of the twentieth century, it was clear that all Asian nations were going to try out various Western political ideologies on their soil.

In addition, some of the people groups that had never functioned at the level of sovereign nations were coercively consolidated into what seemed to them alien countries, despite their strong resistance.[4] Examples include the Naga tribes, who were forced to become a part of India; the Chin, Kachin, and Karen tribes, who were enclosed into Burma (Myanmar); and Tibetans and (inner) Mongolians, who were incorporated into China. In fact, they are sometimes labeled as "nations within a nation." These people groups are markedly different in ethnicity, language, culture, and religion/spirituality and are systemically marginalized and persecuted by their national governments. To this day, these parts of Asia suffer from border disputes, tribal wars, and separatist movements.

Surprisingly, many key political leaders of formally colonized nations embraced Marxism. Marxist revolution swept across most of Asia—from India to Central, Southeast, and Far East Asia. Throughout the latter half of the twentieth century, Asia became the battleground of the Cold War, most notably the Korean War (1950–53), the Vietnam War (1955–75), the Laos War (1953–75), the Cambodian War (1965–75), and the Soviet War in Afghanistan (1979–89). Even though India, Malaysia, the Philippines, Japan, and South Korea were not turned over to Communism, the impact was not minimal. In Malaysia, it was not until 1989 that the Communists (Communist Party of Malaya) laid down their arms. In addition, at the turn of the century, Central Asia faced the collapse of the Soviet Union, and China implemented the Open Door Policy in economics, which has also generated similar changes in Vietnam and Cambodia.

Democracy was another alternative taken by many Asian nations. Singapore and Malaysia modeled their governments after European governments but in combination with indigenous political ideals. Japan, Korea, and Taiwan have successfully transitioned from feudalistic monarchy or dictator regimes to democracy. Unfortunately, the idea of democracy is relatively young, even unfamiliar, to the vast majority of the Asian populace; their governments are heavily corrupt and practice flagrant violations of human rights.

Second, Asians have demonstrated a profound religious consciousness throughout history. Religious beliefs and practices have governed Asian governments, societies, and daily life. Asia's encounter with the Western

Enlightenment thought, however, gave an impetus for secularization.[5] Especially, Marxist philosophy did much to demystify, undermine, and fragment Asian religious consciousness among the intelligentsia, even if they were not Communists. Interestingly, the Communist governments in Asia have imaged their revolutionary heroes as superhuman beings of high virtues and mystique. This is especially true in North Korea, where two of their deceased leaders have been attributed the status of demigods.

The most noteworthy influence of secularism is found in the establishment of secular states—the clearest such examples are China, Japan, Korea, Singapore, and Taiwan. While theocratic ideology of clerics still wields a strong influence, the governments of Bangladesh, Bhutan, India, Indonesia, Malaysia, Myanmar, Nepal, the Philippines, and Thailand are constitutionally declared as secular states. Moreover, despite the resurgence of Islamism and nationalism in the post-Soviet Central Asian countries, their governments have remained constitutionally secular.

Third, much of Asia was preindustrial even as late as the 1960s.[6] The Asian economy has been growing dramatically since the 1970s, rapidly and considerably impacting the global economy. As remarkable and accelerated as the growth is, however, many Asian countries (and areas within a developed country) still remain poor and underdeveloped by global standards. For instance, it would not be uncommon to discover in India or China a village that still maintains a preindustrial lifestyle. In addition, in many of their cities, one would easily find some residents living in a house furnished by modern technology, in stark contrast to their neighbors living without the benefits of running water or electricity. This is not just a problem of the poor cohabiting with the wealthy, although China and India have Asia's wealthiest and poorest people as their citizens. In the case of India, despite the stellar advancements in economy, education, and information technology that have brought the aged nation into the twenty-first century, it is undergoing a state of drastic transition.

Fourth, it was evident that the postcolonial Asia—particularly the cities—was irrevocably transformed by Western education and culture. Unlike the West, however, Asia has never thoroughly walked through the Enlightenment or implemented its implications. Today, Asian societies are in a state of flux in which people of the same time frame are concurrently operating out of premodern, modern, and postmodern ethos and worldviews. Even within a family, the problem of the generational gap is felt more severely than perhaps in Europe because of drastic and frequent changes in educational systems.

Fifth, the postcolonial Asia is also facing a rise of nationalism accompanied by the revival of traditionalism. The demise of colonial rule, economic growth, and more democratic governments are awakening a desire to search for roots and recultivate traditional philosophies, spiritualities/religions, and cultural expressions. And with this revival has come a strong impetus to reinstate centuries-old conventions and customs that embody and reflect Asian spirituality (spiritualities). The restoration of Confucianism and Feng Shui in China, the Saffronization Movement in India, and the rise of fundamental Islamic movements in Central Asia and Pakistan are some of the examples. Moreover, because these nationalists tend to regard globalization as Westernization or Americanism, they vigorously advocate anti-Western and anti-American policies.

Sixth, the contemporary Asia is walking through a process of globalization. Although Latin America and Africa are not exceptions to this phenomenon, the journey has been significantly more rapid and intense in Asia. Globalization in Asia can have two directions. On the one hand, colonization, Western education, media, and the Internet have brought the world to Asia. On the other hand, the Asian labor force and its products are reaching the world. Consequently, globalization has not only contributed to creating common experiences in Asia, but also de-territorialized and scattered Asians around the world. The diaspora or overseas Filipino workers are leading examples of globalization. Every year, more than 150,000 young Chinese students leave their country to study in the United Kingdom and United States alone. The highly homogeneous Japan and Korea have become homes to millions of international students and employees. In recent decades, international marriages in Korea have been increasing noticeably; nearly 35,000 cases of international marriages were reported in 2010.[7]

Seventh, Asia is a continent characterized by great suffering from frequently occurring, massive-scale environmental disasters, poverty, political instability, and gross violations of human rights. The disasters in the Asia Pacific Region are closely linked to the phenomenon of climate change (global warming) and its ramifications.[8] Major and minor scales of recurring earthquakes, volcanic eruptions, tsunamis, floods, cyclones, typhoons, and the rise of sea levels affect Asia more than any other continent. Asia also suffers from drought, deforestation, and pollution due to rapid and aggressive industrialization.

Moreover, behind the triumphal economic success stories reported from Asia lie severe violations of human rights.[9] Deplorable incidents of human trafficking, forced labor, child labor, slavery, genocide, religious and political persecutions and imprisonment, and oppression in general are regularly observed in the majority of Asian nations. Although the Association of South East Asian Nations established the Association of South East Asian Nations (ASEAN) Intergovernmental Human Rights in 2009, its content and effectiveness have been criticized by similar international organizations. Except for a few countries, the environmental crisis and political persecutions are exacerbating poverty, displacement of large people groups, and dangerous migrations.

Asian Ways of Thinking

Communication is indisputably critical to working with people of other regions or nations. In turn, communicating effectively or successfully requires understanding how people think and what they value. This section provides a chart that contrasts the values and thinking patterns of the East and the West. The chart is not meant to be definitively accurate or universally applicable to all of Asia, for it concentrates on the convergent features of East Asia and India.[10]

VALUES AND THINKING PATTERNS OF THE EAST AND WEST		
	East	West
Perception of reality is	in flux, complex, dynamic, flexible, interrelated, harmonious, holistic as a seamless whole	stable, static, constant, discrete/separate/atomic, dualistic with emphasis on the metaphysical world
Perception of time is	circular	linear
Future is	unpredictable (today's misfortune may be the basis of tomorrow's fortune)	providentially structured, logical outcome of the past and present

VALUES AND THINKING PATTERNS OF THE EAST AND WEST (continued)		
	East	**West**
Perceives nature/ environment in terms of	personification/deification, interdependent with the human community, respect, conservation	objectification, exploration (even exploitation)
Ethics is based on	contexts, social history, situation	universal laws
Values are	relative and pluralistic	absolute, noncompetitive
Comfortable with	contradictions, opposites, mystery, changes (there is a place for everything)	logical reasoning, tautology, eliminating what seems to be "out of place"
The content of philosophical analysis or orientation is	practical, concrete	conceptual, abstract
The goal of science is to produce	practical results (e.g., inventions), interconnect- edness of biophysical world	universal principles, classi- fications (taxonomy of the biophysical world)
The goal of scholarship is	receiving tradition, achieving consensus	freedom of expression, making inquiries to satisfy curiosity
Method of instruction is	learning and memorizing tradition	rhetoric, discussion, Socratic (dialogical)
Expectations from an individual are	loyalty, relationship	freedom, independence
Life is	a duty	a gift and an inherent/ fundamental right
Personal freedom is	relative to the group's survival	basic to the person's dignity
Personal identity is based on	family background or social position	the individual's personality and abilities
Makes judgment or decisions based on	collective (especially family) interests and experiences	the individual's convictions, principles, objectivity
When evaluating a situation, empha- sizes or relies on	contexts, personal experiences, intuition, feelings	logic, objectivity, principles, laws, contracts

	East	West
VALUES AND THINKING PATTERNS OF THE EAST AND WEST(continued)		
Group dynamics is governed by	collective interests	independent or autonomous interests
Prefers to work	in groups and with guidance	alone to produce innovative ideas
Style of communication is	indirect, poised, layered, unobtrusive, implicit, reserved (values silence and heavily relies on body language)	direct, expressive, logical, analytical, explicit (relies on what is clearly said)
Resolves tensions and conflicts through	deference to tradition or elders, finding a balance for everything has a place	debate, disputation, process of elimination
In business transactions, emphasizes	revision according to the newly rising contexts	honoring the original contract
In carrying out a mission, emphasizes	context, intuitive judgment	protocols, principles, written procedures and guidelines
Personal disposition to communicate is	modesty, deference, honor, blending in, reserved	prominence, confidence, individuality, transparency, friendliness
When ordering food in restaurants	everyone tends to ask for the same dish	the individual's preference determines what to eat
Social orders or structure is	indirectly expressed and enigmatic to the outsiders	relatively transparent for all to follow
Personal space is	relative	respected, assumed to be granted
Mannerism in a crowd tends to be	impersonal because other people's age or social position is undisclosed	guided by humanism (e.g., social etiquette such as "children and ladies first")
When traffic is congested	situation calls for over-looking some of the rules within reason (Japan and Singapore are notable exceptions)	continue to observe the rules

The Asian Church

Although Asia is most widely known for the origination and practices of Hinduism, Buddhism, and Taoism, its historical exposure to Christianity also goes as far back as the first century, even if one were to exclude Israel from Asia. According to a renowned Asian church historian, Samuel H. Moffett, it is highly probable that Christianity might have reached China at the end of the first century in continuance of Paul's missionary work.[11] There are also convincing mission trails by the apostle Thomas and subsequently by the Nestorians in India and Armenia.[12] Despite its long history, however, Asia is the least evangelized continent.

In recent years, the rise of nationalism and traditionalism accompanied by anti-American and anti-Western sentiments has caused increased persecution against Christian missionaries and local churches.[13] Korea and China have experienced an explosive rate of Christian conversion despite severe persecutions. Nevertheless, the Asian church faces the great challenges of carrying out culturally effective and biblically sound evangelism, protecting the biblical faith from syncretism and heresy, providing a sound theological education, sorting out the non-biblical Western elements, and producing doctrinally and ethically mature Christians.

In conclusion, when a given society encounters an era in which is compounded rapid and multiple dimensions of change, adjustment becomes much more stressful. The contemporary Asia is caught in a vortex of dramatic, complicated, rapid changes that create opportunities as well as threaten regional security. Asia is like a great and strange collage, assembled by the ethos and artifacts from different periods of history. Spiritually, Asia is an intense battleground for ancient spiritualities/religions. Inasmuch, working with Asians (especially Asian Christians) calls for a prophetic and eschatological engagement with the constantly arising new contexts and extremely diverse people.

Key Things to Remember

- Asians prefer the personal and practical. Highlight the practical aspects of a transaction or project rather than conceptualizing.

Take time to use personal experiences and stories rather than emphasizing principles.

- Asians value contexts more than static, absolute, universal principles. Fully pay attention to the changes in contexts and circumstances in the process of making decisions.
- Asian thinking is holistic, nonlinear, and contextual. Carefully observe nuances in conversation and avoid being explicit, head-on, direct. Directness can easily be construed as rudeness or arrogance.
- Asians are highly relational and collective. Earn trust by observing "Asian social protocols":
  - Project an attitude of quiet politeness and respect.
  - Establish personal conversations/relationships before talking about work.
  - Expect long introductions of persons involved before getting to the point of meeting.
  - Respecting the elders and the elder-statespersons is especially important. Do not be offended when asked to reveal your age, for age determines your place in a group.
  - When meeting people for the first time (especially people from Southeast or Southwest Asia), ask about their spirituality/religion, tribal or family heritage or genealogy, and where they live now.
  - Sharing a meal is a good way to begin a new relationship. Don't eat with the left hand, especially in the presence of Hindus and Muslims.
  - Presenting a gift to a visitor is common practice.
  - Avoid causing anyone to "lose face."
  - When in doubt, be low-key.
  - Speak less, listen more, and understand the body language and silence.
- The younger generation of Asians and many Asians who have studied or worked in the West are partially "Westernized." They are likely to manifest combined traits of the East and the West.

Notes

1. *Encyclopaedia Britannica Online*, s.v. "Asia," www.britannica.com/bps/search?query=Asia. Incidentally, in this chapter, Central Asia and the Middle East—though not intentionally or necessarily excluded—will not be specifically taken into account, for they will be covered in chapter 25, "Working with Muslims."

2. Mark T. Berger, *The Battle for Asia: From Decolonization to Globalization* (New York: Routledge Curzon, 2004), 1–36.

3. Xiaoming Huang, *Politics in Pacific Asia: An Introduction* (Sidney: Palgrave Macmillan, 2009).

4. Jacques Bertrand and André Laliberté, *Multination States in Asia: Accommodation or Resistance* (Cambridge: Cambridge University Press, 2010). See also Subir Bhaumick, "Ethnicity, Ideology, and Religion: Separatist Movements in India's Northeast," www.apcss.org/Publications/Edited%20Volumes/ReligiousRadicalism/PagesfromReligiousRadicalismandSecurityinSouthAsiach10.pdf.

5. Lucian W. Pye, *Asian Power and Politics: The Cultural Dimensions of Authority* (Cambridge, MA: President and Fellows of Harvard College, 1985). See also Steven R. Reed, "Analyzing Secularization and Religiosity in Asia," *Japanese Journal of Political Science* 8 (2007): 327–39.

6. Timothy Lee, "Shaping Unity in Diversity: A Missiological Approach to Theological Education in Asia," *Torch Trinity Journal* 11, no. 1 (November 2008): 7–11. See also David Birch, Tony Schirato, and Sanjay Srivastava, *Asia: Cultural Politics in the Global Age* (New York: Palgrave Macmillan, 2001), 25–85.

7. "2010 International Marriage Statistics," http://ref.daum.net/item/49486914.

8. Les Fussell, "The Challenges of a Changing Environment in Asia Pacific Region," *Torch Trinity Journal* 14, no. 1 (May 2011), 4–22.

9. Thomas Davis and Brian Galligan, *Human Rights in Asia* (Cheltenham, UK: Edward Elgar Publishing, 2011).

10. The chart was compiled using information found in Richard E. Nisbett, *The Geography of Thought: How Asians and Westerners Think Differently ... and Why* (New York: Fortress, 2003).

11. Samuel H. Moffett, *A History of Christianity in Asia: Beginning to 1500*, vol. 1 (New York: Harper Collins, 1992), 288.

12. J. Herbert Kane, *A Concise History of the Christian World Mission* (Grand Rapids, MI: Baker, 1978), 12–15.

13. Lee, "Shaping Unity in Diversity," 12–21.

Further Reading

Bautista, Julius, and Francis Khek Gee Lim, eds. *Christianity and the State in Asia: Complicity and Conflict*. New York: Routledge, 2009.

Freedman, Thomas. *The World Is Flat: A Brief History of the Twenty-First Century*. New York: Douglas & McIntyre, 2007.

Jenkins, Philip. *The Lost History of Christianity: The Thousand-Year Golden Age of the Church in the Middle East, Africa, and Asia—and How It Died*. New York: HarperCollins, 2008.

Kingsberry, Damien, and Leena Avonius. *Human Rights in Asia: A Reassessment of the Asian Value Debate*. Sidney: Palgrave Macmillan, 2008.

Mabubani, Kishore. *Can Asians Think? Understanding the Divide between East and West*. South Royalton, VT: Steerforth Press, 2002.

Mitter, Rana. *Modern China: A Very Short Introduction*. Oxford: Oxford University Press, 2008.

Phan, Peter C., ed. *Christianity in Asia*. Blackwell Guides to Global Christianity. Oxford: Blackwell, 2011.

Wolpert, Stanley. *India*. 4th ed. Berkeley: University of California Press, 2009.

Yahuda, Michael B. *The International Politics of the Asia-Pacific*. 3rd ed. New York: Routledge, 2009.

About the Contributor

Miyon Chung, MACSW, MATh, PhD, an associate professor of systematic theology, teaches systematic theology and ethics at Torch Trinity Graduate School, Seoul, Korea. She was born in Seoul but immigrated with her family to the United States in 1979. She received her BA (government/pre-law) from the University of Texas at Austin and subsequently received two master's degrees at Southwestern Baptist Theological Seminary, in church social work and in theology. While working on her PhD in theology at Southwestern Baptist Theological Seminary, Dr. Chung taught classes in systematic theology as a teaching fellow and concurrently served as academic dean of Dallas Korean Seminary and Guatemala Baptist Seminary. Since returning to Korea, Dr. Chung has been serving at Suwon Central Baptist Church as a translator. She also teaches at the church's associated Bible College. Her international ministries include working with Baptist World Alliance, Asia Pacific Baptist Fellowship, Diaspora Track of Lausanne Consultation on World Evangelism, and Global Diaspora Network.

24

Working with Jewish Communities

Myths to Be Unlearned

Rabbi Joseph Potasnik, BA, MS, JD, and
Rabbi Craig Miller, BA, MAFM

This chapter presents a mere tasting of aspects of the Jewish community. A comprehensive guide would extend to hundreds of pages. The scaffolding that we present will equip spiritual leaders with a basic understanding of some of the issues they will confront when interacting with the Jewish community.

Myths to Be Unlearned

Let's start with stating some misconceptions that this chapter, hopefully, will correct. A common narrative that many faiths have about Jews is as follows:

> Jews are followers of the "Old Testament." Their religion is work based, and they believe that their actions lead to salvation. Traditional Jews follow their scripture in the same manner as evangelical Christians, that is, as the unmediated Word of God. Jews are united in uncritical support of Israel, which serves as the headquarters of the Jewish religion.

Over the course of this chapter you will see that each of these preconceptions is wrong and that the reality of the Jewish community is more complex and interesting.

One important note: The Jewish community never refers to itself as Hebrews; we are Jews.

People of the Book

Jews are known as people of the Book. The Book is called in Hebrew the *Torah*. While on one level this refers to the first five books of the Bible (also called the Five Books of Moses), its meaning is much broader. *Torah* also refers to the entire corpus of biblical writings (the Hebrew Bible, which is what is referred to as the Old Testament by Christians), the centuries of rabbinic commentaries (including the Talmud), and the code of laws derived from these writings.

Jewish views of the Bible are extremely nuanced. The most traditional Jews hold that the Five Books of Moses are the direct communication by God to Moses. Other parts of the Jewish community, including the majority of Jews in America, believe it was written under varying levels of divine inspiration.

Jewish tradition holds that at the same time the written text was given, a parallel oral law developed that served to explain and expand on the written text. This oral law was passed down from teacher to student in an unbroken chain of tradition, until it was written down in the Talmud. The Talmud and its commentaries allow Torah to be a living, relevant guide to life according to God's will. The specific actions required of Jews are referred to as mitzvot.

One quick theological point: The goal of Judaism is a relationship with God and the creation of a better world (known in Hebrew as *tikkun olam*). Ours is not a faith of ultimate salvation. Based on our Torah, we presume a relationship with God and seek to improve it. This is done through performance of mitzvot, character development, and developing a stronger faith in God.

Overview of the Jewish Community

It is important to understand that Judaism defines both a religion and a people. One either is born into this community or converts into it. Being a Jew defines a person's status, not his or her beliefs.

No religious community is monolithic. The Jewish community can be categorized in many ways. A common way is by degree of attachment to the traditional understanding of Jewish law.

Roughly this breaks down into the following divisions often called movements:

- **Ultra-Orthodox:** Those who have the strictest interpretation of Jewish law and live their lives accordingly.

- **Orthodox:** Those who hold that the Torah is from God and follow it, but not necessarily with the strictest interpretation.

- **Conservative:** Those who hold that the Torah is divine but not necessarily given by God. They follow Jewish law but seek to incorporate modern understanding into their practice.

- **Reform:** The most liberal end of the spectrum. The Reform movement seeks to fully engage with the modern world and is the most willing to experiment with liturgical changes.

There are a number of other expressions of Judaism. For instance, the Reconstructionist movement has a nuanced approach toward living a Jewish life in the modern world, while Jewish Renewal seeks a more spiritual, from-the-heart approach. Often these movements mix and blend with each other to create innovative worship experiences.

Each of these movements has mechanisms to train and ordain leadership. The two most common positions are the rabbi, who acts as spiritual leader and guide, and the cantor, who is trained in leading the liturgical portions of the service.

Most synagogues retain a large degree of control over their internal and liturgical life, and a great deal of variation exists even among synagogues of the same movement.

In addition to religious organizations, there are many Jewish nonprofit organizations with missions to promote social welfare, community relations, support Israel, and so on.

Who Is a Jew?

Traditionally, a Jew was defined as a person whose mother was Jewish or who converted according to Jewish law. This is known as matrilineal descent. Those born Jewish retain their status regardless of their individual belief system or behavior.

Within the Orthodox and Conservative movements, this standard is retained. In the Reform and Reconstructionist movements, patrilineal descent is accepted and non-Jewish spouses may be given a role in synagogue life.

Sacred Time

Judaism created sacred times, specific periods to commemorate important events in Jewish history. The Jewish calendar is based on the lunar cycle, while the secular one is solar. Because a lunar year is eleven days shorter than a solar one, Jewish holidays will occur at different times of the secular year. Occasionally a leap month is added to adjust the Jewish calendar so the Jewish holidays stay within a three-week band of the secular calendar. It is important to note that the Jewish day begins at sundown, not midnight.

The Sabbath, or Shabbat, is the traditional day of rest. It begins Friday at sundown and extends twenty-five hours to Saturday night. The Sabbath maintains its restful character through a series of positive and restrictive commandments.

The Sabbath is observed with wide variation. For many families, there will be a Friday night family dinner, which may be preceded or followed by attendance at a synagogue. For the more traditional and Orthodox, the Sabbath is literally another world, with no use of cars or turning on or off of electrical appliances. Other Jews may observe their day of rest in less traditional ways.

Besides the weekly Sabbath cycle, there exists a yearly cycle of different holidays. The major holidays are as follows:

- **High Holy Days:** The "Days of Awe" are observed in the early fall, starting with the New Year, **Rosh Hashanah**, and ending ten days later with the Day of Repentance, **Yom Kippur**. Yom Kippur is marked by a daylong fast and very long synagogue services.

- **Passover,** or Pesach, an early spring holiday, commemorates the Exodus from Egypt and is a time when no leavened bread is eaten; instead, matzah (unleavened flat bread) is consumed.

The first two nights are marked by a festive meal at the home known as the seder.

- **Shavuot** takes place seven weeks after Passover and commemorates the giving of the Torah on Mount Sinai.

- **Sukkot,** or Feast of Tabernacles, is an autumn harvest festival commemorating the booths (*sukkot*) used during the forty years spent in the desert after the Exodus from Egypt. *Sukkot* (sing., sukkah) are set up outside to partake of festive meals.

- **Purim** commemorates the story in the book of Esther. This celebration consists of a festive meal and the reading of the book of Esther in synagogue, including loud boos when Haman's, advisor to the King of Persia, name is read; costumes are worn by kids of all ages.

- **Chanukah,** the eight-day festival of lights, is celebrated in early winter. This marks the Jewish liberation of the ancient Jerusalem Temple from the occupying Greek army. The most visible symbol is the candelabra called the menorah. Each night for eight nights an additional candle is lit, and afterwards presents are exchanged.

- **Modern commemorations:** Two modern holidays were developed in the twentieth century: **Yom HaShoah,** Holocaust Remembrance Day, and **Yom HaAtzma'ut,** Israeli Independence Day.

Sacred Living

Kosher Food

Kosher simply means "proper" or "fit." It has nothing to do with whether a rabbi "blessed" the food. Kosher refers to the decree that food adhere to the code of Jewish law. For instance, is the food free of meat from a forbidden animal, such as pig, or shellfish? Was the meat prepared in a prescribed way?

Because milk and meat cannot be mixed under kosher law, there will be a determination of whether the food item is (1) meat, (2) dairy, or (3) neither (i.e., pareve). The laws of keeping kosher are complicated and involved. The more traditional segments of the Jewish community follow a very stringent standard. There are variations in kosher observance among other Jews.

Kosher food production is overseen in most cases by private organizations that supervise to some degree the production of commercial food items. These organizations place a symbol on the packaging to indicate to the consumer that the item was supervised by them. The most well-known symbol is the OU (run by the Orthodox Union).

Prayer

For thousands of years prayer has been central to the Jewish relationship with God. The most common prayers are blessings over food and the *Kaddish*, the prayer said by mourners. Traditionally, Jewish prayer is based on a foundation of three fixed daily services: morning, afternoon, and evening. For many segments of the community, the most frequent time to pray in the synagogue is the Sabbath and the High Holy Days, with the latter having the largest turnout.

The Role of Women

The role of women varies greatly throughout the Jewish community. In most segments, women have full leadership and participatory roles in all institutions. All movements except the Orthodox and ultra-Orthodox ordain women as rabbis.

The Orthodox segments of the Jewish community do not have women in prominent public leadership roles, nor do they ordain women as rabbis. Men and women from the more Orthodox segments will not touch a member of the opposite gender who is not their spouse; this includes shaking hands.

Israel

The rebirth of a Jewish homeland in the Middle East is one of the most defining events for Jews throughout the world.

Israel is a Jewish state and a central focus of concern for the vast majority of Jews worldwide. It is important to note that Israel is not a religious community run for the greater glory of God. Rather, it is a secular democracy, although contention is often along religious and ethnic lines.

Israel faces many internal problems regarding fair economic growth, creation of opportunity, and maintenance of a stable society. Its problems with foreign and internal enemies are well known. While the majority of its citizens are not religious and may be quite secular, its religious community is a strong and very visible bloc.

Israel is in no way the capital of Judaism. There are many respected institutions of advanced Torah learning in Israel, yet none is universally recognized as having control over the Jewish community. In fact, the only world religion whose world headquarters is located in Israel is the Bah'ai, with its large temple in the port city of Haifa.

While the vast majority of the Jewish community is assertively supportive of Israel and its interests, there is by no means uncritical support for every action of the Israeli government. Do not be surprised to find prominent Jewish leaders publicly disagreeing with Israeli government policies.

The Holocaust

How the Jewish community relates to Christian communities in particular and the larger religious world in general is often mediated by a long history of anti-Semitism. The culmination of this was the murder of six million Jews during the Nazi Holocaust of 1933–45. The willful slaughter of innocent men, women, and children solely on the basis of their Jewish identity is more than just history. The Holocaust often serves as a template in how Jews see their political and social situation. Anti-Semitic attacks or threats to Israel often remind Jews about the Holocaust.

Jesus and "Hebrew-Christians"

Jesus in many ways forms the point of separation between the Jewish and Christian communities. No matter how similar we may be in how we relate to God, practice good deeds, or love God, Jesus is not part of our worship or relationship with God.

Often a Jew is asked by Christians, who do you think Jesus is or was? This is often an unfair question that presumes the hearer has a large store of historical and theological information. The more honest question to ask is, who was Jesus not? The Jewish answer is clear, no matter whether one is a Reform, Conservative, Orthodox, or ultra-Orthodox Jew: Jesus was not divine, he was not a unique son of God, he did not fulfill the messianic prophecies, and he did not come to change the content of the Jews' covenant with God. In other words, Jesus does not have theological significance to the content of Jewish thought or practice.

One of the most irritating points of Jewish-Christian relationships involves Christian organizations that claim to be the Jesus-believing part of the Jewish community. While we are famous for disagreeing over almost everything, understand that there is almost unanimous consensus over this: A person cannot accept Christian teachings regarding Jesus and remain part of the Jewish community.

How You Can Effectively Relate to the Jewish Community

From this chapter it should be clear that as a leader you will not be interacting with *the* Jewish community, but rather with a section of it. When you are about to interact with your local Jewish community, either as a local spiritual leader or in some other capacity, do your homework. Find out what you can about the members of the Jewish community you will be working with and where they stand on some of the issues raised.

Will you be working with a Jewish communal organization or with a synagogue? Will the interaction be social, political, or religious? A great place to start is to look at the website of the organization. If your partner will be a rabbi, his or her sermons should be available online; read them through the lens offered in this chapter.

As you can see, our community is complicated and varied. Navigating it can be confusing at times. We hope that this chapter can make your collaboration with our community more meaningful.

About the Contributors

Rabbi Joseph Potasnik, BA, MS, JD, is the former president and presently the executive vice president of the New York Board of Rabbis, the largest interdenominational body of its kind in the world. He is also the senior rabbi at Congregation Mount Sinai in Brooklyn Heights,

New York. He is the cohost, along with Deacon Kevin McCormack, of WABC's Sunday morning talk radio program *Religion on the Line*, and he is the religious commentator for 1010 WINS radio. He also hosts the award-winning television series *Faith to Faith*.

He has served on the New York City Campaign Finance Board, on the New York City Human Rights Commission, and as chaplain of the New York Press Club. As chaplain of the New York City Fire Department and the Fraternal Order of Police, Rabbi Potasnik helped many families cope with the disaster of September 11, 2001.

Rabbi Craig Miller, BA, MAFM, serves as treasurer of the New York Board of Rabbis and as a member of the board of directors of the International Rabbinic Fellowship. Rabbi Miller works in the area of interfaith, disaster chaplaincy, and campus spiritual advising. In the latter capacity, he serves the Jewish community of Baruch College, in New York City. Rabbi Miller was one of the original Red Cross chaplains trained after 9/11, and he was stationed at the Family Assistance Center and Ground Zero.

25

Working with Muslims

Imam Muhammad Hatim, PhD, DMin, and
Shaykh Ibrahim Abdul-Malik, PhD, EdD

A short chapter, by definition, imposes limits on the amount of material it can contain. This limitation is particularly challenging when the assignment is to offer "lessons in leadership" for non-Muslim spiritual leaders who may be unfamiliar with Muslims and have not yet acquired a working knowledge of Islam.

It is undoubtedly true that among the components of effective leadership are knowledge and understanding of the traditions and religious beliefs of those who are being "led," counseled, or advised. It is also true that other equally important factors include compassion, respect, humility, and a desire to learn (as opposed to "I know; so just listen"). In fact, these personal attributes can go a long way toward helping leaders overcome the deficits of not having the knowledge and understanding of their clients' religious beliefs.

It is almost enough that the leader be mindful of Allah's declaration in the Qur'an, a declaration that really puts everything in perspective with respect to our diversity. It is no accident, and it is not designed to promote division and conflict. On the contrary, our very cultural, religious, linguistic, national, and tribal differences are an invitation for us to "know each other," not to despise each other. For in the eyes of Allah, it is only our righteousness that matters:

> O mankind! We created you from a single (pair) of a male and
> a female, and made you into nations and tribes, that ye may

know each other (not that ye may despise each other). Verily, the most honored of you in the sight of Allah is (he who is) the most righteous of you. And Allah has full knowledge, and is well acquainted (with all things). (*Surah* al-Hujurat 49:13)

Yes! The question is not either-or. The truly effective religious leaders enhance these critical attitudes—*respectful, compassionate, humble, patient*—with as sound and comprehensive a knowledge of the clients' beliefs as possible. Accordingly, the rest of this short chapter will offer some basic information about Islam and Muslims, their beliefs and practices.

Who Is the Islamic Community in America?

Islam is the second largest religion in the world and the fastest growing religion in the United States. There are some 1.3 billion Muslims world-wide, an estimated 5 million in the United States. The Muslim community in the United States consists of the indigenous African American Muslims (descendants of formerly enslaved Africans who were forced to immigrate to America) and immigrant Muslim communities (individuals who volunteered to come to the United States for social or economic reasons). Although estimates vary, the American Muslim Council in 1992 suggested that in the United States the African American Muslims were the largest group at 42 percent, followed by South Asians, 24 percent; Arabs, 12.4 percent; Africans, 5.2 percent; and others, 16.4 percent.[1] There are an estimated 1,209 masjids in the United States,[2] and about 70 masjids in New York City.[3]

Islam: Submission to the Will of Allah

In the Arabic language, the word "Islam" has the equivalent meaning to the English concept of submission—submission to the will of Allah. The meaning also implies a sense of surrender and obedience. Those who freely submit their will to the will of Allah are referred to as Muslim. In other words, Muslims are those who give themselves over to the divine command. The word "Islam" comes from the same root as the word *salaam*, which means "peace."

It is in the remembrance of Allah alone that the hearts really find peace. (*Surah* ar-Ra'd 13:28)

A person's intention (*niya*) is significant in Islamic religious practices. Two people completing the same righteous act are not automatically deserving of the reward. The deciding factor is the intention behind the act. Even a "righteous" act can be performed for nefarious reasons:

> But there is no blame on you if ye make a mistake therein. What counts is the intention in your hearts. (*Surah* al-Ahzab 33:5)
>
> Allah will not call you to account for thoughtlessness in your oaths, but for the intention in your hearts. (*Surah* al-Baqarah 2:225)
>
> Actions are but by intention, and every man shall have but that which he intended.[4]

Islamic Faith and Belief

The religion of Islam comprises one point of faith, several points of belief, and a worship system.

Faith[5] and the Oneness of Allah

The one point of faith is *faith in Allah alone*, as the One God, the One and Only. Allah has *no* associates. *La illaha illallah*, "There is no deity/god except Allah." Allah does not beget. Allah was not begotten. Allah is not in need of anything. Allah alone is worthy of worship.

This unique faith is what distinguishes Islam (the religion) and Muslims (the practitioners) from other religions and their adherents. This concept of faith is based upon the revelations of the Holy Qur'an as follows:

> Say: Allah is One.
> Allah is on whom all depend.
> Allah begets not, nor is Allah begotten.
> And none is like Allah.
>
> (*SURAH* AL-IKHLAS 112:1–4)

The worship of anything other than Allah can lead to spiritual distress, grief, and/or other forms of punishment:

> Yet there are men who take (for worship) others beside Allah, as equal (with Allah). For they love them as they should love Allah. *But those of faith are overflowing in their love for Allah.* If only the unrighteous could see, behold, they would see the

punishment: that to Allah belongs all power, and He will strongly enforce the punishment. (*Surah* al-Baqarah 2:165)

Islamic Beliefs

The several points of belief include the following.

BELIEF IN THE ANGELS OF ALLAH

Angels are beings created from light, have no free will, and can only perform the duties as commanded by Allah.

> Angels ... who do not disobey God in whatever He has commanded them, but [*always*] do what they are bidden to do. (*Surah* at-Tahrim 66:6)

Logically, then, angels *cannot* disobey God. From this premise, the concept of "fallen angel" is entirely inconsistent and, indeed, is widely rejected among Muslims. This, despite the view that insists that Iblis (he disobeyed God) was an angel and not a jinn. Angels do, however, have the ability to reason, as explained in the Holy Qur'an:

> And when your Lord said to the angels, I am going to place in the earth a *khalifa* [representative/vicegerent], they said: "What! Wilt Thou place in it such as shall make mischief in it and shed blood, and we celebrate Thy praise and extol Thy holiness?" He said: "Surely I know what you do not know." (*Surah* al-Baqarah 2:30)

Angels have been used to communicate divine revelations to humankind. As examples, Angel Gabriel brought the news of Jesus's impending birth to Mary, and Angel Gabriel also brought to Prophet Muhammad the Qur'an, which was revealed over a period of twenty-three years.

> Say [O Prophet]: "Whosoever is an enemy of Gabriel" (who, verily, by God's leave, has brought down upon thy heart this [divine writ] which confirms the truth of whatever there still remains [of earlier revelations], and is a guidance and a glad tiding for the believers).... (*Surah* al-Baqarah 2:97–98)

BELIEF IN THE BOOKS OF ALLAH

The books of Allah are the Torah (*Taurat*), the Psalms of David, the Gospel (*Injeel*) of Jesus, and the Qur'an.

This is *The Book*; in it is guidance sure, without doubt, to those who
fear Allah, who believe in the Unseen, are steadfast in prayer, and spend
out of what We have provided for them. (*Surah* al-Baqarah 2:2–3)

He has revealed to you the Book ... and He revealed the *Taurat* and the *Injeel*. (*Surah* al-i'lmran 3:3)

Behold, We have inspired thee [O Prophet] just as We inspired
Noah and all the prophets after him

... *and as We vouchsafed unto David a book of divine wisdom*. (*Surah* an-Nisaa 4:163)

BELIEF IN THE MESSENGERS OF ALLAH

Some of the messengers of Allah were Noah, Abraham, Moses, Jesus,
and Muhammad (peace and blessings be upon them), and many of
them are not known to us by name. According to the Qur'an, Muhammad is "the Seal of the prophets," that is, he is the *final* link in the long
chain of messengers whom Allah has sent to humankind.

Muhammad is not the father of any of your men, but he is the
Messenger of Allah, and the Seal of the prophets. And Allah has
full knowledge of all things. (*Surah* al-Ahzab 33:40)

As Muslims, we make no distinction among any of Allah's prophets,
who were all *only* human, men and women. They were Allah's filters,
through whom the message could be cleanly transmitted without its
being affected by any interference or pollution. What qualified them
most for their mission was that all of them had risen to a high level of
morality and spiritual consciousness in relation to their people.

Many of us are familiar with the big names: Abraham, Isaac, and
Ishmael, the older brother who is the progenitor of the Islamic peoples.
Here are three lesser knowns, as recorded in the Qur'an:

And unto [the tribe of] 'Ad [*We sent*] *their brother Hud*. He said: "O
my people! Worship God [alone]: You have no deity other than Him.
[As it is,] you are but inventors of falsehood!" (*Surah*, al-Araf 7:65)

And unto [the tribe of] Thamud [*We sent*] *their brother Salih*.
He said: "O my people! Worship God alone; you have no deity
other than Him." (*Surah* al-Araf 7:73)

And unto [the people of] Madyan [*We sent*] *their brother
Shu'ayb*. He said: "O my people! Worship God alone; you have
no deity other than Him." (*Surah* al-Araf 7:85)

As Muslims, we honor Prophet Jesus (*Isa*), who, with his mother, Mary, is highly revered in the Qur'an. Indeed, *surah* 19 (Maryam) is named for the mother of Jesus. Here are some of the Qur'an's words about Jesus and Mary:

> His name will be Christ Jesus, the son of Mary, held in honor in this world and the Hereafter, and of (the company of) those nearest to Allah. (*Surah* al-i'lmran 3:45)
>
> To Jesus the son of Mary, We gave clear (Signs), and strengthened him with the Holy Spirit. (*Surah* al-Baqarah 2:253)
>
> O Mary! Allah hath chosen [you], and purified [you]; chosen [you] above the women of all nations. (*Surah* al-i'lmran 3:42)
>
> And (remember) her who guarded her chastity. *We breathed into her of Our Spirit*, and *We made her and her son a Sign for all peoples*. (*Surah* al-Anbiyaa 21:91)

BELIEF IN JINN BEINGS

Jinns are beings that were created before humans, from smokeless flames (fire).

> And indeed, We have created man out of sounding clay, out of dark-slime transmuted, whereas the invisible beings We had created, long before that, out of the fire of scorching winds. (*Surah* al-Hijr 15:26–27)

In the Holy Qur'an, jinns are described as rational beings who can hear, discern, appreciate truth, and correct sinful behavior. Among the jinns, there are those who submit to the will of Allah and those who do not. Therefore, jinns will ultimately be judged, like humans, on the Day of Judgment. Contrary to popular beliefs, not all jinns are inherently devilish or evil.

> Say: "It has been revealed to me that some of the unseen beings gave ear to this divine writ, and thereupon said [unto their fellow-beings]: 'Verily, we have heard a wondrous guiding toward consciousness of what is right; and so we have come to believe in it. And we shall never ascribe divinity to anyone beside our Sustainer.'" (*Surah* al-Jinn 72:1–2)
>
> But [as for those who refuse to avail themselves of divine guidance,] that word of thy Sustainer shall be fulfilled: "Most certainly will I fill hell with invisible beings, as well as with humans, all together." (*Surah* Hud 11:119)

Human beings are different from jinns. Allah gave humans mercy from Allah to Adam, then commanded the angels and jinns to bow down to Adam. They all did, except Iblis, a jinn, who was also identified as a *shaytan* (devil). The name *Iblis* implies one who is proud or haughty. The word *shaytan* is used to refer to someone who rebels against Allah's commandments. It also connotes the idea of perversity or enmity.

BELIEF IN THE LAST DAY—THE DAY OF JUDGMENT— AND IN THE HEREAFTER

This is the belief that the life of humans is not without a meaningful end and that death is certain. It also suggests that life, as we understand it, will one day cease to exist, and Allah will confront everyone with a record of the life they have lived while on earth. Then, depending on the weight of evil and good deeds of each individual, Allah will determine whether to grant each person the reward of paradise or the punishment of hell.

> And know, O man, that *the last hour is bound to come, beyond any doubt*, and that God will indeed resurrect all who are in their graves. (*Surah* al-Hajj 22:7)

BELIEF IN DIVINE ORDINANCE

Allah's laws operate in every phase of our lives. When we obey those laws, we are rewarded. When we violate them, we suffer the consequences.

Islamic Worship System (Ibadah)

Islam consists of a unique set of religious acts. They include, but are not limited to, the following:

Bearing Witness to the Oneness of Allah and to the Messengership of Muhammad

This is usually expressed in the words *La illaha illallah, Muhammadan rasul allah*, "There is no god but Allah, Muhammad is a messenger of Allah." These words constitute the *shahaadah*, which is the public declaration of faith.

In a certain sense, the *shahaadah* could be thought of as a "rite of passage" through which a non-Muslim passes to become a Muslim.

Clearly, the process requires much more than the mere recitation of a few words. At the very least, the person will have studied the essentials of Islamic faith, belief, and worship, and the recitation represents the person's sincere acceptance of and commitment to them. Persons born into a Muslim family typically do not take the *shahaadah*.

Performing the Five Daily Prayers (*Salaat*): Morning (*Fajr*), Noon (*Dhuhr*), Afternoon (*Asr*), Evening (*Maghrib*), Night (*Isha*)

Allah created all living things for the purpose of worshipping Allah. Through regular prayer, people keep themselves in tune with the universal scheme of creation.

Before Muslims engage in any of these formal prayers, they must perform ablutions called *wudu*. For the believer, *wudu* is more than mere washing of the appropriate body parts. It is done with a prayerful attitude, in preparation for the impending communication with the Almighty.

The prayers may be said in congregation or alone. In either situation, the worshippers face toward the Kaaba in Mecca. Muslim males are also required to attend the Friday congregational prayers (*salaat-ul-jumah*). Muslim women are urged to and do attend, but attending is not an obligation for them. *Salaah* is a ritual performed according to a prescribed sequence, in the same way as it was done by Prophet Muhammad. All formal prayers are recited in Arabic.

Muslims also pray informally, whenever and wherever they desire, as many times as they choose, sitting, walking, lying down, speaking whatever language they select. These informal prayers are called *du'a*.

Paying the Religious Tax (*Zakat*)

Zakat is often mistakenly translated only as "charity." Its root word has the meaning "to purify." Muslims are required to pay a specified amount of tax to the Islamic community or state in which they are members. This exemplifies the fact that Muslims must be "formal members" of a Muslim collective in order to meet their religious obligations. The payment of *zakat* not only economically supports the community, but also acts to purify the soul of the payer.

Keeping the Fast of the Holy Month of Ramadan

Muslims are required to fast each day during the month of Ramadan, from dawn to dusk. The fast requires that the person refrain from all food and drink (including water) and from all sexual activity during the daylight hours. These abstentions are minimal, however. The much deeper meaning of the fast is spiritual. It is an opportunity for all believers to deepen their spiritual practices and to emerge from the month-long involvement better equipped spiritually to face the challenges of the ensuing year.

Making a Pilgrimage to the Holy City of Mecca

During the hajj season, Muslims are required to perform the pilgrimage to the holiest shrine in Islam—the Kaaba, which is located in the city of Mecca, Saudi Arabia. It is obligatory on all Muslims to make the pilgrimage at least once in their lifetime. Exemptions are made for those persons who are not physically and/or economically equipped to make the journey. The Kaaba is also known as the "House of Allah." Tradition says that it was built by Prophet Abraham (Ibrahim) and his son Ishmael (Ismail).

Engaging in Jihad—Struggle, Striving

In the popular mind, the word "jihad" means "holy war," implying Qur'anic sanction of an aggressive war waged by Muslims against non-Muslim societies. Against this distortion, we offer two facts that clearly state the Qur'an's answer to the misrepresentation.

First, Muslims are permitted to defend themselves; that is, they have the right to fight back when they are attacked, and they may engage only in defensive wars to protect the faith. But we are warned not to be excessive in our response. And further, the moment the enemy stops fighting and seeks peace, we are instructed to end all hostilities.

> Fight, in the cause of Allah, those who fight you. *But do not transgress limits*; for Allah loveth not transgressors. (*Surah* al-Baqarah 2:190)
>
> To those against whom war is made, permission is given (to fight), because they are wronged. And verily, Allah is most powerful for their aid. (*Surah* al-Hajj 22:39)

> But if they cease, *let there be no hostility*, except to those who
> practice oppression. (*Surah* al-Baqarah 2:193)
>
> But if the enemy incline toward peace, *do [you] (also) incline
> toward peace*, and trust in Allah; for Allah is the one that heareth
> and knoweth [all things]. (*Surah* al-Anfal 8:61)

Second, the much more important meaning of the word "jihad" is
"struggle" or "striving." And indeed, this meaning represents the *greater*
jihad. For the struggle is within oneself and refers to the great effort it
requires to put God's will into practice at every level—personal, social,
and political. This struggle is a constant in our daily living.

> The strong is not the one who overcomes the people by his
> strength, *but the strong is the one who controls himself while in
> anger*. (*Hadith* al-Bukhari 8:135)
>
> Behold! As for those who attain to Faith, and do righteous
> deeds, We do not fail to requite any *who persevere in doing good*.
> (*Surah* al-Kahf 18:30)

Finding and exercising the courage to speak truth to power, that is
jihad. Doing the difficult thing (because it is morally right), as opposed
to taking the easy way that would violate your moral principles, that
is jihad. Working to relieve the suffering of victims of injustice or to
improve the living conditions in the society, that is jihad.

Muslim Education and Leadership

The existing professional routes by which a person can become
an imam include mentorship under a *shaykh* (or *shaykha*; a title of
respect, usually accorded to elders and leaders in the community) or
Islamic scholar, graduation from or matriculation at an Islamic school/
university, or being assigned leadership roles by an individual community through acclamation, in order to meet the specific needs of that
community.

The traditional Islamic education typically equips imams with a
good knowledge of Qur'an and hadith. It typically falls short in preparing them for leadership and surely for dealing with contemporary
American Issues. There is a palpable need for additional training in
areas such as administering nonprofit organizations and providing pastoral care/counseling.

Additionally, there is an increasing question as to whether imams in local masjids will/should play a role in chaplaincies such as in hospitals, prisons, and other settings. Even as the questions continue, some imams are already volunteering or are employed as professional chaplains.

Role of the Imam

Literally, the word "imam" means "he who stands in front of others," hence the person who leads a congregational or group prayer. In actual practice, an imam is an Islamic religious leader. Generally, she/he is the leader of a congregation, although that is not a necessary condition for being an imam.

Surprised? Are you thinking that "she/he" was a mistake? Well, think again. Yes, Muslim women can serve as imams to female congregations. Only Allah knows when they will not be so restricted. Meanwhile, Muslim women are serving at many levels of leadership throughout their communities.

The role of the imam varies. Imams can function as the charismatic leaders of a masjid, as chief executive officers hired by a board of directors, or as per diem workers/volunteers, who perform Friday congregational (*jummah*) and other prayers for a community. In any event, the imam often has no employee benefits, such as health or life insurance or a retirement plan.

Imams, by virtue of being the imam, are perceived by many in their congregations as qualified to offer advice on a variety of issues outside of Qur'an and hadith. And soon enough, they find themselves advising (counseling) individuals, men and women, on a wide range of topics, including domestic violence, spousal infidelities, addictions, loss of faith, and more. Many imams are undoubtedly qualified to play this role. Some are not. But even for the qualified, the challenge is to recognize when the situation before them is beyond their skill set and to make a referral to a more skilled professional.

Wa llahu a'lam (And Allah knows best).

Notes

1. Fareed H. Nu'man, *The Muslim Population in the United States* (American Muslim Council, 1992).

2. Ihsan Bagby, Paul M. Perl, and Bryan T. Froehle, *The Mosque in America: A National Portrait* (Washington, DC: Council on American-Islamic Relations, 2001).

3. *New York Times*, May 4, 1993, citing Dawud Assad of the Muslim World League in New York City.

4. An-Nawawi, *Forty Hadith*, trans. Ezzedin Ibrahim and Denys Johnson-Davies, hadith 1 (Jakarta, Indonesia: Dar al-ilm), 26.

5. It is common in English translations to use the word "iman" to refer to the Arabic word for faith. However, to make the distinction between "faith" and "belief," we have chosen to use the word *tawhid* (oneness) to emphasize the unique aspect of faith: *Faith is for Allah only*. Our only faith-based relationship is with Allah. Other relationships are based upon belief, that is, evidence (e.g., touch, hearing, experience).

About the Contributors

Imam Muhammad Hatim, PhD, DMin, is Imam Warith Deen Muhammad Professor of African American Muslim Studies at the Graduate Theological Foundation in Mishawaka, Indiana. He has more than twenty years of experience in the informal resolution of equal employment opportunity (EEO) issues. As an imam with the Admiral Family Circle Islamic Community (Admiral Family) in New York City, he headed its justice ministry and the UN Summer Internship Program in Human Rights in Geneva, Switzerland; he is also co-founder of the Malik Shabazz (Malcolm X) Human Rights Institute. He sits on several interfaith committees and is a chaplain with Disaster Chaplain Services in New York City. He holds a BS in industrial arts education, an MS in transportation planning and engineering, a PhD in civil engineering (environmental), and a DMin from the Graduate Theological Foundation and is a certified alcohol and drug counselor (CADC) in New Jersey. He is a contributor to the book *Disaster Spiritual Care: Practical Clergy Response to Community, Regional, and National Tragedy* (SkyLight Paths Publishing).

Shaykh Ibrahim Abdul-Malik, PhD, EdD, earned his first doctor's degree in science and education at Harvard University and his second in Islamic studies from the Graduate Theological Foundation. Following a twenty-five-year career with the New York City school system, Dr. Ibrahim became a science advisor at UNESCO. In that capacity, he organized and headed the first junior college in the Islamic Republic of Maldives. Shaykh Ibrahim has been part of the adjunct faculty in the School of English, Philosophy, Humanities, and Religious Studies at Fairleigh Dickinson University since 2003. His written works include *Islam and Muslims: Twenty-Five Questions and Answers* (a widely distributed information booklet written in the aftermath of the 9/11 tragedy); *Islam and Muslims: Fifty Questions and Answers*; *Ramadan: A Primer*; and *Prayer in Islam: A Guide for Beginning Muslims, an Introduction for Non-Muslims.*

26

Working with Catholics

Rev. Monsignor Richard Arnhols, MDiv, and
Anne Masters, MA

In this chapter we will briefly introduce you to the Roman Catholic Church, its self-understanding, structure, and leadership roles. It is our expectation that the primary audience for this chapter is someone who is not Catholic who would like to collaborate with the Catholic Church in some way at the local level, which could mean a parish, (arch)diocese,[1] the whole United States, or some portion of it. More will be said about this below. Any statements of faith are made strictly to increase the reader's knowledge of the beliefs of the church.

The Catholic Church is more than two thousand years old, with a worldwide membership of more than one billion. Although it is an organization with a concrete structure that is observable, with set procedures and policies, from the perspective of a Catholic at least, it is so much more, and yet can also be quite messy at times, as is the case with any relationship-based group. So we will provide a general orientation of structures and models of operation, as well as a general orientation about sacraments, tradition, and scripture within it.

Concise Summary of Beliefs and Mission

The Catholic Church, having been founded in the life of Christ, who was the visible form of the invisible God, is called to be a sign of God's saving activity in the world through Christ, in effect, to be

311

a sacrament of God's presence in the world, to be formed and animated by the life of Jesus the Christ, reaching out to all humanity and seeking unity. We believe that all people are created in the image of God and affirm the inherent dignity of all persons from conception to natural death; that creation is good; that we are called to be stewards of creation. By extension of this, we also proclaim a preferential option for the poor, which can be witnessed in the life of Christ, who reached out to those in the margins of society in his day. The church's mission is focused both inward in the building up of its members and outward, sharing the Gospel with the world, inspiring attention to the will of God, and responding as a healing presence where there is pain and need.

Sacraments in the Catholic Church

All the faithful (clergy and laity) are united to Christ and to one another, nurtured by God's Word in the Bible, and nourished by the grace of the seven sacraments, founded in the life of Christ (often referred to as "instituted by Christ"). Sacraments are central to Catholic identity. Through the use of tangible signs and prescribed rituals, the sacraments celebrate the grace-filled presence of Jesus Christ in the midst of his people. There are seven sacraments officially celebrated: baptism (typically in infancy), reconciliation, Eucharist, confirmation, matrimony, holy orders, and anointing of the sick. Briefly stated, they are an outward sign of God's presence and activity within. They are the healing presence of God through the ministry of Jesus in the ordinary moments of life: birth, reconciliation and forgiveness, meals, vocation and station, and sickness.

Sunday Eucharist, the Mass, is particularly important for Catholics. It is when we gather to hear God's Word and to be nourished and strengthened by the Eucharist to live God's will in our lives. We believe it is important that we gather together, rather than simply maintaining our personal devotions: to celebrate God's presence in our lives and to draw strength from that, with and through each other; to remember who and what we are called to be; and to experience the enhanced presence of Christ with us when gathered in his name (Matthew 18:20).

Models of the Church Describe a Multifaceted Nature

We will draw on Cardinal Avery Dulles's *Models of the Church*, which provides helpful insights into the multidimensional nature of the church.[2] The models Dulles describes are the church as institution, mystical communion, sacrament, herald, servant, and community of disciples.

The church as sacrament acknowledges the call to be what we proclaim in our actions, both when we gather as a people and in the world at large. It implies that the felt impact of the church as the healing presence of God is experienced within itself and without. At the same time, we acknowledge that we do not always do this as we should.

The church as a mystical communion refers to the interconnectedness through space and time of the church as the body of Christ. The proclamation of the Word is at the center of church as herald, which recognizes the importance of this activity in community worship and life. Saint Francis of Assisi is supposed to have said, "Preach the Gospel always, and when necessary, use words," indicating the connectedness of our worship, proclamation, and actions in life.

The church as servant draws on the teachings of Jesus found in scripture that call us to love one another as he has loved us (John 13:34) and indicates that when we feed the hungry, visit the sick, all that we do for the least of us, we are doing it for him (Matthew 25:40), as we live our mission in service. The church as sacrament and servant are difficult to separate at their best, both calling us to be Christ's presence in the world today.

The Catholic Church is an institution and, as such, has a visible structure that is hierarchical in nature. Yet it is not just an institution; it is much more than that. Its organization provides structure to enable its activity and mission in the world. Most people who are not Catholic are aware of its hierarchical structure, yet they do not understand its implementation. It provides a chain of command, and at the same time, it does not operate in the same way a business or government structure works. At its best, the church as institution allows for an emphasis on the pastoral aspects of leadership, in which the ordained, as well as installed, may nurture and guide the community.

Scripture and Tradition: Single Source of Revelation

Scripture and tradition together are the single deposit of revelation; liturgy and the lived expression of our faith are that dynamic of ongoing interaction between the two. Tradition is dynamic, not static; it is both content and process.

Although the Bible has many different books, Catholics hold them in tension together. The Catholic Bible, with the Hebrew Bible and Christian Scriptures, is understood to present the faith of the early church that was inherited from the People of Israel and handed on by the apostles. It begins with God's early activity in our world, calling the People of Israel, and continuing with the ministry of Jesus in the Gospel and activity of the early church. It contains additional Hebrew text that is not in the Protestant Bible, referred to as either Apocryphal or deuterocanonical books.

Tradition and scripture in the Catholic Church draws on the Bible's history as an oral tradition. Once the canon was set, the process of tradition continued in interpreting scripture within the context of our faith. This process continues to this day. Tradition is both noun and verb, coming from Latin, *tradition, traditio*, the content of beliefs and the handing on of the beliefs. Catholics believe that revelation is complete, but there can be a growth in our understanding of its meaning. All the bishops of the world, in communion with the pope, constitute the teaching authority of the Catholic Church. Any new teaching must be consistent with the inherited Tradition of the faith. Although there are four authors of the Gospel, we believe there is one Gospel, and all is held together in tension.

Tradition with a "T" refers to official teachings of the church; tradition with a "t" refers to practices, devotions, and rituals, such as Advent wreaths, praying the rosary, and so forth. Within our Tradition, there is a large body of information. While we hold it all to be true, not all truths are of equal importance, referred to as a hierarchy of truths. The highest levels of truths are directly related to the central teachings of our faith regarding God present most fully in the person of Jesus the Christ and that though God is one, God is three in the three persons of the Trinity: God the Father, God the Son, God the Holy Spirit (Creator, Redeemer, Sanctifier).

Local Church, Universal Church

There is one Catholic Church, but two locations: the local church and the universal church. The most local level is the parish, a single community that gathers in a particular location for worship and other activities, such as catechesis (religious education) for children and teens, sacrament preparation, ongoing faith formation of all ages, scripture study, social outreach, and so on.

The clergy are men who are ordained as either priests[3] or deacons. The pastor is a priest. He may be the only priest in the parish, or there may be others. Only a priest may preside at Mass; deacons assist the presider. Priests are not married; deacons typically are, though not always, and often coordinate a ministry in the parish.

Additionally, men and women in religious orders, referred to as "brother" and "sister," work in many of the church's ministries, in parishes, schools, diocesan offices, or the community at large.[4] There are usually also laypeople on the parish staff, referred to as lay ecclesial ministers, though the official titles may be parish catechetical leader, director of religious education, or pastoral associate. There is also a parish secretary. Other roles may or may not include director of operations, a handyman/janitor/groundskeeper, accountant, and so on.

In addition to people on staff, most parishes have a number of laypeople leading and participating in different ministry activities in the parish, which you can find listed on the parish bulletin. In fact, it is helpful to know that a parish bulletin provides insight into a particular parish community. You can easily gain a sense of its activity and focus by how much or how little is contained in it, as well as what the content is. Another good indication would be the parish website.

Parishes are organized within a diocese and come under the jurisdiction of a bishop,[5] who is also referred to as the pastor of the diocese. However, the bishop's focus is typically on needs of the entire diocese and the work of the college of bishops. In the United States, dioceses tend to consist of several counties in a particular state, presided over by a bishop, and the largest diocese by population is generally considered an archdiocese, presided over by an archbishop. Archdioceses may also have auxiliary or regional bishops assisting an archbishop.

Each pastor/parish/diocese has its own personality, identity, and mission. It is a human community and therefore varied in nature and style. Some pastors are very involved in details; others are not. Although I (Arnhols) tend to be a hands-on person by nature, at the same time I have always embraced the model of the church as a community of disciples, recognizing that, though institutionally I am ultimately responsible for what goes on in my parish, realistically I rely on the gifts, talents, and sacrifices of others to get everything done that serves our diverse community. I have been pastor to a small, poor, inner-city parish as well as a much larger suburban parish of close to thirty-five hundred families born in fifty-five countries of the world, with the predominant languages being English, Spanish, and Tagalog (leading language in the Philippines). We have about fifty organizations, ministries, groups, and societies led by faith-filled individuals of varying position, both clergy and lay.

Each diocese has its own particular structure and organization, with each office reflecting the overall mission of the church in some way, fully or in part. The structures have evolved over time in its particular location. Although changes are made, as will be seen in one example below, the changes are made based on the needs of that particular local church at the diocesan level. For example, some dioceses are organized into vicariates, some into secretariats. Also, particular offices can be located differently within the structure. For example, ministry with persons with disabilities may be in the Vicariate for Pastoral Life, Office of Pro Life, or Office for Catechetics. Diocesan websites are a helpful indication of organization, as well as the diocesan newspaper, which is usually available through its communications office.

The Catholic Church is represented in America by the United States Conference of Catholic Bishops (USCCB). Headquartered in Washington, DC, and working in cooperation with the Papal Nuncio from the Vatican to the church in the United States, bishops work collaboratively to provide unity and direction for the faithful of the country among themselves and in unity with the pope, the bishop of Rome. Also called the "Holy Father," the pope is seen as the Vicar of Christ on earth. As pope, he is the leader of the universal church. As bishop of Rome, he is leader of the local church in Rome. The balancing of roles of the local and universal church tends to be the most confusing to people who are not Catholic. As one church, we are united in mission and faith, yet also individual in its implementation.

Ways of Engagement

In my work as director of Pastoral Ministry with Persons with Disabilities, I (Masters) work with clergy and lay leaders in the parishes and archdiocesan offices to develop structures of support for the participation of individuals with disabilities to the extent that each is able and desires to. The teachings of the Catholic Church, its Tradition, affirm the inherent dignity of all persons. This means also valuing and honoring the participation of every person baptized, regardless of ability or disability, and there is full pastoral allowance to adapt based on need. Yet, the lived reality of that is not so easy at the local level. Therefore, I am frequently involved in conversations about balancing needs.

Education may be needed about specific church teaching that is supportive or about supportive strategies. It may be the parish leadership that needs the education, or it may be the person in the pew, in which case, parish leadership needs support in educating the parish. This can be done in various ways. One is simple explanatory announcements from the altar or in the parish bulletin. For example, when a child with autism is learning to attend Mass, there may be some noises and behaviors people are not used to experiencing during liturgy. A brief explanation of the situation that expresses appreciation for the parish's faithfulness as disciples of Christ supporting the effort goes a long way. It reminds people of who we are called to be as Christians, and it explains the need. How I work with a given parish really depends on the dynamics of that parish, but the goal is always to work together as disciples of Christ, each with our own gifts to contribute.

The very existence of the department within the Newark Archdiocese Vicariate for Pastoral Life grew out of the need to provide guidance and leadership to parishes in this area. An earlier version of the ministry used to operate out of a Catholic social service agency in the archdiocese. Due to budgetary issues, it and another office, Ministry with the Deaf, faced closure. However, believing that both works needed to continue, I (Arnhols) gathered with other department heads (Catechetics, School Office, and Family Life) to evaluate the options and make a recommendation to Archbishop Myers. Although we also faced tight budget constraints, there was the recognition that both offices participated in unique ways to advance the mission of the church. The institutional and communal natures of the church are easily seen operating in this example.

Pertinent to the focus of this book, interfaith collaboration, the Catholic Church affirms the value of this for the benefit of humanity.[6] The development of a Clergy Emergency Outreach Group in Bergenfield, New Jersey, is an example of this. One of the members of the local interfaith clergy association initiated the call for this group in response to a high number of teen suicides that was, quite understandably, troubling the town. The schools and police in the town knew about the group and how to contact for clergy support in crisis situations. Years after its inception, the group was reactivated on September 11, 2001, to be on hand to provide support for children impacted by the events of that day. It developed out of the recognition of a shared responsibility for the community on some issues by the different faith communities. Although this group was active on a conditional basis, areas of ongoing engagement around social areas of need, in particular but not exclusively, are very practical opportunities for collaborative activities.

Key Things to Remember

- The local church and universal church, though united in mission and faith, are individual in its implementation.
- The Catholic Church is multifaceted in structure and operation and is open to collaborating with people of goodwill in the service of humanity.
- Possible parish contacts for local community activity: pastor, parish catechetical leader, director of religious education, social outreach, parish secretary, relevant ministry leader listed in the church bulletin.

- Possible diocesan contacts for county- or diocesan-wide activity: director of relevant ministry found in church directory or website, vicariate/secretariat head for relevant office, office of the bishop for direction.

- Sources to learn about the structure and mission of a parish or diocese: parish bulletin, parish website, diocesan directory, diocesan website, newspaper. Internet presence varies greatly but is increasing in general.

Notes

1. For ease of reading, (arch)diocese, which refers to archdiocese or diocese, will simply be referred to as "diocese" unless it is important to reference archdiocese specifically.
2. Avery Dulles, *Models of the Church,* expanded ed. (New York: Auckland Image Books/Doubleday, 1987). Although originally published in 1974, expanded and republished in 1987 and 1991, it is still an excellent resource for understanding the multifaceted dimensions of the workings of the church and its faith precepts.
3. Priests are either diocesan, reporting directly to the bishop and ordained by him for service within his diocese, or religious order (e.g., Franciscan, Jesuit, Benedictine, Dominican), who take vows of poverty, chastity, and obedience, live in community, and have a direct religious superior. Priests who are involved in diocesan or other service beyond or in addition to parochial duties may be honored with the title "Monsignor."
4. These men and women have also taken vows of poverty, chastity, and obedience, live in community, and have a direct religious superior. In addition to previous examples of orders, two women's orders are Sisters of Charity and Daughters of Mercy.
5. Archbishop is in the case of an archdiocese. Some bishops who oversee more significant dioceses or who directly assist in the papal offices in Rome may be honored with the title "Cardinal."
6. "Dogmatic Constitution on the Church," Vatican II. (1) "Pastoral Constitution on the Church in the Modern World" (3) in *Vatican Council II: The Basic Sixteen Documents, Constitutions, Decrees, Declarations; A Completely Revised Translation in Inclusive Language,* ed. Austin Flannery (Northport, NY / Dublin, Ireland: Costello Publishing Company / Dominican Publications, 1966).

Further Reading

Catechism of the Catholic Church. 2nd ed. Washington, DC: United States Catholic Conference, 2000.

Dulles, Avery. *Models of the Church.* Expanded ed. New York: Image Books/Doubleday, 1991.

Flannery, Austin, ed. *Vatican Council II: The Basic Sixteen Documents, Constitutions, Decrees, Declarations; A Completely Revised Translation in Inclusive Language.* New York: Costello Publishing Company, 1996.

Handbook for Today's Catholic: Fully Indexed to the Catechism of the Catholic Church. 3rd ed. Liguori, MO: Liguori Publications, 1994.

Himes, Michael J. *The Mystery of Faith: An Introduction to Catholicism.* Cincinnati: St. Anthony Messenger Press, 2004.

Kendzia, Mary Carol, ed. *The 5 W's of Our Catholic Faith: Who, What, Where, When, Why ... and How We Live It.* Liguori, MO: Liguori Publications, 2011.

Madges, William, and Michael J. Daley, eds. *Vatican II: Forty Personal Stories.* Mystic, CT: Twenty-Third Publications, 2003.

Marthaler, Bernard L. *Introducing the Catechism of the Catholic Church.* New York: Paulist Press, 1994.

McBrien, Richard P. *Catholicism.* Rev. ed. San Francisco: HarperOne, 1994.

Place, Michael, and Rev. Sammie Maletta. *Life in Christ: A Catholic Catechism for Adults.* Chicago: ACTA Publications, 1995.

Walter, Mares, and Rosemary Gallagher. *Faith for the Future: A New Illustrated Catechism.* Liguori, MO: Liguori Publications, 1998.

Websites

FOR INFORMATION ABOUT CATHOLICISM AND THE CATHOLIC CHURCH

New Advent, Catholic online encyclopedia that is a good online source for general information: www.newadvent.org.

United States Conference of Catholic Bishops: www.usccb.org.

Vatican: www.vatican.va.

EXAMPLES OF PARISH WEBSITES

St. Bartholomew the Apostle, Scotch Plains, NJ: www.stbartholomewchurch.org.

St. John the Evangelist, Bergenfield, NJ: www.sjrc.org.

St. Joseph, Maplewood, NJ: www.stjosephmaplewood.org.

EXAMPLES OF DIOCESAN WEBSITES

Camden Diocese: www.camdendiocese.org.

Metuchen Diocese: www.diometuchen.org.

Newark Archdiocese: www.rcan.org.

Paterson Diocese: www.patersondiocese.org.

About the Contributors

Rev. Monsignor Richard J. Arnhols, MDiv, is pastor of St. John the Evangelist Roman Catholic Church in Bergenfield, New Jersey. He is also vicar for pastoral life for the Roman Catholic Archdiocese of Newark, overseeing more than fifteen departments geared to pastoral service, and is a member of the College of Consultors and Presbyteral Council. He is a regular contributor to the "Seeing and Believing" column of *The Catholic Advocate*, the official biweekly periodical of the archdiocese. As former pastor of the inner-city St. Patrick's Church in Elizabeth, New Jersey, he wrote the foreword to the recently released *The Grand Old Man of the Port: Dean Martin Gessner, the American Catholic Church, and Parish Life in the Nineteenth Century*, written by Carl Ganz Jr.

Anne Masters, MA, is the director of the Department for Pastoral Ministry with Persons with Disabilities, Roman Catholic Archdiocese of Newark; president of the Religion and Spirituality Division of the American Association of Intellectual and Developmental Disabilities; and board member of the New Jersey Coalition for Inclusive Ministries. She has worked in various areas of pastoral ministry as a lay ecclesial minister in the San Francisco Bay Area and northern New Jersey and is a workshop presenter on inclusive religious education and pastoral practices. She has a master's degree in theology from the College of St. Elizabeth. Her published works include "Inclusive Faith Practices for Children with Autism," *Autism and Faith: A Journey into Community*, and a book review of *Autism and Your Church* in the *Journal of Religion, Disability, and Health*.

27

Working with Protestants

Rev. Rose Niles, MDiv, DMin, and
Rev. Kevin Park, MDiv, PhD

Our challenge is to be nimble, flexible, and agile, moving with the
Spirit of God, always grounded in the Word of God....[1]

What is Protestantism? In simple to understand language, it is a group of Christian communions tracing their heritage from the European revolution that broke with the hierarchy of the Roman Catholic Church in the sixteenth century. They hold in common belief in historic Christian doctrines (such as the Trinity) and adhere to early shared creeds such as the Nicene and Apostle's Creeds.

The largest American Protestant branches are the Southern Baptist Convention and the United Methodist Church, and the fastest growing branches are the Pentecostal denominations such as the Assemblies of God. Despite declines in membership, mainline Protestant churches continue to be a significant force, numerically and spiritually.[2]

Understanding the Roots and Branches of the Protestant Tree

Believers in the Triune God—Creator God, Jesus Christ, and the Holy Spirit—Protestants emerged in at least seven streams in the Protest movement of the 1500s. Lutheran, Reformed, Anglican, Free Church, Quaker, Methodism, and Pentecostal streams are all under the Protestant umbrella. Specific church situations can be understood by referencing background in excellent resources such as the *Yearbook of American and Canadian Churches*, published by the National Council of Churches USA; it provides a specific overview and contact entry points for any specific Protestant branch.

Three Major Common Principles of the Protestant Reformation

- *Sola scriptura*—by scripture alone: The belief in the centrality of the Bible (with Hebrew and Christian "Testaments," sixty-six canonical books) as the sole authority for faith and practice. Reformers took the Bible seriously, though not always literally. It was considered the source of authority in all matters of faith. Numerous stories are told illustrating that the Bible, a complex document more like a library than a single book, is not in this tradition to be an idol to be worshipped, but a living document accessible to all. Thus, multiple translations and a complex history of interpretation inevitably took root. An excellent resource for this critical area is found in Rev. Dr. Peter Gomes's *The Good Book: Reading the Bible with Mind and Heart*.

- *Sola fide*—by faith alone: The belief that God's free gift of grace, by faith and not dependent on good works, is the agency of salvation.

- **Priesthood of all believers:** The belief that each person has free access to God without the intermediation of a religious interpreter.

Understanding Protestantism Today

Protestants are Christians formed historically in the crucible of the European revolution known as the Protestant Reformation, reacting against Roman Catholic Church strictures, hallmarked by an unease with any authority other than scripture, any sovereign other than God, any pathway to salvation except through faith, by grace, and any priesthood other than the priesthood of all believers.

Despite a dominant and influential role on the historical stage and notwithstanding that there are many vibrant life-giving and transformative congregations, many mainline Protestant communions give voice to a strong sense of exile, of wilderness journeys, of huge movements of cultural shifts moving the tectonic plates of the religious landscape requiring transformation. Mainline Protestant churches have counted many years of membership decline and experience no longer being in the mainstream of contemporary culture. Greatest growth is reported from Pentecostal denominations such as the Assemblies of God among Protestants worldwide and especially in the "global South." We are not and cannot be what we have been, and we are not yet what we will be.

In considering the dynamics of leadership within any specific branch, we will no doubt weigh considerations of faith, order, and practice. Leaders will explore by asking an array of open-ended questions. What do they confess and profess to believe? How do they order their common life and make decisions? Is their practice in worship strictly liturgical with a set form to follow, or is it unstructured, open, and free flowing? How often and with what liturgical elements do they celebrate the two biblically based out of seven original sacraments held up as authentic in the Protestant tradition: baptism and the Lord's Supper, also termed Holy Communion, or Eucharist? Sacraments are important signs and seals of the covenant with God as revealed in the Bible; they are enacted signs giving meaning in the community of faith. What ethos of the Protestant Reformation might drive and inform leadership in contemporary contexts? Communions shaped in protest and strongly embracing the personal right and responsibility for discernment of the Divine may well support new communal empowerment models of leadership.

Tools for Understanding

Below are some suggested considerations and tools that are effective ways to navigate and explore what must seem complex and to translate an understanding of these core shared beliefs into effective leadership in the Protestant context.

- Establish advising and mentorship opportunities with leaders
  - Find a mentor you are comfortable with, such as an established member of the church governance structure or longtime church schoolteacher.

- Explore dimensions of faith, order, and practice together. Create a map together of how the core principles come to life for that church community.
- Be curious and ask open-ended questions.
- Explore connectedness
  - Engage in sacred conversation as community-building praxis. Utilize models such as World Café and Community Building to encourage voices of leaders in community together.
  - Attend a leadership peer support group. Help create one if there is not one already ongoing that you can participate in. Whether you are a member of the laity or clergy, this will help you understand the leadership culture of the church or Protestant organization.
  - Participate in a peer study group. Again, help create one if there is not one already ongoing that you can participate in.
  - Attend the denomination's regional and annual gatherings. Study the profile of leaders and how they lead.

Twenty-First-Century Issues of Leadership in the Protestant Context

As we have seen, for diverse sets of Protestant communions, leadership is a core concern. Through effective mentoring and coaching, an aspiring leader needs to learn to engage in communal coversations with appropriate curiousity and skills to ask informed questions that can develop into an appreciative inquiry. As such areas of inquiry are developed, an understanding of nuances of diversity and the current discourse about leadership for the twenty-first-century should be engaged.

Engaging Diversity: Multicultural Leadership

Church and spiritual leadership in the twenty-first century in the Protestant context must take into account the ever-increasing migratory nature of the globalized world. Immigration is changing the world such that many countries are becoming radically multicultural. This is true of the United States. And yet the churches in the United States, especially the Protestant mainline churches, have not adjusted their leadership to reach out to the multicultural population, nor have they empowered multiethnic leadership in tandem with the demographic shift. A quick comparison between the racial demographics of the United States and mainline denominations points out the discrepancy in racial ethnic diversity between the general population and the church population:

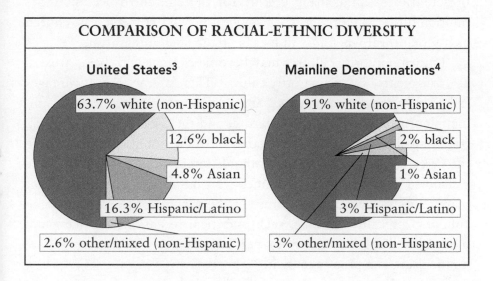

It is fair to say that all of the mainline denominations are not only aware of this discrepancy but are also engaged in various programs, including outreach and new church developments for new immigrants and racial ethnic communities. The danger of such programmatic response is that this becomes a way of "ornamentalizing" races rather than empowering them to become an essential part of the larger denominational ecclesial community. By ornamental multiculturalism we mean treating minority racial ethnic groups as ornaments that enhance the perceived value of the dominant culture. Ornaments do not exist on their own merit, but they exist to enhance something else. In ornamental multiculturalism, cultures are valued insofar as they contribute to the overall value of the dominant culture and race. In ornamental multiculturalism, minority cultures are celebrated by the dominant culture largely through rhetorical flourish, aesthetics, and tolerance without effecting a deeper change to the whole cultural system of the church. A casual perusal of any mainline denominational periodical or promotional materials will show that the presentation of denominations in such forums exaggerates their racial diversity. An outsider will easily conclude that any mainline denomination is a racially mixed and integrated church from looking at the covers of church magazines and posters that depict racial ethnic peoples in inordinate frequency. At best, such presentation is an aspiring gesture for the church to become more multicultural. At worst, it is a disingenuous way to depict the church as multicultural when it is in fact far from such integration.

In turn, minority cultures may become content with being treated as "ornaments" by the majority culture. There are, in fact, advantages to being treated as "ornaments." Special attention is given to racial ethnic minorities by the majority culture, and they are treated as special, fragile symbols and commodities that have the potential of increasing the perceived value and status of the denomination. Such attention is welcomed by minority communities who have experienced the brunt marginality of living as minorities in the very nationalistic American culture. Ironically, however, such uncritical reception of ornamental multiculturalism by minorities perpetuates the unfortunate virtual multiculturalism promoted by it.

We need a sound and faithful biblical theology of multicultural theology that will not only critique and unmask utilitarian and programmatic responses like ornamental multiculturalism but also provide an alternative theological/biblical vision. One possible avenue is to understand that a multicultural vision of God's kingdom is embedded in the biblical narrative. From God's first directive to humans, "Be fruitful and multiply and fill the earth" (Genesis 1:28) to the Spirit's gathering of people from all nations at Pentecost to the vision of the New Jerusalem in Revelation where the "glory and the honor of the nations" (21:26) will participate in God's glory, the multicultural and multiracial reality of the biblical witness of God's world and kingdom must be part and parcel of the leadership vision of the church for the twenty-first century. Therefore, participating in the leadership toward this vision of multicultural ministry is not merely for the sake of church growth or denominational survival, but for nothing less than bringing glory to God.

Leadership That Will Inspire Youth

> In the view of American teenagers, God is more object than subject,
> an Idea but not a companion. The problem does not seem to be that
> churches are teaching young people badly, but that we are doing
> an exceedingly good job of teaching youth what we really believe:
> namely that Christianity is not a big deal, that God requires little,
> and the church is a helpful social institution filled with nice people
> focused primarily on "folks like us"—which, of course, begs the
> question of whether we are really the church at all.[5]

The Protestant churches in America have largely failed to inspire our
youth with the Gospel of Jesus Christ. The Protestant leadership in the
twenty-first century must take into account the sobering reality that too
many of our churches are without young people. Like the issue of multicultural ministry, the leadership for youth cannot be solved by merely
engaging at the programmatic level of ministry. The reason the youth
are not attracted to church is largely our fault. We have, intentionally
or not, communicated to our youth that Christianity itself is an ornament to decorate our lives rather than God's way of transforming our
lives through the Good News of Jesus Christ by the Holy Spirit. Our
failure to reach the youth with the Gospel is our failure to live the Gospel. Before we can launch into exciting youth ministry with programs
that we think will "wow" the young people, church leaders must turn
to God and repent of our lukewarm, casual lives that have replaced the
robust Christian life revealed in the life and death of Jesus Christ.

Furthermore, youth ministry in the twenty-first century will require
"incarnational" ministry where leaders are willing to learn and embrace
the language, culture, and fabric of youth culture in order to demonstrate
the love of Jesus for them. No longer can we merely rely on powerful
speakers and extravagant events and programs to communicate the Gospel to our young people. They are looking for deeper connectional community that embodies the love of Christ in real life. Only such authentic
"incarnational" leadership supported by authentic Christian communities can hope to demonstrate the life-changing Gospel of Jesus Christ.

Thanksgiving

Thanksgiving is at the heart of Christian life. To give thanks is to live a
God-centered life. We give thanks because God is good and we belong

to God in life and in death by the costly grace of Jesus Christ through the Holy Spirit. However, for more than two decades the mainline denominations as well as other Protestant churches have been preoccupied with anxiety-producing statistics of relentless decline in membership and funding, as well as fragmentation of all kinds. When we are deep in anxiety, we are focused on ourselves and our situation, thus not on God and what God is doing in the midst of us. The church is in danger of having its life of thanksgiving replaced by a life of anxiety. Paul, in his letter to the Philippians, writes:

> Rejoice in the Lord always; again I will say, Rejoice. Let your gentleness be known to everyone. The Lord is near. Do not worry about anything, but in everything by prayer and supplication with thanksgiving let your requests be made known to God. And the peace of God, which surpasses all understanding, will guard your hearts and your minds in Christ Jesus. (Philippians 4:4–7)

Paul's exhortation not to worry about anything but instead engage in a life of prayer and thanksgiving in joy is remarkable given his situation. He is writing in a Roman prison; he does not know if he is going to live or die tomorrow. Paul also writes in 1 Thessalonians 5:18, "Give thanks in all circumstances...." From these passages and many others, we learn that thanksgiving is more than a cordial acknowledgment of mutual benefit or a kind of thankful feeling. Thanksgiving, according to Paul, is focusing our whole lives solely on God. This has several important implications for the Protestant church leadership in the twenty-first century:

1. We give thanks acknowledging that God is continuing to restore and renew the church for God's glory.

2. We continue to give thanks for God's faithful accompaniment and God's steadfast love for the church as well as for the privilege of participating in God's mission in the past, the present, and the future.

3. We give thanks affirming that the Protestant churches are part of God's church founded by Christ in the Holy Spirit. We give thanks and praise in all circumstances because we belong to God and the hope that we have through the resurrection of Christ.

4. "I am about to do a new thing; now it springs forth, do you not perceive it?" (Isaiah 43:19) We give thanks anticipating the new and unfamiliar ways that God will renew the church for God's mission. We give thanks that God may renew the church in ways that may be hidden to us, but we will continue to trust that God will finish the good work God started in us.

Notes

1. Joint Committee on Leadership Needs, *Raising Up Leaders for the Mission of God: A Report of the Presbyterian Church (USA)*, April 2009, 7, www.presbyterysd.org/docs/resources/JCLN_Raising_Up_Leaders_Final.pdf.
2. Eileen W. Lindner, *Yearbook of American and Canadian Churches* (New York: National Council of Churches USA, 2011), 11.
3. US Census Bureau 2010, http://quickfacts.census.gov/qfd/states/00000.html.
4. "US Religious Landscape Survey," *Pew Forum on Religion and Public Life*, http://religions.pewforum.org/portraits.
5. Kenda Creasy Dean, *Almost Christian: What the Faith of Our Teenagers Is Telling the American Church* (New York: Oxford University Press, 2010), 11–12.

Further Reading

Baker, Dori Grinenko. *Greenhouses of Hope: Congregations Growing Young Leaders Who Will Change the World*. Herndon, VA: Alban Institute, 2010.

Dean, Kenda Creasy. *Almost Christian: What the Faith of Our Teenagers Is Telling the American Church*. New York: Oxford University Press, 2010.

Gomes, Peter. *The Good Book: Reading the Bible with Mind and Heart*. New York: William Morrow, 1996.

Lindner, Eileen W., ed. *Yearbook of American and Canadian Churches*. New York: National Council of Churches USA, 2012.

Merritt, Carol Howard. *Tribal Church: Ministering to the Missing Generation*. Herndon, VA: Alban Institute, 2007.

Prothero, Stephen. *Religious Literacy: What Every American Needs to Know—and Doesn't*. San Francisco: HarperSanFrancisco, 2007.

Putnam, Robert D., and David E. Campbell. *American Grace: How Religion Divides and Unites Us*. New York: Simon and Schuster, 2010.

Rendle, Gil. *Journey in the Wilderness: New Life for Mainline Churches*. Nashville: Abingdon Press, 2010.

Smith, Christian. *Souls in Transition: The Religious and Spiritual Lives of Emerging Adults*. New York: Oxford University Press, 2009.

Tickle, Phyllis. *The Great Emergence: How Christianity Is Changing and Why.* Grand Rapids, MI: Baker Books, 2008.

Walker, Williston, Richard A. Norris, David W. Lotz, and Robert T. Handy, eds. *History of the Christian Church*. 4th ed. New York: Charles Scribner's Sons, 1985.

About the Contributors

Rev. Rose Niles, MDiv, DMin, currently serves as the associate for theological education and seminary relations for the Presbyterian Church (USA) General Assembly Council (GAC). She previously served as the head of staff of First Presbyterian Church of Mount Vernon, New York, and as pastor of Emmanuel Presbyterian Church in Manhattan. At the New York Theological Seminary, she has taught in multiple programs, including the doctor of ministry program, and has taught in their master's degree program at Sing Sing Correctional Facility. Dr. Niles currently leads the Theological Education Fund effort for the Presbyterian Church (USA) seminaries. As the primary staffperson for the National Seminary Support Network, she coordinates connecting congregations, presbyteries, and synods to Presbyterian seminaries.

Rev. Kevin Park, MDiv, PhD, is the associate dean for Advanced Professional Studies at Columbia Theological Seminary in Decatur, Georgia. Previously, he was a pastor of a multicultural church in New Jersey and worked as the assistant director of the Office of Asian American Program at Princeton Theological Seminary.

28

Leading a Multifaith Disaster Response Group

Rev. Julie Taylor, MDiv, CTR, EMT-B

We need not think alike to love alike.
FRANCIS DAVID, SIXTEENTH-CENTURY
UNITARIAN PREACHER AND MARTYR

For ten years I have been part of Disaster Chaplaincy Services, a multifaith, multicultural, multilingual disaster response organization in the New York metropolitan area. This chapter is a case study in leading multifaith groups, using this multifaith disaster response organization as an example.

I began my work with Disaster Chaplaincy Services in early 2002. At the time I was volunteering as a chaplain at St. Paul's Chapel, which was acting as a respite center for recovery workers at the World Trade Center site. I met a few Disaster Chaplaincy Services chaplains when they would come across the street to St. Paul's to take their breaks from working at the temporary disaster morgue. These chaplains came from many faith traditions and communities. They did not espouse the same theologies but were committed to providing spiritual care for the victims and the responders of this tragedy. I was invited to take the Disaster Chaplaincy Services training and to join the ranks. So I did. I started out as a volunteer chaplain, later rising to the Leadership Team, and was hired as the organization's second executive director in 2005. I remained the executive director until 2010, when I stepped down and began to work with Disaster Chaplaincy Services as their consultant for training and deployment. In that time, I have learned from my experience with Disaster Chaplaincy Services that multifaith groups require a vision of something larger than themselves, much time and energy, willingness to share leadership, and humility in order to be successful.

Disaster Chaplaincy Services is a pre-9/11 organization. Its roots were begun in January of 2000, when a working relationship with the American Red Cross of Greater New York (ARC-GNY) was established. The original intention for creating what would become Disaster Chaplaincy Services (then called Disaster Spiritual Care Services) was to have a cadre of endorsed, screened, and trained chaplains from a broad range of local faith communities ready to respond to aviation disasters in the New York metropolitan area. It has been important in New York City to have "buy-in" from a wide variety of local faith communities to work together in an organized way *before* an incident occurs in order to best serve the needs of the public. This principle applies outside New York City as well. Those who are already connected, who already have power and a voice, lead the response. Rabbi Stephen B. Roberts led the initial outreach to local faith groups. The partnership with ARC-GNY was finalized the first week of September 2001. The first response for Disaster Chaplaincy Services was to the terrorist attacks on the World Trade Center one week later.

Disaster Chaplaincy Services had more than 850 volunteer chaplains working shifts at multiple locations 24/7 during the nine-month response and recovery to the September 11th attacks. At that time our volunteer disaster chaplains were Muslim, Jewish, Roman Catholic, Lutheran, Unitarian Universalist, Baptist, United Church of Christ, Presbyterian, United Methodist, Buddhist, Interfaith, nondenominational Christian, Christian Orthodox, Episcopalian, and Pentecostal, among others. Faith communities that don't ordinarily dialogue came together to work alongside one another in response to this tragedy.

Here lies the first element I have found for successfully leading multifaith groups: when there is *a common cause, larger than dialogue, that cause brings multifaith communities together to effect change.* I will go into this in greater detail later in the chapter.

Since 2001, Disaster Chaplaincy Services volunteers have provided more than sixty-four thousand hours of direct spiritual care to those affected by disasters, crises, and emergencies. Beyond the 9/11 response, Disaster Chaplaincy Services has been deployed to such varied events as weather-related disasters like hurricanes (both local and national deployment to Hurricanes Katrina and Rita, local response to Hurricane Irene), floods, tornadoes, blizzards, and heat emergencies; apartment fires and mandatory vacates; uniformed services line-of-duty deaths; and transportation incidents, including fatal bus crashes and multiple airline disasters (both commercial airlines and commuter planes). These events have affected Buddhists, Muslims, Christians, Jews, the Yoruba, Unitarian Universalists, Hindus, Native Americans, Sikhs, atheists, agnostics, and the list goes on. Disasters do not discriminate; anyone can be affected by a human or natural disaster. Because we never know who will be affected by an incident we are called to, it is imperative that a response group be multifaith, multicultural, and multilingual to best care for those in need.

Currently, Disaster Chaplaincy Services has 170 chaplains from 31 faith traditions, speaking 29 different languages. All Disaster Chaplaincy Services chaplains volunteer their time to take care of others during times of disaster, crisis, and emergencies. Disaster Chaplaincy Services partners with many agencies in the New York City government, as well as agencies from other municipalities and nongovernmental organizations, to ensure an integrated and seamless response in times of need. We do not self-deploy but are written into disaster response plans and are recognized by our partner agencies as the lead chaplaincy response organization in this area. As a result, spiritual care becomes part of a multidisciplinary approach to response and recovery, ensuring the best outcome for those affected by a crisis.

A Common Cause

Working with multifaith groups is different from being part of an interfaith or multifaith dialogue. While there is a place for dialogue, it does not bring about significant or lasting change in and of itself. Being part of a group that has a job to do, a focused goal where a symphony of voices, hands, and hearts are necessary to create success—that's what makes change happen.

Multifaith groups work when there is an issue to rally around. Dialogue groups generally have a shorter life span, because people cannot sustain just talking. After a period of time, energy is needed elsewhere, usually to see to issues affecting communities. Dialogue groups become a luxury and tend to fall by the wayside either temporarily or permanently, depending on the resolution of concrete issues.

Disaster Chaplaincy Services is a successful example of an organization that goes beyond dialogue. Asking thirty-one faith groups to come together to dialogue about our traditions and beliefs surrounding tragedy would have been a disaster in itself. Nothing would get done and no one would be helped. But instead we recognize a need in our community that faith leaders can fulfill by showing up and working together. It is powerful and it has lasted.

Asking the Questions, Doing the Work

A second element I have found in successfully working with multifaith groups: *it takes a lot of internal and external work*. In my experience, working with multifaith groups requires more effort than most people are willing to undertake. When beginning such work, it is important to ask yourself the following questions:

- Why work with multifaith groups? What is your motivation to lead a multifaith group? If it is to garner status for yourself or your organization, stop right here. Efforts of this type will fail to ring true. I have seen this over and over again, whether it be faith leaders, politicians, or municipal agencies; when they need something to further their status, they go out into the community for the photo ops, as if to say, "See, I care about you," and then as soon as the election is over or the grant has been given, they are nowhere to be found. It will be ineffective at best, destructive at worst.

- Is there a reason for you to be there? Is there a common cause that will allow connection with other faith communities and faith leaders? Is it a cause you are willing to invest your time, talent, and likely your treasures in? If not, perhaps it is time to reconsider. Forming a multifaith group in order to have a multifaith group sounds good, but it is not likely to last, and opportunities for real relationships may be squandered. It is better to form a group for an important and urgent purpose that will effect change or fill an actual need for a community than to start one that will disappear.

- What is all this work? What's so hard about calling a meeting? Truly leading a multifaith group is more than meetings; the work is external as well as internal. Commitment to a cause and to change within yourself requires attention, humility, and perseverance. It is unlikely a person would be willing to delve into those depths for dialogue, and certainly not for long.

Inclusivity

To be truly multifaith, a group must be intentionally inclusive. Leaders must go beyond the local council of churches or ministers' groups to create this. In such gatherings, we are likely to find a few different mainline Christian denominations and perhaps even few rabbis or imams. This may be ecumenical, but it is not multifaith. The reality is that a twenty-first-century America includes hundreds of faith traditions, ethnicities, and immigrant groups. Working in a multifaith way means moving out of our comfort zone and intentionally seeking out others, others who may be marginalized and probably hard to find.

For a group to reach out to all of these people equally, leaders must get out into the streets. This may be difficult for those of us who tend to be more introverted. Outreach includes talking with people, going to new restaurants, and attending cultural events listed in local newspapers. If we know people or faith leaders from other communities, we can ask to be invited to celebrations or events important to them and the people they serve and network. Most important, we must have a task, an initiative, or a project in mind that is vital to the community. Finally, as frustrating as it may be, we have to recognize that this takes time. Becoming welcome in new communities takes effort, consistency, and dedication so that they will know that we are sincere rather than opportunistic.

To do this, leaders must be teachable and be in relationship. In the past years there has been a push in schools, health care, and business to become "culturally competent." The cultural competency "trainings" I have attended and read are often quite general and mostly unhelpful. I don't believe any of us can become "culturally competent" in all the cultures we encounter on a daily basis. Culture goes beyond ethnicity or race; it encompasses religion, regionalisms, language, age, and experience. Always keep in mind that there is a great diversity within cultures as well.

Let's take a (seemingly) simple example of American youth as a culture. If you don't think of youth as a culture, try reading texts, tweets, and e-mails young people send; they have their own language. Youth can be considered a cultural designation, but if you were working with youth, you would need to become "competent" in more than just the general category of "youth." Remember back to your own high school days. I would venture to bet there was a diverse array of subcultures just within your school. These youth cultures came with their own dress codes, attitudes, belief systems, and behaviors. To know one was not to know them all. To know one is certainly not to understand them all.

The best way to become culturally competent is not to simply read all the books or go to all the lectures, but instead to be willing to personally engage with people of another culture. Be willing to be in relationship with the other, vulnerable in asking questions and being asked questions. Be willing to make a mistake and then humble enough to honestly apologize and stay in relationship to one another.

We can't become experts in the multitude of faith groups we may work with, let alone come into contact with. True competence comes from flexibility, humility, and communication.

Confronting Privilege

There are special requirements for those of us with positions of privilege (this means you if you are any of the following: white, male, Christian, heterosexual, able-bodied, economically or class privileged).

This may not be a comfortable notion, but leaders who fall into any one or several of the above-mentioned categories hold power, freedoms, and favor that if unchecked can be counterproductive to working in a multifaith group. The first requirement is to acknowledge that privilege; the second is to do the internal work required to step out of that privilege.

Privilege is almost always invisible to those who hold it. Recognizing our own privilege can be difficult and painful. I grew up as a missionary kid in Native American and First Nation communities and reservations in the northwestern United States and Canada. In some of the towns we lived in, generally I was in the minority as a white kid going to powwows, in the neighborhood, and in school. When I got a little older, we moved to a larger city in Oregon where whites were the majority, and later I went to New York City for college. I always had friends of different races and never thought about myself as being white. I didn't think I wasn't white; I just didn't think about it at all. It was years later at seminary that I first learned the term "white privilege" and was hit with how clueless I had been to what that meant. "White privilege" is a term used to describe the advantages white people receive in society that are not available to people of color.

It was a shock to my system to realize and then metabolize that I have been complicit in a system that has given me power and favor since the day I was born. It doesn't matter that I was raised to respect other people regardless of race or religion or that I have not taken part in overt racism, to the best of my knowledge. By the fact of being born with white skin I am advantaged, I have privilege. My personal work on this has included internal learning and reflection in combination with external actions, both in learning and in antiracism advocacy. In order for me to be a more conscious member of society and certainly to remain a relevant and useful leader in multifaith settings, I need to be vigilant in my awareness of my privilege (be it white, class, or otherwise) and actively work to expose and dismantle systems of privilege and oppression where I can. This will ultimately result in my giving up power.

In multifaith groups, the privilege wielded by the majority is particularly important. In American society, Christians are in the majority, and it is easy to miss what favor that garners. As leaders wishing to lead multifaith groups, it is imperative to recognize the plurality of faith communities and their needs as being legitimate. Over these ten years as a leader with Disaster Chaplaincy Services, I have seen how something as seemingly simple as planning a meeting can either alienate or welcome. As an example, a secular organization we work with was planning a year's worth of training exercises for disaster response. Each training was scheduled on a Saturday. I went to the planning team and asked if it was possible to have some exercises on Sundays as well. The initial response from the leaders was that people need to have Sundays free for church. I pointed out that many of the Disaster Chaplaincy Services' volunteers were rabbis and Seventh-Day Adventists, as well as the employees and volunteers from other organizations who were Jewish and observed their holy day on Saturday. If every training exercise were held on Saturday, these folks would never have the opportunity to gain the benefit of the training and working with their peers. I don't believe the folks on this planning committee were anti-Semitic; I believe it had not occurred to them to think outside of their own context.

Those of us who have privilege need to be aware of our tendencies to take over. This is particularly difficult when privilege is compounded by personality traits that bring us to leadership positions. By definition, leaders often fall into the "type A" personalities, being ambitious, competitive, and high achieving. While these traits bring tools needed to get work done, they can also make it difficult to recognize when we are bulldozing over the top of someone else. When a person with privilege does this, the message (intended or not) is that regardless of any invitation to inclusion, the same old rules apply: we are in charge, you are not. An important skill in leading multifaith groups is the willingness to step back and follow.

I was able to experience this firsthand while leading Disaster Chaplaincy Services. In response to the 2010 earthquake that devastated Haiti, Disaster Chaplaincy Services was asked to assist the National Association of Jewish Chaplains (NAJC) in providing support to the Haitian community in New Jersey. Upon receiving that request, my first call was to one of our volunteer chaplains who is originally from Haiti and a current resident of New Jersey, Noster Montas. Chaplain Montas not only had important insights that were needed to create the best program to assist with the grieving process, but he also knew how to navigate within the New Jersey Haitian community, a community that would likely have remained closed to "outsiders" like Disaster Chaplaincy Services or the NAJC. Once the programs were in place, Chaplain Montas led them in both English and Haitian Kreyol, with me as an assistant. A caring and effective multifaith response to this tragedy was made possible by those with power intentionally bringing others in to lead.

Rewards

As complicated, time-consuming, and difficult as working with this multifaith disaster response agency has been at times, the rewards have been tremendous. The Yoruba, Santeria, and Afro-Caribbean religious communities have been much maligned in the United States and therefore remain largely under the radar to outsiders. Through the Disaster Chaplaincy Services network of volunteers, we were introduced to a leader in the New York City Yoruba community. Over a series of meetings and meals together, we set up a training for the spiritual leaders of these communities. Only two attended this initial training that I led. It became clear by the end that they were sizing me up, as well as Disaster Chaplaincy Services as a whole, to find out whether we were serious about having them be a part of the organization, or if this was a way to weasel our way into their community to either exploit or harm it. Because of our dedication to a common cause, our willingness to ask questions and cede authority, and the humility we brought to the table, a relationship was established and they joined our team. These Yoruba chaplains have been indispensable in the ability for Disaster Chaplaincy Services to respond to the needs of this very discriminated-against community.

Tragedy struck two families in the Bronx, recent immigrants from the African country of Mali, when a fire ripped through their building on a March day. Ten people died in that fire, nine children and one mother. The families were active members in their Malian Muslim community. A member of the Disaster Chaplaincy Services Leadership Team, Nurah Amat'ullah, a Muslim sister and chaplain, responded to the fire and acted as a liaison between the local community and the various municipal and nongovernmental organizations that were offering help. Chaplain Amat'ullah has stated of her involvement, "It was an opportunity for me to serve as a chaplain in my own community, but servicing everyone at large to provide support during a huge event [sic]."[1] Through the leadership of Chaplain Amat'ullah, not only were the spiritual needs of the families and community seen to, but she was able to facilitate the interface between the community and various agencies providing secular services as well.

In this as in other events, multifaith leadership has proved rewarding to us as well as to those we serve. Those affected by the disaster trusted Chaplain Amat'ullah as an insider in her community to lead that interface. For me the reward is in knowing that there is a web of trained spiritual care responders ready to heed the call of neighbors in trouble. I also experience the rewards of being part of something bigger than myself—that because of the intentional work to make it a multi-faith effort responding to a multifaith need, it will continue beyond my immediate participation. Our theologies don't have to agree for us to agree to work together to ensure an appropriate response to people during their greatest need.

Disaster Chaplaincy Services is a truly multifaith organization, and I am proud of that. We still have further to go. There are hundreds of faith communities in the greater New York metropolitan area, and we continue to work to bring more faith groups in. This chapter brings a comma and comment rather than a period to the work of Disaster Chaplaincy Services. I look forward to participating in and bearing witness to the changes for individuals and for the larger New York metropolitan community that Disaster Chaplaincy Services will provide.

Notes

1. Disaster Chaplaincy Services video, "Responding to the Call," www.disasterchaplaincy.org/about-2.

Further Reading

Barndt, Joseph. *Dismantling Racism: The Continuing Challenge to White America.* Minneapolis, MN: Augsburg Fortress, 1991.

Disaster Chaplaincy Services, www.disasterchaplaincy.org.

Eck, Diana L. *A New Religious America: How a "Christian Country" Has Become the World's Most Religiously Diverse Nation.* New York: HarperSanFrancisco, 2002.

McIntosh, Peggy. "Unpacking the Invisible Knapsack." In *Peace & Freedom.* Philadelphia: Women's International League for Peace and Freedom, 1989.

Patel, Eboo, and Patrice Brodeur, eds. *Building the Interfaith Youth Movement.* Lanham, MD: Rowman & Littlefield, 2006.

Pluralism Project. www.pluralism.org.

Smith, Chip. *The Cost of Privilege: Taking on the System of White Supremacy and Racism.* Fayetteville, NC: Camino Press, 2007.

Wise, Tim. *White Like Me: Reflections on Race from a Privileged Son.* Brooklyn, NY: Soft Skull Press, 2008.

About the Contributor

Rev. Julie Taylor, MDiv, CTR, EMT-B, is a Unitarian Universalist minister specializing in critical incident response, trauma, and disaster spiritual care. She served for five years as the executive director for Disaster Chaplaincy Services, located in New York City. During the 9/11 recovery, Rev. Taylor was a chaplain at St. Paul's Chapel at the World Trade Center site and has continued to respond to local and national crises, including floods, building collapses, fatal shootings, and airline disasters. In addition to her work with Disaster Chaplaincy Services, Rev. Taylor serves as a board member and a responder with the Unitarian Universalist Trauma Response Ministry, is a member of the Hudson Valley CISM Team, and is a volunteer EMT with the Central Park Medical Unit. She is a certified trauma responder through the Association of Traumatic Stress Specialists (ATSS) and a board-certified chaplain through the National Association of Veterans Affairs Chaplains (NAVAC). She received her master of divinity degree from Union Theological Seminary in New York City.

Final Words

Phyllis Harrison-Ross, MD

I am deeply honored to write the epilogue to this powerful and needed text. Throughout my years, the topics explored in this book have been of great importance to me. I previously authored two books on child development and coauthored several textbook chapters and articles on prison health, most recently regarding the fastest growing incarcerated group—women prisoners. I served as moderator of a parent-education television series called "All about Parents" in the early 1970s. Currently, I co-host a radio talk show, *Ethics on the Air* and am a member of the editorial board of the *New York Amsterdam News*.

I find it remarkable how Rev. Dr. Willard Ashley and the contributors to this volume have brought the issue of skilled leadership to my consciousness in new ways—reminding me of the leadership skills that have proven crucial for me to learn over the years, in every professional, academic, and volunteer position in which I have found myself. By calling on his unique and talented cadre of family, friends, and colleagues, it is clear to me that he has amassed and presented sound guidance to help recognize what all of us—as potential or actual leaders—must know, do, and protect about our lives and work in varied communities.

Serving as secretary/trustee and chairperson of the Social Service Board of the New York Society for Ethical Culture, I am particularly struck by the fact that this book, like the Social Service Board, focuses on learning about, enabling, and empowering our communities, congregations, and students in order to adapt their worldviews to the realities of the twenty-first century—an effort that is very important to me.

I am pleased by the ways it encourages speaking out from the soul, even if one is struggling to overcome a learned sense of inferiority and inadequacy. This is a key part of mentoring and facilitating leadership skill development for younger colleagues, or even seasoned elders such as myself (I learned so much from Rev. Dr. Ashley over the course of my career such as the effectiveness of the collaboration of pastoral care with psychiatric care). I found the advice on how to survive and thrive as an organization with limited resources, operating alongside larger greater advantaged competitors, of particular resonance. It is something I have dealt with often in my own personal work helping underserved persons—including families with disabilities and children of undocumented immigrants, like those described in the text—in a culturally proficient manner.

I believe that *Learning to Lead* has professionally and astutely highlighted the most important issues one faces at each new leadership juncture. Part I explores the foundations of spiritual leadership, including how to share and grow from personal experiences; to learn from the strengths of others; to focus on bringing out the best in others; and to put "deed before creed" by helping others. Part II follows up on this strong foundation by providing insights on how to evaluate complex situations that potential leaders may find themselves in as they work to find and implement outside of the box solutions. As a physician who has worked for many years with a wide range of diverse, difficult-to-reach, and underserved populations, I greatly appreciate the third part of this book's focus on the care of others. In particular, I find this section's ideas—on how better to serve those so often known in society as the least of us—to be meaningful. Finally, part IV contains information that is increasingly crucial in the world of care giving: how to encourage collaboration across specific religious traditions by better understanding who they are and what their actual needs may be; how to form new, socially, and culturally diverse partnerships; and how to make peace with the rapidly expanding technological world.

I, along with Rev. Dr. Ashley and the contributors to this crucial text, all embrace the edict, "care for the caregivers" and I would like to close by emphasizing the importance of loving and caring for oneself. As a physician and psychiatrist, I understand how important this is on a cerebral and professional level—but it has taken the spiritual nurturing, love, and support of the leaders in this volume and many others, to continually make this a living and dynamic part of my own spirituality.

I profoundly believe that you will find this text of use and inspiration as you proceed in the essential work you do, and that it will help you work more professionally, with greater skill, and with a deeper sense of satisfaction with yourself as a spiritual being along the way.

About the Contributor

Phyllis Harrison-Ross, MD, is trustee, secretary of the New York Society for Ethical Culture (NYSEC) and chair of the Social Service Board for United Social Services, Inc., a NYSEC social action affiliate. She is a trustee and member of the supporting organization for the Ethical Culture Fieldston School. She practices child and adult psychiatry, is emeritus professor of psychiatry and behavioral health sciences at New York Medical College, emeritus attending psychiatrist/chief of psychiatry at Metropolitan Hospital Center and founder and managing partner of Black Psychiatrists of Greater New York. Currently, she serves fulltime as commissioner for the NYS Commission of Correction and chair of the Commission Medical Review Board, which oversees the operation and management of local and state correctional facilities and secure residential juvenile treatment centers operated by the Office of Children and Family Services.

She is a past president of Black Psychiatrists of America and received the American Psychiatric Association's Solomon Carter Fuller Award. The All Healers Mental Health Alliance (AHMA), an organization that Dr. Harrison-Ross, along with the NYSEC and the Social Service Board, was instrumental in forming, received an award for public health leadership at the American Public Health Association meeting in Washington, DC. It was bestowed for AHMHA's work to bring hope and healing to survivors following the 9/11 World Trade Center tragedy and the devastation caused in the mid-south/Gulf Coast by Hurricane Katrina and Hurricane Rita, the BP oil spill, and the Haitian earthquake. She was recently appointed to the International Advisory Board of the Auschwitz Institute for Peace and Reconciliation.

Index

Inspiration

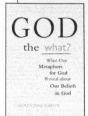

Finding Time for the Timeless: Spirituality in the Workweek
By John McQuiston II
Offers refreshing stories of everyday spiritual practices people use to free themselves from the work and worry mindset of our culture.
5⅛ x 6½, 208 pp, Quality PB, 978-1-59473-383-3 **$9.99**

God the *What?*: What Our Metaphors for God Reveal about Our
Beliefs in God *by Carolyn Jane Bohler*
Inspires you to consider a wide range of images of God in order to refine how you imagine God.   6 x 9, 192 pp, Quality PB, 978-1-59473-251-5 **$16.99**

How Did I Get to Be 70 When I'm 35 Inside?: Spiritual Surprises of
Later Life *by Linda Douty*
Encourages you to focus on the inner changes of aging to help you greet your later years as the grand adventure they can be.   6 x 9, 208 pp, Quality PB, 978-1-59473-297-3 **$16.99**

Restoring Life's Missing Pieces: The Spiritual Power of Remembering
& Reuniting with People, Places, Things & Self *by Caren Goldman*
A powerful and thought-provoking look at reunions of all kinds as roads to remembering and re-membering ourselves.
6 x 9, 208 pp, Quality PB, 978-1-59473-295-9 **$16.99**

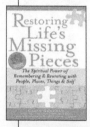

Saving Civility: 52 Ways to Tame Rude, Crude & Attitude for a Polite Planet
By Sara Hacala
Provides fifty-two practical ways you can reverse the course of incivility and make the world a more enriching, pleasant place to live.
6 x 9, 240 pp, Quality PB 978-1-59473-314-7 **$16.99**

Spiritually Healthy Divorce: Navigating Disruption with Insight & Hope
by Carolyne Call
A spiritual map to help you move through the twists and turns of divorce.
6 x 9, 224 pp, Quality PB, 978-1-59473-288-1 **$16.99**

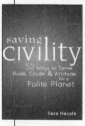

Who Is My God? 2nd Edition
An Innovative Guide to Finding Your Spiritual Identity
by the Editors at SkyLight Paths
Provides the Spiritual Identity Self-Test™ to uncover the components of your unique spirituality.   6 x 9, 160 pp, Quality PB, 978-1-59473-014-6 **$15.99**

Journeys of Simplicity
Traveling Light with Thomas Merton, Bashō,
Edward Abbey, Annie Dillard & Others
by Philip Harnden
Invites you to consider a more graceful way of traveling through life.
PB includes journal pages to help you get started on
your own spiritual journey.
5 x 7¼, 144 pp, Quality PB, 978-1-59473-181-5 **$12.99**
5 x 7¼, 128 pp, HC, 978-1-893361-76-8 **$16.95**

Or phone, mail or e-mail to: SKYLIGHT PATHS Publishing
An imprint of Turner Publishing Company
4507 Charlotte Avenue • Suite 100 • Nashville, Tennessee 37209
Tel: (615) 255-2665 • www.skylightpaths.com
Prices subject to change.

Spirituality

Gathering at God's Table: The Meaning of Mission in the Feast of Faith
By Katharine Jefferts Schori
A profound reminder of our role in the larger frame of God's dream for a restored and reconciled world.   6 x 9, 256 pp, HC, 978-1-59473-316-1 **$21.99**

The Heartbeat of God: Finding the Sacred in the Middle of Everything
by Katharine Jefferts Schori; Foreword by Joan Chittister, OSB
Explores our connections to other people, to other nations and with the environment through the lens of faith.   6 x 9, 240 pp, HC, 978-1-59473-292-8 **$21.99**

A Dangerous Dozen: Twelve Christians Who Threatened the Status Quo but Taught Us to Live Like Jesus
by the Rev. Canon C. K. Robertson, PhD; Foreword by Archbishop Desmond Tutu
Profiles twelve visionary men and women who challenged society and showed the world a different way of living.   6 x 9, 208 pp, Quality PB, 978-1-59473-298-0 **$16.99**

Decision Making & Spiritual Discernment: The Sacred Art of Finding Your Way *by Nancy L. Bieber*
Presents three essential aspects of Spirit-led decision making: willingness, attentiveness and responsiveness.   5½ x 8½, 208 pp, Quality PB, 978-1-59473-289-8 **$16.99**

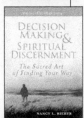

Laugh Your Way to Grace: Reclaiming the Spiritual Power of Humor
by Rev. Susan Sparks   A powerful, humorous case for laughter as a spiritual, healing path.   6 x 9, 176 pp, Quality PB, 978-1-59473-280-5 **$16.99**

Bread, Body, Spirit: Finding the Sacred in Food
Edited and with Introductions by Alice Peck   6 x 9, 224 pp, Quality PB, 978-1-59473-242-3 **$19.99**

Claiming Earth as Common Ground: The Ecological Crisis through the Lens of Faith
by Andrea Cohen-Kiener; Foreword by Rev. Sally Bingham
6 x 9, 192 pp, Quality PB, 978-1-59473-261-4 **$16.99**

Creating a Spiritual Retirement: A Guide to the Unseen Possibilities in Our Lives
by Molly Srode   6 x 9, 208 pp, b/w photos, Quality PB, 978-1-59473-050-4 **$14.99**

Creative Aging: Rethinking Retirement and Non-Retirement in a Changing World
by Marjory Zoet Bankson   6 x 9, 160 pp, Quality PB, 978-1-59473-281-2 **$16.99**

Keeping Spiritual Balance as We Grow Older: More than 65 Creative Ways to Use Purpose, Prayer, and the Power of Spirit to Build a Meaningful Retirement
by Molly and Bernie Srode   8 x 8, 224 pp, Quality PB, 978-1-59473-042-9 **$16.99**

Hearing the Call across Traditions: Readings on Faith and Service
Edited by Adam Davis; Foreword by Eboo Patel
6 x 9, 352 pp, Quality PB, 978-1-59473-303-1 **$18.99**; HC, 978-1-59473-264-5 **$29.99**

Honoring Motherhood: Prayers, Ceremonies & Blessings
Edited and with Introductions by Lynn L. Caruso
5 x 7¼, 272 pp, Quality PB, 978-1-58473-384-0 **$9.99**; HC, 978-1-59473-239-3 **$19.99**

The Losses of Our Lives: The Sacred Gifts of Renewal in Everyday Loss
by Dr. Nancy Copeland-Payton   6 x 9, 192 pp, HC, 978-1-59473-271-3 **$19.99**

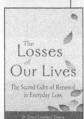

Renewal in the Wilderness: A Spiritual Guide to Connecting with God in the Natural World *by John Lionberger*
6 x 9, 176 pp, b/w photos, Quality PB, 978-1-59473-219-5 **$16.99**

Soul Fire: Accessing Your Creativity
by Thomas Ryan, CSP   6 x 9, 160 pp, Quality PB, 978-1-59473-243-0 **$16.99**

A Spirituality for Brokenness: Discovering Your Deepest Self in Difficult Times
by Terry Taylor   6 x 9, 176 pp, Quality PB, 978-1-59473-229-4 **$16.99**

A Walk with Four Spiritual Guides: Krishna, Buddha, Jesus, and Ramakrishna
by Andrew Harvey   5½ x 8½, 192 pp, b/w photos & illus., Quality PB, 978-1-59473-138-9 **$15.99**

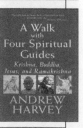

The Workplace and Spirituality: New Perspectives on Research and Practice
Edited by Dr. Joan Marques, Dr. Satinder Dhiman and Dr. Richard King
6 x 9, 256 pp, HC, 978-1-59473-260-7 **$29.99**

Women's Interest

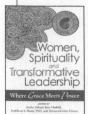

Women, Spirituality and Transformative Leadership
Where Grace Meets Power
Edited by Kathe Schaaf, Kay Lindahl, Kathleen S. Hurty, PhD, and Reverend Guo Cheen
A dynamic conversation on the power of women's spiritual leadership and its emerging patterns of transformation. 6 x 9, 288 pp, Hardcover, 978-1-59473-313-0 **$24.99**

Spiritually Healthy Divorce: Navigating Disruption with Insight & Hope
by Carolyne Call A spiritual map to help you move through the twists and turns of divorce. 6 x 9, 224 pp, Quality PB, 978-1-59473-288-1 **$16.99**

New Feminist Christianity: Many Voices, Many Views
Edited by Mary E. Hunt and Diann L. Neu
Insights from ministers and theologians, activists and leaders, artists and liturgists who are shaping the future. Taken together, their voices offer a starting point for building new models of religious life and worship.
6 x 9, 384 pp, HC, 978-1-59473-285-0 **$24.99**

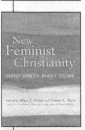

New Jewish Feminism: Probing the Past, Forging the Future
Edited by Rabbi Elyse Goldstein; Foreword by Anita Diamant
Looks at the growth and accomplishments of Jewish feminism and what they mean for Jewish women today and tomorrow. Features the voices of women from every area of Jewish life, addressing the important issues that concern Jewish women.
6 x 9, 480 pp, Quality PB, 978-1-58023-448-1 **$19.99**; HC, 978-1-58023-359-0 **$24.99***

Bread, Body, Spirit: Finding the Sacred in Food
Edited and with Introductions by Alice Peck 6 x 9, 224 pp, Quality PB, 978-1-59473-242-3 **$19.99**

Dance—The Sacred Art: The Joy of Movement as a Spiritual Practice
by Cynthia Winton-Henry 5½ x 8½, 224 pp, Quality PB, 978-1-59473-268-3 **$16.99**

Daughters of the Desert: Stories of Remarkable Women from Christian, Jewish and Muslim Traditions
by Claire Rudolf Murphy, Meghan Nuttall Sayres, Mary Cronk Farrell, Sarah Conover and Betsy Wharton
5½ x 8½, 192 pp, Illus., Quality PB, 978-1-59473-106-8 **$14.99** Inc. reader's discussion guide

The Divine Feminine in Biblical Wisdom Literature
Selections Annotated & Explained
Translation & Annotation by Rabbi Rami Shapiro; Foreword by Rev. Cynthia Bourgeault, PhD
5½ x 8½, 240 pp, Quality PB, 978-1-59473-109-9 **$16.99**

Divining the Body: Reclaim the Holiness of Your Physical Self
by Jan Phillips 8 x 8, 256 pp, Quality PB, 978-1-59473-080-1 **$18.99**

Honoring Motherhood: Prayers, Ceremonies & Blessings
Edited and with Introductions by Lynn L. Caruso
5 x 7¼, 272 pp, Quality PB, 978-1-58473-384-0 **$9.99**; HC, 978-1-59473-239-3 **$19.99**

Next to Godliness: Finding the Sacred in Housekeeping
Edited by Alice Peck 6 x 9, 224 pp, Quality PB, 978-1-59473-214-0 **$19.99**

ReVisions: Seeing Torah through a Feminist Lens
by Rabbi Elyse Goldstein 5½ x 8½, 224 pp, Quality PB, 978-1-58023-117-6 **$16.95***

The Triumph of Eve & Other Subversive Bible Tales
by Matt Biers-Ariel 5½ x 8½, 192 pp, Quality PB, 978-1-59473-176-1 **$14.99**

White Fire: A Portrait of Women Spiritual Leaders in America
by Malka Drucker; Photos by Gay Block 7 x 10, 320 pp, b/w photos, HC, 978-1-893361-64-5 **$24.95**

Woman Spirit Awakening in Nature: Growing Into the Fullness of Who You Are
by Nancy Barrett Chickerneo, PhD; Foreword by Eileen Fisher
8 x 8, 224 pp, b/w illus., Quality PB, 978-1-59473-250-8 **$16.99**

Women of Color Pray: Voices of Strength, Faith, Healing, Hope and Courage
Edited and with Introductions by Christal M. Jackson
5 x 7¼, 208 pp, Quality PB, 978-1-59473-077-1 **$15.99**

The Women's Torah Commentary: New Insights from Women Rabbis on the 54 Weekly Torah Portions *Edited by Rabbi Elyse Goldstein*
6 x 9, 496 pp, Quality PB, 978-1-58023-370-5 **$19.99**; HC, 978-1-58023-076-6 **$34.95***

* A book from Jewish Lights, SkyLight Paths' sister imprint

Spiritual Practice

Fly-Fishing—The Sacred Art: Casting a Fly as a Spiritual Practice
by Rabbi Eric Eisenkramer and Rev. Michael Attas, MD; Foreword by Chris Wood, CEO,
Trout Unlimited; Preface by Lori Simon, executive director, Casting for Recovery
Shares what fly-fishing can teach you about reflection, awe and wonder; the benefits
of solitude; the blessing of community and the search for the Divine.
5½ x 8½, 160 pp, Quality PB, 978-1-59473-299-7 **$16.99**

Lectio Divina—The Sacred Art: Transforming Words & Images into
Heart-Centered Prayer *by Christine Valters Paintner, PhD*
Expands the practice of sacred reading beyond scriptural texts and makes it
accessible in contemporary life. 5½ x 8½, 240 pp, Quality PB, 978-1-59473-300-0 **$16.99**

Writing—The Sacred Art: Beyond the Page to Spiritual Practice
By Rami Shapiro and Aaron Shapiro
Push your writing through the trite and the boring to something fresh, something
transformative. Includes over fifty unique, practical exercises.
5½ x 8½, 192 pp, Quality PB, 978-1-59473-372-7 **$16.99**

Dance—The Sacred Art: The Joy of Movement as a Spiritual Practice
by Cynthia Winton-Henry 5½ x 8½, 224 pp, Quality PB, 978-1-59473-268-3 **$16.99**

Everyday Herbs in Spiritual Life: A Guide to Many Practices
by Michael J. Caduto; Foreword by Rosemary Gladstar
7 x 9, 208 pp, 20+ b/w illus., Quality PB, 978-1-59473-174-7 **$16.99**

Giving—The Sacred Art: Creating a Lifestyle of Generosity
by Lauren Tyler Wright 5½ x 8½, 208 pp, Quality PB, 978-1-59473-224-9 **$16.99**

Haiku—The Sacred Art: A Spiritual Practice in Three Lines
by Margaret D. McGee 5½ x 8½, 192 pp, Quality PB, 978-1-59473-269-0 **$16.99**

Hospitality—The Sacred Art: Discovering the Hidden Spiritual Power of Invitation
and Welcome *by Rev. Nanette Sawyer; Foreword by Rev. Dirk Ficca*
5½ x 8½, 208 pp, Quality PB, 978-1-59473-228-7 **$16.99**

Labyrinths from the Outside In: Walking to Spiritual Insight—A Beginner's Guide
by Donna Schaper and Carole Ann Camp
6 x 9, 208 pp, b/w illus. and photos, Quality PB, 978-1-893361-18-8 **$16.95**

Practicing the Sacred Art of Listening: A Guide to Enrich Your Relationships
and Kindle Your Spiritual Life *by Kay Lindahl* 8 x 8, 176 pp, Quality PB, 978-1-893361-85-0 **$16.95**

Recovery—The Sacred Art: The Twelve Steps as Spiritual Practice *by Rami Shapiro;*
Foreword by Joan Borysenko, PhD 5½ x 8½, 240 pp, Quality PB, 978-1-59473-259-1 **$16.99**

Running—The Sacred Art: Preparing to Practice *by Dr. Warren A. Kay; Foreword by*
Kristin Armstrong 5½ x 8½, 160 pp, Quality PB, 978-1-59473-227-0 **$16.99**

The Sacred Art of Chant: Preparing to Practice
by Ana Hernández 5½ x 8½, 192 pp, Quality PB, 978-1-59473-036-8 **$15.99**

The Sacred Art of Fasting: Preparing to Practice
by Thomas Ryan, CSP 5½ x 8½, 192 pp, Quality PB, 978-1-59473-078-8 **$15.99**

The Sacred Art of Forgiveness: Forgiving Ourselves and Others through God's Grace
by Marcia Ford 8 x 8, 176 pp, Quality PB, 978-1-59473-175-4 **$18.99**

The Sacred Art of Listening: Forty Reflections for Cultivating a Spiritual Practice
by Kay Lindahl; Illus. by Amy Schnapper 8 x 8, 160 pp, b/w illus., Quality PB, 978-1-893361-44-7 **$16.99**

The Sacred Art of Lovingkindness: Preparing to Practice
by Rabbi Rami Shapiro; Foreword by Marcia Ford 5½ x 8½, 176 pp, Quality PB, 978-1-59473-151-8 **$16.99**

Sacred Attention: A Spiritual Practice for Finding God in the Moment
by Margaret D. McGee 6 x 9, 144 pp, Quality PB, 978-1-59473-291-1 **$16.99**

Soul Fire: Accessing Your Creativity
by Thomas Ryan, CSP 6 x 9, 160 pp, Quality PB, 978-1-59473-243-0 **$16.99**

Spiritual Adventures in the Snow: Skiing & Snowboarding as Renewal for Your Soul
by Dr. Marcia McFee and Rev. Karen Foster; Foreword by Paul Arthur
5½ x 8½, 208 pp, Quality PB, 978-1-59473-270-6 **$16.99**

Thanking & Blessing—The Sacred Art: Spiritual Vitality through Gratefulness
by Jay Marshall, PhD; Foreword by Philip Gulley 5½ x 8½, 176 pp, Quality PB, 978-1-59473-231-7 **$16.99**

Judaism / Christianity / Islam / Interfaith

Professional Spiritual & Pastoral Care Resources

Professional Spiritual & Pastoral Care
A Practical Clergy and Chaplain's Handbook
Edited by Rabbi Stephen B. Roberts, MBA, MHL, BCJC
An essential resource integrating the classic foundations of pastoral care with the latest approaches to spiritual care, specifically intended for professionals who work or spend time with congregants in acute care hospitals, behavioral health facilities, rehabilitation centers and long-term care facilities.
6 x 9, 480 pp, HC, 978-1-59473-312-3 **$50.00**

Disaster Spiritual Care
Practical Clergy Responses to Community, Regional and National Tragedy
Edited by Rabbi Stephen B. Roberts, BCJC, and Rev. Willard W.C. Ashley, Sr., DMin, DH
The definitive guidebook for counseling not only the victims of disaster but also the clergy and caregivers who are called to service in the wake of crisis.
6 x 9, 384 pp, HC, 978-1-59473-240-9 **$50.00**

Learning to Lead
Lessons in Leadership for People of Faith
Edited by Rev. Williard W.C. Ashley Sr., MDiv, DMin, DH
In this multifaith, cross-cultural and comprehensive resource for both clergy and lay persons, contributors who are experts in the field explore how to engage spiritual leaders and teach them how to bring healing, faith, justice and support to communities and congregations.
6 x 9, 384 pp, HC, 978-1-59473-432-8 **$40.00**

How to Be a Perfect Stranger, 5th Edition
The Essential Religious Etiquette Handbook
Edited by Stuart M. Matlins and Arthur J. Magida
The indispensable guidebook to help the well-meaning guest when visiting other people's religious ceremonies. A straightforward guide to the rituals and celebrations of the major religions and denominations in the United States and Canada from the perspective of an interested guest of any other faith, based on information obtained from authorities of each religion. Belongs in every living room, library and office. Covers:
African American Methodist Churches • Assemblies of God • Bahá'í Faith • Baptist • Buddhist • Christian Church (Disciples of Christ) • Christian Science (Church of Christ, Scientist) • Churches of Christ • Episcopalian and Anglican • Hindu • Islam • Jehovah's Witnesses • Jewish • Lutheran • Mennonite/Amish • Methodist • Mormon (Church of Jesus Christ of Latter-day Saints) • Native American/First Nations • Orthodox Churches • Pentecostal Church of God • Presbyterian • Quaker (Religious Society of Friends) • Reformed Church in America/Canada • Roman Catholic • Seventh-day Adventist • Sikh • Unitarian Universalist • United Church of Canada • United Church of Christ

"The things Miss Manners forgot to tell us about religion."
—*Los Angeles Times*

6 x 9, 432 pp, Quality PB, 978-1-59473-294-2 **$19.99**

The Perfect Stranger's Guide to Funerals and Grieving Practices
A Guide to Etiquette in Other People's Religious Ceremonies
Edited by Stuart M. Matlins
6 x 9, 240 pp, Quality PB, 978-1-893361-20-1 **$16.95**

Jewish Pastoral Care, 2nd Edition
A Practical Handbook from Traditional & Contemporary Sources
Edited by Rabbi Dayle A. Friedman, MSW, MAJCS, BCC
6 x 9, 528 pp, Quality PB, 978-1-58023-427-6 **$30.00**
(A book from Jewish Lights, SkyLight Paths' sister imprint)

Caresharing: A Reciprocal Approach to Caregiving and Care Receiving in the Complexities of Aging, Illness or Disability
by Marty Richards
6 x 9, 256 pp, Quality PB, 978-1-59473-286-7 **$16.99**; HC, 978-1-59473-247-8 **$24.99**

InterActive Faith
The Essential Interreligious Community-Building Handbook
Edited by Rev. Bud Heckman with Rori Picker Neiss
6 x 9, 304 pp, Quality PB, 978-1-59473-273-7 **$16.99**; HC, 978-1-59473-237-9 **$29.99**

About SKYLIGHT PATHS Publishing

SkyLight Paths Publishing is creating a place where people of different spiritual traditions come together for challenge and inspiration, a place where we can help each other understand the mystery that lies at the heart of our existence.

Through spirituality, our religious beliefs are increasingly becoming a part of our lives—rather than *apart* from our lives. While many of us may be more interested than ever in spiritual growth, we may be less firmly planted in traditional religion. Yet, we do want to deepen our relationship to the sacred, to learn from our own as well as from other faith traditions, and to practice in new ways.

SkyLight Paths sees both believers and seekers as a community that increasingly transcends traditional boundaries of religion and denomination—people wanting to learn from each other, *walking together, finding the way.*

For your information and convenience, at the back of this book we have provided a list of other SkyLight Paths books you might find interesting and useful. They cover the following subjects:

Buddhism / Zen	Global Spiritual	Monasticism
Catholicism	Perspectives	Mysticism
Children's Books	Gnosticism	Poetry
Christianity	Hinduism /	Prayer
Comparative	Vedanta	Religious Etiquette
Religion	Inspiration	Retirement
Current Events	Islam / Sufism	Spiritual Biography
Earth-Based	Judaism	Spiritual Direction
Spirituality	Kabbalah	Spirituality
Enneagram	Meditation	Women's Interest
	Midrash Fiction	Worship

Or phone, mail or e-mail to: SKYLIGHT PATHS Publishing

An imprint of Turner Publishing Company

4507 Charlotte Avenue • Suite 100 • Nashville, Tennessee 37209
Tel: (615) 255-2665 • www.skylightpaths.com

Prices subject to change.